Hemingway, the Red Cross, and the Great War

Steven Florczyk

The Kent State University Press   Kent, Ohio

© 2014 by The Kent State University Press, Kent, Ohio 44242

All rights reserved

Library of Congress Catalog Card Number 2012048475

ISBN 978-1-60635-162-8

Manufactured in the United States of America

Library of Congress Cataloging-in-Publication Data

Florczyk, Steven.

  Hemingway, the Red Cross, and the Great War / Steven Florczyk.

    pages cm

  Includes bibliographical references.

  ISBN 978-1-60635-162-8 (hardcover) ∞

  1. Hemingway, Ernest, 1899–1961. 2. American Association of the Red Cross—
Biography. 3. Authors, American—20th century—Biography. 4. World War,
1914–1918—Literature and the war. I. Title.

  PS3515.E37Z59414 2013

  813'.52—dc23

  [B]

                          2012048475

18 17 16 15 14   5 4 3 2 1

For Kathy and Stan Florczyk

Contents

Acknowledgments

This project began after a conversation with Tim and Ginny Bliss, who told me about the connection between Robert W. Bates and Ernest Hemingway. Tim and Ginny shared with me stories of the famous writer that had become part of local lore, stories known mostly to Bates's descendants and some farmers in central California where Bates eventually settled after volunteering with the American Red Cross in World War I. Thanks to Tim and Ginny for telling me about Bates and those who knew him, and, along with the Bliss's children, Tory and Teddy, thanks for the numerous ways they have supported me ever since.

Many special thanks go to Bates's grandson John Evans for his hospitality in inviting me into his home so I could learn more about his grandfather. I am also grateful for his willingness to share his grandfather's papers with me and his permission to publish excerpts. Pat Evans's kindness and helpfulness is also much appreciated, as is the assistance I received from the Evans's daughters, Juliette, Kathryn, and Suzanne. Likewise, my research for this project benefited greatly from conversations with R. W. Bates Jr., Julia Bates, Stephen Bates, George Bliss, Tony and Johnny Brown, Juliette Grey, and Robbie Hutto.

I am also indebted to the many scholars whose influence and advice significantly shaped this study. Much gratitude goes to James Nagel, whose mentorship, expertise, encouragement, and continued guidance have been essential in helping me complete this book. Many thanks also to H. R. Stoneback for inspiring me to take on the project in the first place and his invaluable advice and support over the years. I would also like to express my appreciation to Richard Davison, Allen Josephs, Donald Junkins, Robert W. Lewis, Jim Meredith, Linda Miller, and Rena Sanderson for supporting my work. Thanks as well to Richard Menke, Hugh Ruppersburg, Robert Trogdon, and Steven Trout for their helpful comments in guiding my revisions. For additional valuable insights and suggestions, I am also grateful to Doug Anderson, Nicole Camastra, Bob

Clark, Marinella Garatti, Angela Green, Mary Holland, Dan Kempton, Hubert McAlexander, Brad McDuffie, Patrick McGinn, Gwen Nagel, Tom Olsen, Alan Przybyla, and Alex Shakespeare.

I greatly appreciate funding from The Hemingway Foundation and Society, The Jane and Harry Willson Center for Humanities and Arts, The University of Georgia Department of English, and The University of Georgia Graduate School. I would also like to acknowledge help from librarians at the Harry Ransom Center at the University of Texas at Austin, the Hemingway Collection at the John F. Kennedy Library, the Firestone Library at Princeton University, the Library of Congress, the Lilly Library at Indiana University, and the National Archives at College Park. Likewise, I am grateful for assistance provided by staff at the interlibrary loan departments at the Sojourner Truth Library at SUNY New Paltz and the Main Library at the University of Georgia. Many thanks as well to Sandra Stelts at the Special Collections Library at Pennsylvania State University for help transcribing letters, to Charles Machon for sharing his knowledge of the Missouri National Guard, and to Don Vogel for locating articles that appeared in Hemingway's high school newspaper.

Much gratitude goes to the Hemingway Foundation for permission to quote Ernest Hemingway's letters and to Kirk Curnutt and Sandra Spanier for help with permissions requests. I would also like to express my appreciation to everyone at the Kent State University Press who worked on this book, especially Joyce Harrison for her encouragement and expert advice.

Many others helped with this project in immeasurable ways, and I would especially like to acknowledge interest and support from Mark Bellomo, Larry Cappelletti, Dan, Kim, Jake, and Justin Ellithorpe, David Hyman, John Langan, Carl McGrath, Paul and Debra Meehan, Ed Meisel, Len Monachello, Ivan Scrivner, Brad Sikes, Josh Sternlicht, Sparrow Stoneback, Brandt Temple, Roger and Anne Thomas, Thomas Vigliotta, and Ryan Vogel. Much heartfelt gratitude also goes to Mary Ashby Brown for her invaluable advice and enthusiasm as I worked to bring the volume to press.

Finally, I would like to express my deepest thanks to my family—especially Lori, Stas, and my parents, Kathy and Stan, to whom this book is dedicated.

Introduction

In chapter 4 of *Green Hills of Africa,* Ernest Hemingway describes his free associations reading Leo Tolstoy's *Sevastopol* during a respite from hunting, noting in particular that he thought

> about what a great advantage an experience of war was to a writer. It was one of the major subjects and certainly one of the hardest to write truly of and those writers who had not seen it were always very jealous and tried to make it seem unimportant, or abnormal, or a disease as a subject, while, really, it was just something quite irreplaceable that they had missed.[1]

By 1935, when Hemingway first published his reflection on this "major" subject, his fame had been established in large part as a result of his literature that derived from participation in the Great War.[2] After *A Farewell to Arms* appeared in 1929, Malcolm Cowley commented that Hemingway "expressed, better than any other writer, the limited viewpoint of his contemporaries, of the generation which was formed by the war and which is still incompletely demobilized."[3] T. S. Matthews concurred, noting that "the description of the War, in the first part of *A Farewell to Arms,* is perhaps as good a description of war just behind the front as has been written."[4] Moreover, John Dos Passos indicated that Hemingway's portrayal of the retreat from Caporetto had been likened with some of the best prose "written since there was any English language."[5] Indeed, Hemingway's emerging reputation on the topic indicates his ability to transform a relatively brief experience as a noncombatant in the American Red Cross into some of the best fiction portraying World War I and its aftermath.

The extent to which Hemingway's oeuvre deals with the Great War is impressive. Prior to *A Farewell to Arms,* he wrote on the topic in each of his preceding volumes: *Three Stories & Ten Poems* (1923), *in our time*

(1924), *In Our Time* (1925), *The Torrents of Spring* (1926), *The Sun Also Rises* (1926), and *Men Without Women* (1927). Although *A Farewell to Arms* came to represent the culmination of his World-War-I literary output, he continued to produce fiction related to the conflict throughout his entire career. "A Way You'll Never Be," published among the short stories of *Winner Take Nothing* (1933), for example, stands as his most direct treatment of the Italian front in the summer of 1918. Much later, *Across the River and Into the Trees* (1950) included another portrayal of that locale, to which Colonel Cantwell returns in 1948 to bury the memory of his previous wounding once and for all.

Hemingway's nonfiction works have also very much relied on the war. Early articles such as "How to Be Popular in Peace Though a Slacker in War" and "A Veteran Visits Old Front, Wishes He Had Stayed Away" added to his growing reputation as a journalist as did much of his writing for the *Toronto Star* between 1920 and 1924.[6] In *Death in the Afternoon* (1932), a treatise on bullfighting that surprised a readership expecting new fiction, Hemingway essentially introduced the book as it grew out of a fascination that originated with his tour in Italy: "The only place where you could see life and death, i.e., violent death now that the wars were over, was in the bull ring and I wanted very much to go to Spain where I could study it."[7] "A Natural History of the Dead," published in the same volume, includes one of his most significant treatments of initiation into the horrors of wartime destruction.

The American Red Cross service, out of which Hemingway cultivated his reputation, has been well documented by scholars. Charles A. Fenton's *The Apprenticeship of Ernest Hemingway: The Early Years* (1954) includes a chapter that established many of the distinguishing features of Hemingway's experience in Italy: his journey to war, stint with an ambulance section, enlistment with a canteen unit, and subsequent wounding on July 8, 1918.[8] Carlos Baker's *Ernest Hemingway: A Life Story* (1969) presents a thorough discussion of the Italian episode in the writer's life from the very beginning until his tragic death in 1961.[9] Relying greatly on descriptions from Hemingway's letters as well as accounts by those who knew him, Baker's volume marked the most comprehensive biographical study at the time. Indeed, *A Life Story* continues to serve as a crucial point of reference for the several biographies that followed: Scott Donaldson's *By Force of Will: The Life and Art of Ernest Hemingway* (1977), Jeffrey Meyers's *Hemingway: A Biography* (1985), Peter Griffin's *Along with Youth:*

Hemingway, the Early Years (1985), Kenneth Lynn's *Hemingway* (1987), and James Mellow's *Hemingway: A Life Without Consequences* (1992).[10] Although the portraits of the subject differ greatly, the scholarly record has nonetheless firmly established the Italian experience as a formative period in Hemingway's life.

Other scholarship stands out for calling attention to the Red Cross service in more detail, but influential studies during the 1970s came to favor approaches that relegated the experience to Hemingway's reading about the Italian front and the development of his literary technique. For example, in *Hemingway's First War: The Making of "A Farewell to Arms"* (1976), Michael Reynolds acknowledges the Red Cross milieu as relatively minor source material for the novel, which he discusses more thoroughly in the context of historical accounts of the 1920s.[11] Reynolds's study, however, necessarily laid out what became the seminal argument for combating previous criticism that suggested Hemingway was only a reporter of personal exploits. Bernard Oldsey's *Hemingway's Hidden Craft* (1979) bolstered that claim, discussing the complex ways that memoir and fiction sometimes intersect but concluding that the writer's "form of literary art demanded that he take substance from actuality, provide it with mimetic reflection, and produce his own form of combining fiction—but fiction, in these specific instances, not auto-biography."[12] Robert W. Lewis's article "Hemingway in Italy: Making It Up" commented further on these notions, questioning the value of interpretive exercises based on the application of biographical material while also establishing G. M. Trevelyan's *Scenes from Italy's War* (1919) as a significant influence on the writing of *A Farewell to Arms*. Lewis's essay underscores the argument that Hemingway's extensive reading inspired the composition of the novel.[13]

Additional studies eventually acknowledged the Red Cross as more significant in shaping Hemingway's complex point of view on war. Although Peter Griffin's *Along With Youth: Hemingway, the Early Years* (1985) benefited from the recollections and contemporaneous letters of former ambulance driver Bill Horne, the volume also relied on Hemingway's fiction for biographical information, a practice which diminishes its overall value. However, the first two books in Michael Reynolds's impressive five-volume biographical study, *The Young Hemingway* (1986) and *Hemingway: The Paris Years* (1989), provide extremely helpful insights on the subject. Not only did Reynolds supply useful historical context for Hemingway's fiction related to the Red Cross, but his work also became recognized alongside that of Carlos Baker as essential for future inquiry into the life and literature of the famed writer. Subsequent to Reynolds, Henry Villard, another former ambulance driver, and James Nagel contributed a wealth of information in *Hemingway in Love and War: The Lost Diary of Agnes von Kurowsky* (1989), which provided the fullest picture yet regarding Hemingway's service and convalescence, as well as a careful consideration of the biographical puzzle about which scholars had previously debated. Indeed, Villard's reflections, contemporaneous documents from 1918, as well as Nagel's essay "Hemingway and the Italian Legacy," all make the volume an indispensable resource for the study of this phase of Ernest's development. With the exception of Griffin's work, the later studies of the Red Cross period reaffirmed Reynolds's earlier argument that the fictional themes, although inspired by the events of 1918, are considerably distinct from Hemingway's personal experience in the war.

Scholarship that has confirmed Hemingway's supreme achievement as a literary craftsman is central to understanding the correlation between the writer's life and work, but some of these interpretations have led to a backlash with respect to the biographical record. Indeed, arguments claiming the importance of Hemingway's power of imagination have, perhaps sometimes unintentionally, obscured the historical circumstances out of which the literature developed in the first place. This confusion is especially apparent in studies that show too much favor toward dismissing the significance of the writer's firsthand experience as a source for the fiction. Scholars, of course, cannot effectively argue for Hemingway's artistry as distinct from personal reportage if the life story becomes muddled.

Charles M. Oliver's essay in *Teaching Hemingway's "A Farewell to Arms"* (2008) serves as case in point. Oliver begins his contribution to the "Backgrounds and Context" section of the volume by overstating the conclusion reached by Reynolds:

> One of the most interesting yet often misunderstood facts about Hemingway's *A Farewell to Arms* is that it was written not so much from personal experience as from research. The author was wounded badly while driving ambulances for the American Red Cross in support of the Italian Army, and he apparently had a love affair with a

nurse; that is more or less the extent of his personal life that went into the novel. The rest is a mix of research and imagination.[14]

Oliver's point about Hemingway's thorough investigation of his subject in combination with powers of invention is a valid one, but he misconstrues the biographical data. As scholars have clearly established, Hemingway was wounded not while driving ambulances but as a volunteer in the canteen service. Oliver's subsequent summary of "Hemingway's actual experiences" is equally misleading:

> He arrived in Italy on June 4, 1918; was wounded on July 8; arrived at the American hospital in Milan on July 17; spent the rest of the summer and early fall recuperating from two operations; and was discharged from the Red Cross service on January 4, 1919, leaving for home that day, barely six months after his arrival in Italy.[15]

In fact, Hemingway did not enter Italy until June 7, 1918. He had arrived at the Red Cross hospital by July 14, was released from the ambulance service on November 16, and boarded a steamship bound for New York on January 4, 1919, after having stayed in Italy to receive mechanical therapy treatments for his leg.

Moreover, although it is true that Hemingway's active duty effectively ended after the wounding on July 8, the totality of his Italian experience nonetheless turned out to be one of the most formative periods of his life. Oliver's account not only tampers with the accuracy of the biographical record but fails to appreciate the richness of Hemingway's adventure. Episodes from those six months suggest not only source material for *A Farewell to Arms* and other fiction about Italy but many of Hemingway's themes related to subsequent wars as well. Frederic J. Svoboda, in the "Background and Context" section of *Teaching Hemingway's "A Farewell to Arms,"* reasonably explains that students should be aware of "the novel's importance as a reaction to the Great War."[16] Indeed, it is crucial to know exactly what Hemingway was reacting against when he began the serious endeavor of creating his fiction in the twenties.

Works such as those by Reynolds and Nagel provide excellent references suitable for following Svoboda's suggestion, but previously unexamined materials offer even more helpful details about Hemingway's American Red Cross service. Among these, the diary of the commanding officer, Captain Robert W. Bates; official reports documenting the ambulance and canteen services; section newspapers published by volunteers; as well as additional contemporaneous accounts, taken in conjunction with the established biography, clarify aspects of Hemingway's involvement that have been unclear or not entirely accurate in previous scholarship. Moreover, these records show that the author drew on his war experience as source material in ways that have not yet been fully appreciated. The documents shed light on the writer's initial naiveté as a young volunteer and point to the ways in which he transformed that experience in his fiction according to a more sophisticated attitude toward war that he worked out in the 1920s. The shift he underwent led him to "tell the truth," as he later called the "writer's job," by using complex literary techniques to portray the wartime adventures of his youth from the vantage point of the postwar era.[17] Indeed, it was Hemingway's brief involvement with the Red Cross that ultimately led to some of the finest American literature on the Great War.

One *Esprit de Corps*

The story of Ernest Hemingway's involvement in the Great War begins
with the formation of volunteer ambulance services at the outbreak
of hostilities in August of 1914. During the summer before Hemingway's sophomore year in high school, Americans in charge of the hospital in the Paris suburb of Neuilly instituted a plan to provide aid for
wounded soldiers on the Western front.[1] As Arlen Hansen explains in
*Gentleman Volunteers: The Story of the American Ambulance Drivers in the
Great War, August 1914–September 1918*, the service eventually developed
into three separate groups operating in France. Each one of them came
to be led by influential figures: H. Herman Harjes, Senior Partner of the
Morgan-Harjes Bank in Paris; Richard Norton, archeologist and son of
the esteemed Harvard professor of art history, Charles Eliot Norton;
and A. Piatt Andrew, a former assistant professor of economics at Harvard who went on to direct the United States Mint and later assumed
the role of assistant secretary of the Treasury. The volunteers affiliated
with the Harjes and Norton corps eventually merged under the spon-
sorship of the American Red Cross in 1917, and Andrew's organization
developed into the American Field Service, by far the most extensive
group of volunteers aiding wounded soldiers in France.[2]

The ambulance service, as James Nagel has commented, "had a literary and academic dimension that is at times astonishing."[3] Not only did
the corps eventually include John Dos Passos, E. E. Cummings, Malcolm
Cowley, Harry Crosby, Dashiell Hammett, and Louis Bromfield among
other writers, but literary figures were also instrumental in its inception.
In 1914, Henry James volunteered to write a pamphlet praising the work
of Richard Norton to help enlist others in the cause. James's essay appeared as an "open letter" in "a variety of journals in the United States,"
and the esteemed novelist offered to write additional tracts to promote
the service as well.[4] In early 1917, prior to emerging as one of the most
influential figures in the postwar Parisian literary milieu, Gertrude Stein

volunteered to drive her Ford, nicknamed "Auntie," to cart supplies and soldiers along the Western front.[5] When the Red Cross developed their ambulance corps in Italy in the fall of 1917, the American Poets Committee was among the first groups to offer its support, donating fifty vehicles.[6] Afterward, Robert W. Bates recorded an anecdote about an Austrian's response of disbelief when, after having been captured by the Italians, the prisoner of war noticed insignia on vehicles affiliating the Red Cross workers with writers. As Bates explained, an Italian captain responded to his enemy's surprise by assuring him that his observation was correct: "So you see," the captain told him, "you have the entire world against you, even the American poets."[7] The goading comment, delivered partly in jest, nonetheless calls attention to a significant distinguishing feature of the volunteer organizations that derived major support from a wide array of writers.

The backing for ambulance services reflects important values related to the Allied cause that were instrumental in leading to Hemingway's involvement. The men who formed the units often exhibited, as Charles Fenton has explained, "a spirit of humanitarianism" that compelled them to ameliorate the horrific conditions endured by wounded soldiers who waited for medical treatment.[8] After Richard Norton accepted Bates for service in France, for example, the latter notified his family to say that his "ambulance dream has been realized," explaining that

> I cannot bear to sit by idly while the greatest conflict man has ever known and probably will know is devouring the world. I cannot bear to be part of this oasis of peace while the world is suffering and struggling madly about me. I have got to take some small part in it and if I cannot be of the world as well as in it my life is not worth thinking much about.[9]

Bates, like many other volunteers, was inspired by the writings of Leslie Buswell, a driver from France whose publications during the war served to characterize ambulance work as "grandly" altruistic and in vital need of support from ambitious philanthropists.[10] Despite later cynicism expressed by some writers toward the units, the contemporaneous documents overwhelmingly show, as Fenton has discussed, that "the vast majority of volunteers sustained throughout the war and into the peace a firm belief in the validity and necessity of their conduct."[11] Hemingway later came to identify with similar ideals as he became involved with the Red Cross in Italy.

Fenton's emphasis on the selflessness associated with ambulance driving is well-founded, but volunteers were also undoubtedly inspired by the opportunity for thrill-seeking. In addition to expressing his desire to offer assistance abroad, for example, A. Piatt Andrew, well before he took charge of the largest outfit serving on the Western front, wrote his parents about an opportunity to haul wounded men, telling them about "the possibility of having even an infinitesimal part in one of the greatest events in all history" as well as the chance for "witnessing some of the gravest scenes in this gravest of spectacles."[12] Malcolm Cowley, who served as camion driver in Andrew's Field Service, noted that many college students volunteered "feeling certain that it would bear us into new adventures."[13] Although his account of the experience in *Exile's Return: A Literary Odyssey of the 1920s* is steeped in postwar disillusionment, Cowley was, like several others, "eager to get into action."[14] Stories relating the daring work undertaken by drivers, such as those published in *The Harvard Volunteers in Europe* (1916), motivated potential recruits as much as the testimonials describing the work as a chance to perform acts of good will.[15]

Even so, when Hemingway began exploring possibilities for involvement in the Great War in the fall of 1917, the ambulance service in France was not an option. Several months after the United States declared war on Germany on April 6, 1917, the units that operated along the Western front were militarized.[16] Because of his defective vision, he was ineligible for enlistment according to army regulations; moreover, he was too young to join an armed force without parental consent, which his father and mother were unwilling to provide.[17] At the same time he began his assignment as cub reporter for the *Kansas City Star* in October, however, front-page headlines reported the disastrous outcome of the Battle of Caporetto that led to the need for a new corps of ambulance drivers on the Italian front.[18]

Beginning on October 24, 1917, a week after Hemingway arrived for work at the *Kansas City Star*, the changing conditions in Italy commanded the world's attention. German and Austrian soldiers broke through the lines on the Isonzo River, and soon the enemy was in control of a significant amount of territory in the vicinity of the Bainsizza Plateau. "It is Italy's Verdun," one article announced.[19] The ensuing retreat of Italian soldiers developed into a wholesale evacuation of the region. Italy's third and second armies were separated, and the Austrians who occupied the breach employed a "cunning device." Similar to the sequence of events that leads to suspicion of Frederic Henry as an enemy infiltrator in *A Farewell to Arms*, soldiers were

> dressed in Italian uniforms so as to permit them to spread out over the country or mingle with the Italian forces on both sides of the gap. The Austrians thus garbed were enabled to advance unopposed and then opened fire with machine guns on retreating parties. Some of the Austrians were smuggled forward in motor lorries and then turned against the westward-moving forces.[20]

Refugees dispersed through points south, and estimates indicated that the population in Rome had increased by one million as a result of the displaced people from towns above the Piave River, where the Italians finally hindered the enemy's advance. By November 10, the newspaper had published a map of Italy's new front. General Luigi Cadorna had been replaced by General Armando Diaz, and British and French troops arrived to help reinforce the new positions. The Piave was expected to be the site of the next major battle of the war.[21] At the end of November, an article reported that the threat was still a grave one, but German forces were digging in for the winter. Over the next several months, Italy continued to suffer from the aftermath of the tremendous defeat, and the Allies were required to plot a new course of action for the coming year.[22]

By the first week of November, Italian officials petitioned the United States to declare war on Austria-Hungary, asking Americans to lend the "greatest service to Italy and to the cause of the Entente during the critical events of the present time."[23] Officials grew increasingly concerned that the Central Powers might achieve continued success in Italy, gaining a significant advantage over the Allies. Maps were printed in the *Kansas City Star* indicating that if the Piave line did not hold in the coming battles of 1918, the enemy might advance to Vicenza and eventually the Po River, a position that would enable them to conquer the entire northern region.[24] Meanwhile, Austria had been showering the countryside with "peace bombs," propagandistic leaflets suggesting that Italy was a mere pawn, disregarded by the United States and controlled by the interests of Great Britain and France. Using a phrase that Hemingway later employed about protagonists who renounce their commitment to war, the newspaper reported that the tracts encouraged Italian soldiers to declare a "separate peace," a tactic that had also been employed with Belgium and Russia. The Central Powers were attempting to capitalize on internal strife within enemy states by debilitating them to the point of complete failure, leading those countries to negotiate their own truces independent of the Allied Cause. Such an agreement in Italy, war strategists feared, would allow Germany to concentrate forces more effectively on the Western front.[25]

These concerns proved influential in the findings of the American Senate Foreign Relations Committee as its members weighed potential strategies for the coming months. Their report, printed on the front page of the *Kansas City Star*, announced that "as a result of this situation, the Allies have rushed aid to Italy, and the United States is sending ships, money and supplies, and will probably send troops, who will be facing and making war on Austrian soldiers."[26] The following day, December 7, the United States issued a formal declaration of war on Austria-Hungary. Thomas Nelson Page, American ambassador to Italy, promised an enthusiastic crowd, who gathered at the U.S. embassy in Rome, that "it is to Italy, lover and champion of liberty, in her hour of distress, that my people come as one man, pledging every resource for her relief; and be sure we will not stop until we have won."[27] Although members of the Allied Cause had not yet agreed upon a specific timetable for the commitment of armed forces in Italy, even the promise of troops carrying the Stars and Stripes into the region had increased optimism throughout the war-torn country.

Headlines announced news of the disastrous circumstances during the retreat from the Isonzo River, while at the same time feature articles in the *Kansas City Star* romanticized the Italian front. Burris Jenkins, a local minister who had spent time in Europe, published a series of essays describing the theater of operations as "the most dramatic, the most spectacular battle line in Europe."[28] Unlike the topography of the Western front, "the Alps lift the whole line up and hang it in festoons over their shoulders. You can look down upon the evening's guns, watch their fire, trace their projectiles, hear and see them fall and explode."[29] Indeed, the mountainous combat zone seemed "hung like a picture on the wall."[30] According to one article, King Victor Emmanuel III made frequent visits to the "common man" in the trenches, and the transports full of soldiers motoring to the lines resounded with song, details that would also appear in *A Farewell to Arms* minus the exuberance of Jenkins's account. Another report describes a field hospital under the able command of an exemplary and high-spirited surgeon overseeing the wounded, bloody, and bandaged that are well-served by British Red Cross workers, who "lend a hand to brothers in arms."[31] Perhaps "America can lend a hand" too, he suggests.[32] The "most romantic of the battle fronts," Jenkins maintained, "here war retains something of its old glamour."[33] Steve Paul writes that Hemingway could have been "primed by" these remarks, not only as they might have inspired him to enlist but also because the writings suggest an influence on later portrayals of landscapes in his fiction.[34] Hemingway never referred to the articles as an inspiration, but the features nonetheless demonstrate how idealized accounts about the emerging significance of the Italian front served to promote U.S. involvement in aiding her distressed ally. Publicity asserting the validity of that cause was a major factor resulting in Ernest's involvement with the American Red Cross.

Three months before the Battle of Caporetto, Americans had already initiated a plan for aid to Italy. Henry P. Davison, chairman of the Red Cross War Council, dispatched a temporary commission in late July of 1917 under the direction of George F. Baker Jr. vice president of the First National Bank. Baker's group included philanthropic businessmen, experts in health-related professions, and, according to the *Red Cross Bulletin*, "one of the leading authorities in this country on Italy," Harvard professor Chandler R. Post.[35] Their mission was "to investigate conditions" and report "how activity can best be utilized to meet needs of the suffering soldiers and the civilian population of Italy."[36] After a tour of several cities and the frontline trenches, the men returned to the United States on October 2.

As Charles Bakewell recalls in *The Story of the American Red Cross in Italy*, the report they carried on their journey back to Washington proved to be "out of date almost before their vessel landed." As "the very fate of the allies hung in the balance," according to Bakewell, organizers hurriedly revised their strategy in response to the conditions that developed in late October.[37] Italian-sponsored relief societies allocated resources in the aftermath of the retreat, but local agencies proved inadequate. Ambassador Page communicated with Paris and Washington to procure more help, and by early November, the American Red Cross began the emergency organization of a full-scale relief effort that came to have a significant presence in Italy not only through the end of the war but also for several months thereafter.[38]

Initial support focused on hospitals and aid to refugees, but when workers at the transportation headquarters in Paris learned of the need for relief, they made plans to send the first ambulance sections to Italy. Michael Reynolds describes the situation in *Hemingway's First War*:

> For the Norton-Harjes drivers who remained in France, the Italian di-saster at Caporetto presented a reprieve from joining the U.S. Army. The Red Cross had hastily assembled in Paris three sections of ambu-lances to be ferried over the Alps into Italy. By December the cars were ready, but there were no experienced drivers available.[39]

Although Reynolds acknowledges the "ambulance drivers who served with Hemingway" as "identifiable sources who contributed to" *A Fare-well to Arms*, some of the information he provides is not entirely accu-rate.[40] Indeed, Andrew's American Field Service had been taken over by the army, and the unemployed Norton-Harjes men, who spurned militarization in a show of support echoing Norton's dislike of U.S. of-ficers, became pioneers of the American Red Cross service in Italy.[41] In-stead of ferrying three sections over the Alps, however, the headquar-ters in Paris sent two groups by train preceded by an initial convoy that departed for Milan on November 18.[42] According to George Buchanon Fife, who served as a correspondent with the American Red Cross in 1917, there was no shortage of seasoned drivers either: "No sooner did it become known that the Red Cross was sending an ambulance divi-sion to Italy than its headquarters in the rue François 1er were overrun by applicants for enlistment."[43] After the disruption of many positions during militarization, the emergency organizers had a large pool of ex-perienced men to choose from, and they were able to staff three sec-tions of thirty-five men apiece, with the names of thirty-five to forty more volunteers placed on a waiting list.

Since officials anticipated intense work in Italy, they sought an expe-rienced crew that could handle the difficult task. The terms indicated a six-month period of enlistment, five hundred lire per month ("roughly $96," as Nagel indicates) for "personal expense except clothing and medical attention," as well as a "willingness on the part of the men to do whatever work assigned to them in the ambulance in Italy."[44] As Fife explains,

> it was made clear at the outset that for this service only those who had actual ambulance service at the front would be acceptable and, preferably, those who had had much of it, because there had been many intimations that the work of the corps in Italy would be a severe test even of men well acquainted with hazards and hardships and a never ended day's work.[45]

One of the initial organizers, Beverly Myles, spoke of not only a preference for men with knowledge of operating, maintaining, and repairing the "machines" but also having a desire for volunteers with plenty of experience in battle zones.[46] Many of the enlistees, therefore, had hauled wounded on shell-pocked roads in France amid enemy gunfire in regions such as the Somme, the Marne, and Verdun, where workers became inured to the atrocities of the western front.

The story of Section One's departure from Paris reveals much about the character of the men who initiated the service. "Paris was still asleep," Fife wrote, when the drivers prepared to set off from the *rue François 1er* in the early hours of a mid-November morning:

> It was cold and foggy, with a haze about the few, far-spaced street lights. In the cobbled courtyard of the transportation building, once the home of the United States Embassy and still bearing the National Arms cut deeply in the stone of a high gate-post, a number of the cars were parked; others were lined along the curbing to the vanishing point. And moving about among them with swinging lanterns to stow their kits and duffle, the men of the section, in short bulky jackets lined with sheep's wool, or in hairy, goatskin great coats, were grotesque shadows in the mist.[47]

In addition to his impressions of the drivers' hardened nature, Fife was also in awe of the oversized fur coats that became something of a trademark of their unique demeanor. Reynolds has likewise noted that these men "dressed in somewhat non-regulation uniforms with cigarettes dangling from their mouths," traits that marked them as "not your spit-and-polish young soldiers off to make the world safe for democracy." Accordingly, they were "accustomed to working hard when there was work to be done, but in the slack periods they did not maintain military discipline unnecessarily."[48] Fife's inclination to describe these men in sensational terms, along with Reynolds's descriptions, reflects the extent to which Section One was a selective group that held a mystique. Indeed, the volunteers who paved the way for Hemingway's unit were hardened veterans and something of a maverick crew.

Section One's trip to Italy reflects the degree to which the drivers exuded unconventionality. Even before the unit had left Paris, the staff car had shed its muffler, and the "unholy noise" that ensued earned it the nickname "Old Firecrackers." The vehicle, according to Fife, wreaked havoc throughout the countryside as the convoy journeyed south until the car was finally "demolished against a pillar" not far from Avignon. One car burned up in the street during a refueling pit stop in Marseilles and had to be salvaged for parts. Two other vehicles became inoperable and needed to be pulled in order to keep them moving, a system of travel that proved just as challenging for the driver doing the towing as for the man "condemned" to ride behind.[49] After seventeen days and roughly two-thousand kilometers of dusty roads and constant repairs, Section One arrived in Milan on December 5.[50] Major problems notwithstanding, most of the vehicles were in relatively good form, a testament to the perseverance of the group and their skills in repairing cantankerous vehicles on the fly. One of the drivers later summed up the trip by saying that "twenty-one convoys, each consisting of one car, have arrived at the Italian front for service. Several of the convoys made the entire trip without becoming separated. Most of them were completely separated, however, some of them being nigh well disemboweled."[51] Despite Section One's eccentricities, it was nonetheless a dependable outfit that could be relied on to get the job done in the most difficult of circumstances.

Besides enlisting as ambulance drivers, these men, perhaps unwittingly, also became representatives for the American people. When they arrived at the Italian border town of Ventimiglia, the warm welcome of United States support became abundantly clear. Passport checks were waived, and the road was literally strewn with flowers and cheering locals all the way to Milan.[52] By mid-December, after two additional sections of drivers and vehicles arrived, all three units were involved in a formal presentation of their services to the Italian Army. The ceremony was attended by civil and military officials and included flag waving, speech making, and a formal review of the ambulance corps by General Gastaldello.[53] The reception acknowledged the drivers as "tangible proof of the assistance which is coming to Italy from the United States" and solidified the bond between America and its beleaguered ally.[54]

After their formal presentation in Milan, the Red Cross drivers, now three sections strong, continued another two-hundred-and-fifty kilometers to locations near the Austro-Italian front. By December 23, they were housed in "comfortable villas a few miles from Padua," and in the absence of heavy fighting, other than helping with the occasional case of a soldier with frozen feet, the men were mostly working "to get their equipment in order before moving forward to take up their serious work still nearer the front."[55] In other words, they had quite a bit of downtime, and without a clear sense of work to occupy them, instead of polishing their boots and keeping careful account of fuel consumption, they tended to do as they pleased.

The names of those listed with the first three ambulance sections include several men that Hemingway later came to know. George Utassy, originally leader of Section One, was eventually promoted to quartermaster general of the corps and became a key figure in the recruitment effort that resulted in Ernest's enlistment. Meade Detweiler assigned Hemingway and Ted Brumback, also of the *Kansas City Star*, to Section Four upon their arrival in June and later visited Ernest at the hospital in Milan.[56] Coles van B. Seeley was admitted as a patient the same time as Hemingway, and the two developed a friendship over the course of their recovery.[57] James Baker, Charles Griffin, and Edward Welch Jr. later transferred to Hemingway's Section Four.[58] John Dos Passos, who was initially separated from the first group but subsequently arrived at the front all the same, became friends with Ernest during the twenties in Paris when they recalled their time in the Red Cross amid the postwar literary scene.[59]

Over the course of their first few weeks in Italy, the drivers from France received their direction from temporary leaders, but plans soon developed for a permanent supervisor at the front. Vernon S. Prentice and Gordon Sarre, along with Captain Felice Cacciapuoti, the Italian liaison officer, initially worked on equipping the units, setting up their accommodations, and coordinating efforts with the Italian government. As the sections established themselves, the need for an overseer became quickly apparent. Myles noted as much in his report to Prentice on January 1, 1918: "It is recommended that one man be selected for administrator and that the formation of field staff, the office administration, and the coordination of the sections be left entirely to him. . . . He must have not only the responsibility but also the authority to deal with all matters pertaining to the ambulance service." The director should operate from a base behind the lines "taking whatever trips are necessary to the front for inspection, and occasionally going back to the headquarters and Milan to conduct new sections to the front." Recognizing the profound impact such a position would have on the service as a whole, Myles noted that "it is of utmost importance that the administrator be recognized head of this service. On the character, initiative, diplomacy and resources of the man selected for this position will depend more than any other factors the success of the service." Not all of the duties would be as glamorous, however, since they also needed a bureaucrat with a talent for pushing paper and collating section leaders' reports "showing the numbers of wounded carried, approximate number of miles covered by each car, financial accounts, and requisition of supplies for the sections." Even so, Myles imagined the leadership position to be vital in establishing an organization that the members would be proud to call their own, an outfit similar to the ambulance units founded on the Western front:

> The *esprit de corps* of the service must be built up if the greatest efficiency is to be gotten from the men. They must be made to feel that they are part of a crack organization and that they have its reputation to uphold. This *esprit de corps* depends more than any other factor on the man who is at the head of the service.[60]

Indeed, Red Cross organizers had high expectations for the newly arrived ambulance units preparing for action over the next several months, and they emphasized the person in charge as integral to their success.

On January 25, Bates, with experience as a driver and section leader in France, wrote in his diary about accepting the job:

> They asked me to take charge of the field service and promised me a free hand. Utassy, one of my old Section 63 men is to be in charge of the office work as Quartermaster General, and although our work is parallel, Utassy is head of his own department, it is understood that

there can be but one head of the service and that I shall be that head. I am delighted with this arrangement. It is the identical position that Norton occupied in the old service and the very one of all that I hoped to have.[61]

Bates has been identified by Carlos Baker as the "inspector of ambulance services," but the importance of his role in the corps and subsequent influence on Hemingway has never been fully discussed.[62] Not long after arriving on the Italian front and setting up headquarters in Vicenza, the newly installed captain found that he had unprecedented authority in shaping some of the most significant work being accomplished by the Red Cross at the time. As the Permanent Commission to Italy took form in the early months of 1918, Bates was considered as the "ranking American officer in active service" on the Italian front.[63]

Bates's letters and reports reflect not only the humanitarian mission abroad but also the role of the Red Cross in promoting rapport between volunteers and the people of their host country. In a missive to H. Nelson Gay, of the American Poets Committee in Rome, Bates responded to an inquiry about general operations at the front. His reply suggests the increasing importance associated with ambulance drivers in the absence of United States troops:

We are also painting a small American flag on each side of the cars, and on the ambulances which we brought from France we are changing the "Croix Rouge Américaine" to "Croce Rossa Americana." We recognize the importance of the propaganda element in our work and wish to leave nothing undone to mark us as Americans. To this end, in addition to the above, we are changing from the old French Ambulance Service, English-cut uniform, to the regulation American uniform with "U.S." on the collar, and a small red cross. For every American seen in Italy, "rumor" gives 10 more. At no time were there more than 100 ambulance men in Milan; and yet a Milanese whom I met in Rome told me that one of his friends had written him there were at least 3000 American troops in the city and that the uniform had already ceased to attract attention.[64]

In *The Best Times*, John Dos Passos later criticized this policy. Recalling an encounter with two Red Cross officials who "rubbed me the wrong way by declaring in a fit of winey candor that we were at the Italian front only as a propaganda gesture to help keep the Italians in the war," Dos Passos noted his idealistic perceptions prior to learning about that objective: "What I liked to think I was doing was dragging the poor wops out from under fire, not jollying them into dying in a war that didn't concern them."[65] In the spring of 1918, however, the Red Cross mission had been clearly defined in terms of bolstering morale on the faltering Italian front. After Austrians had previously donned uniforms of their rival to defeat the enemy during the retreat from Caporetto, Red Cross workers planned to wear American military garb to encourage their ally in the fight.

The bond that developed between Americans and Italians also resulted in officer privileges for ambulance drivers. Sections on the western front included French lieutenants through whom American volunteers were required to clear their directives, but the Italian service allowed for more leeway. "There are no Italian lieutenants in the Sections," Bates wrote, "and our American leaders are allowed to wear the Italian insignia of rank (1st Lieut.). . . . In addition to all this, as if this were not enough, we are all regarded as having the rank of officers and are treated accordingly."[66] This meant that general workers were granted the rank of honorary second lieutenant while commanding officers attained a level of distinction one grade higher. The point clarifies Bill Horne's uncertainty as expressed to Hemingway's sister Marcelline about volunteers' roles with the foreign service. Regarding the status of honorary second lieutenant, Horne told her "how true that was I don't know—but it makes good sense."[67] Bates's letter not only explains the issue of rank but shows that the newly installed captain considered this situation as a remedy to problems that occurred in France, "where the lieutenant was always saying that our men could do this, that, and the other thing, because the French *poilu* [soldier] did it and that we were no better than they."[68] Accordingly, the privilege indicates the extent to which drivers enjoyed unprecedented standing as token members of the foreign army while still retaining autonomy outside of the military.

Even so, volunteers were required to adhere to restrictions put in place by the official censor, another integral component of the propaganda objective. "Every line of our letters is read," Bates wrote in a missive, "and the Italians are very sensitive; that is why you will notice that if I happen to mention them in my letters it is always in terms of admiration. The French and English show a certain tendency to look down on them and they feel it keenly." These circumstances led Bates to discipline his men on several occasions: "Our boys have been putting very unflattering comments in their letters home and it is causing us a great deal of trouble. . . . Have had to fire one man for this and before we get thru I expect to fire some more. It's inexcusable."[69] Not long before Hemingway's arrival, Bates intercepted a letter written by Dos Passos expressing "pacifist ideas" to a friend in Spain that violated the censorship policy.[70] Even though Bates recommended a dishonorable discharge, administrators settled the matter instead by barring Dos Passos from service after his enlistment expired at the end of May. The incident shows not only the extent to which Italian support became crucial prior to Hemingway's involvement but also the friction that developed between Bates and some of the jaded members who populated the corps during its inception.[71]

By late February of 1918, the Red Cross had begun a recruitment campaign to enlist new drivers for additional sections anticipated for the increase in activity during the summer. In strategizing for the work to come, Bates did not regard the crew from France with the same sense of awe as did Fife, nor did he envision them as integral to the future of the corps: "The old crowd," as he called them, "were for the most part malcontents and misfits who had failed to get into a regular service when the French sections were taken over. They were a hard crowd to handle." Therefore, he was eager to enlist new workers who might conform to Red Cross policy: "I hope to be able to pick my own men," he wrote, "the kind of men we ought to have for this service instead of putting up with a lot of bum material that is sent over by someone else."[72] Although Bates explained that he cancelled what he considered to be extravagant allowances in an effort to save money, he also mentioned that it helped to hasten the departure of drivers from France upon the expiration of their enlistments, noting in his diary that his action had the "desired result: it saved the R. C. a large sum of money monthly and got rid of practically all the old crowd."[73] Indeed, Section Two threatened to walk out even before the administration had their replacements. When Bates wrote his report on the subject of reenlistment, he noted that "in Section 1 about ten men are reenlisting, in Section 2 about five men and in Section 3 four men." Furthermore, he noted that "the failure of the men to reenlist has been primarily due to the lack of active work on this front," but there were "some, however, who maintained that they did not reenlist because of the suppression of the expense account."[74] By the time Hemingway's crew signed on, recruits were "furnished with lodging and mess free" but expected to pay their own transportation expenses. None of them were allotted additional funds as were the original personnel.[75] The changes reflected Bates's goal to enlist workers on "a purely voluntary basis," adhering to principles associated with the "gentleman volunteers" who established ambulance sections on the Western front.[76]

As in *A Farewell to Arms*, where Frederic Henry states that he "was always embarrassed by the words sacred, glorious, and sacrifice and the expression in vain," the impetus for Hemingway's enlistment with the Red Cross developed amid a climate dominated by demonstrations of idealism inspiring various forms of involvement in the war, not the least important of which had been that of ambulance driving.[77] Gwendolyn Shealy has described the era of World War I as a period in which the American Red Cross completed a significant shift from a relatively limited humanitarian aid establishment to a sizeable corporate entity with an unprecedented amount of economic power over which the United States government held significant sway. The bureaucracy as well as propaganda measures, she claims, are at least two indicators of this transition in terms of the role of the organization as a "tool of the government," especially in terms of "boosting Italian morale with the message of American friendship."[78] The culmination of activities arising as a result of these conditions occurred at the same time Hemingway began his enlistment process and lasted throughout his entire period of service.

Paul Fussell's *The Great War and Modern Memory*, the benchmark study establishing irony as the main outgrowth of reactions to the horrors of the European catastrophe that rendered initial wartime values obsolete, notes *A Farewell to Arms* as a quintessential example of the postwar literature that abandoned earlier notions of optimism: "It was not until eleven years after the war," Fussell writes,

> that Hemingway could declare in *A Farewell to Arms* that "abstract words such as glory, honor, courage, or hallow were obscene beside the concrete names of villages, the numbers of roads, the names of rivers, the numbers of regiments and the dates." In the summer of 1914 no one would have understood what on earth he was talking about.[79]

Fussell makes a valuable point about the passage of time necessary for Hemingway's growth as a writer, but George Monteiro, echoing Robert Lewis's comments in *"A Farewell to Arms": The War of the Words* (1992), offers a more profound statement on the sophisticated depictions that Hemingway produced in the twenties. "Arguably," Monteiro states, "it is Hemingway's hidden but never expunged idealism that provides the basis for a true understanding of Frederic Henry's denunciation."[80] Indeed, the same can be said for much of Hemingway's war fiction as a whole. Even more, Fussell's citation of Henry's famous phrase as a reaction to a wide array of circumstances leading to the escalation of World War I is more readily understood in terms of Hemingway's decision to enlist with the American Red Cross in Italy as the fighting intensified during the spring and summer of 1918.

Two Journey to War

Ernest Hemingway describes the naïve disposition of a novice heading off to combat in his introduction to *Men at War:* "When you go to war as a boy you have a great illusion of immortality. Other people get killed; not you. It can happen to other people; but not to you. Then when you are badly wounded the first time you lose that illusion and you know it can happen to you."[1] On the night of May 11, 1918, Hemingway himself was a boy leaving for war holding many of his romantic illusions intact. After being accepted for Red Cross service in Italy, he boarded a train to New York where he took passage on the *Chicago* on his way to the frontlines via Bordeaux, Paris, and Milan. Although scholars have provided several chronicles of the burgeoning writer's entry into the Great War, additional documents help clarify aspects of Hemingway's enlistment process and the early stage of his adventure abroad. The portrait of Hemingway that emerges reaffirms the ways in which his fiction contrasts with the personal experience on which it was based. Indeed, the beginning of Ernest's involvement with the Red Cross shows him to be an eager participant amid wartime fanfare promoting the cause in Europe, a point of view that he later altered significantly in his fiction.

At the end of October, 1917, as Red Cross organizers were responding to the needs in Italy in the aftermath of the Battle of Caporetto, Hemingway was writing about an idea he had for entering the military despite his defective vision. As Steve Paul has pointed out, within a few weeks of joining the staff at the *Kansas City Star,* Ernest wrote his sister about an unlikely option for volunteering on the Western front.[2] He explained that

> I intend to enlist in the Canadian Army soon but may wait till spring brings back Blue days and Fair. Honest kid I cant stay out much longer, the Canadian Mission Down here are good pals of mine and I intend to go in. Major Biggs and Lieut. Simmie are the officers in charge. If you enlist in the Canadian forces you are given as much time as you

specify and then go to either Toronto or Halifax and then to London and in three months you are in France. They are the greatest fighters in the world and our troops are not to be spoken of in the same breath. I may even wait untill the summer is over but believe me I will go not because of any love of gold braid glory etc. but because I couldnt face any body after the war and not have been in it.[3]

His plan was being conducted on the sly. The circuitous route Hemingway suggested for entering the trenches via the "greatest fighters" of the Canadian Army was not "for Family consumption," he wrote, but it never materialized just the same. His comment explaining that he would join because "I couldnt face anybody after the war," however, equates a lack of participation in the conflict with a mark of dishonor that he seemed unwilling to bear.

By the week after he had written, Hemingway had chosen another option. The Missouri Guard, with origins like those of the regiment in which his grandfather Anson had served in the Civil War, offered men a chance to receive martial training in addition to performing domestic duties such as the "guarding of the water works."[4] A temporary force authorized by the governor to operate until the return of the National Guard, which had been called up on August 5, 1917, the state militia was a provisional army regulated by the same laws of the federal service, "in so far as the same may be applicable," but with one notable exception: in addition to the increase of the maximum age limit to fifty years, the "rigid physical qualifications required for enlistment in the National Guard were not insisted upon."[5] This meant that Hemingway, poor eyesight notwithstanding, could become a soldier, albeit temporary and unable to serve in Europe.[6] The alternative to foreign duty was also more amenable to his parents, who were opposed to Ernest's plan to enter the conflict overseas.[7]

Hemingway's letters indicate that he signed up with the Home Guard in early November of 1917. Although Michael Reynolds has written that Ernest was not accepted until January of 1918, a missive Hemingway wrote to his parents on December 6, 1917, as James Nagel has noted, shows that "he had just received his uniform and was, presumably, already a member of the unit."[8] Indeed, Ernest's postscript to Marcelline, written on November 6, 1917, confirms that he had "joined the Mo. National Guard for State service only," as Peter Griffin has explained, "less than three weeks after he arrived in Kansas City."[9] Hemingway has been described as being "a member of the 7th Missouri Infantry, a temporary Home Guard that was organized when the entire Kansas City National Guard left for France,"[10] but in November of 1917, Ernest's regiment was known as the "2nd Missouri Home Guards."[11] It was not until March that he joined the Seventh Infantry when his regiment was incorporated into the National Guard.[12]

Despite its homebound status, the militia offered Hemingway a rudimentary military experience as well as an introduction to ideals motivating participants in the Great War. Some six thousand men served from the state, and drills ranged by regiment from one-to-three times per week. Adjutant General Harvey C. Clark reported an 80 to 90 percent attendance rate. At first, instructors were hard to come by because of the call to arms in Europe, but eventually retired officers and even veterans of the Spanish American conflict and Civil War volunteered. The men who joined were highly praised: "Not only did they furnish police protection for the state, but they rendered a very great service in stimulating interest in all war activities, in keeping alive the spirit of patriotism and in stamping out any semblance of disloyalty on the part of certain elements of our population."[13] In February, the governor reviewed Hemingway's regiment and called attention to the Guard's role in training men for overseas duty and motivating an increase in enlistments as well.[14]

Hemingway's letters from Kansas City often contain enthusiastic reports of his involvement with the Second Regiment. On November 5, 1917, he described himself as a "beautiful soldier, and much to be admired."[15] The next day, he informed Marcelline that he had "a 40 buck uniform and 50 dollar overcoat. Some youth."[16] At first, he had to borrow khakis from a friend, but he anticipated winter attire that would be, other than the Missouri-state shield on the hat, "just like Regular Army," as he told his parents in mid-November. In the same letter, he wrote that "all the Guard were ordered to report Tuesday and we had an all day maneuver and sham battle in the woods outside of town we marched and skirmished and had bayonet charges and sent out spies and all." The exercises included "regular army officers" as judges, "and it was very thrilling and instructive too."[17] Over the next few weeks, he continued to write about the military garb as well as a pair of army shoes from his father.[18] When the wool-winter outfits finally arrived, he reminded Clarence that they "are the same as the regular Army except have Mo. State Shield on the collar instead of U.S."[19] As his correspondence attests, Hemingway often equated the experience with that of real soldiering and expressed a sense of pride in his involvement with the organization.

Home Guard experience notwithstanding, Hemingway continued to write about searching for a unit that would send him overseas. In November, as Kenneth Lynn has noted, he told his parents that "I will plan to work here until Spring and then get in one more good summer before enlisting. I couldn't possibly stay out of it any longer than that under any circumstances. It will be hard enough to stay out until then."[20] Paul has referred to another resolution Ernest made after New Year's Day. Along with friends Bill Smith and Carl Edgar, Hemingway planned to "enlist together in the Marines in the fall unless I can get into aviation when I am 19 and get a commission."[21] Even though Ernest was disqualified for service in an armed force in Europe, he repeatedly expressed intentions to enter the war as a soldier.

On February 22, the *Kansas City Star* presented an alternative.[22] Inserted next to an illustration of the Home Guard in review before the governor, an article titled "Red Cross Calls Men" announced that "experienced business men not of draft age or who are physically exempt from army duty, and women without relatives in the American army are called by the American Red Cross to volunteer for immediate service in France and Italy."[23] Charles P. Pettus, a Red Cross official headquartered in St. Louis, was authorized to enroll personnel from the Southwestern Division. He ensured that "some of the positions to be filled are at the front and dangerous."[24] The article indicated several openings for posts in France, but at the bottom of the list of vacancies, the request specified "four ambulance drivers" and "one man for rolling canteen work in Italy."[25] Hemingway submitted his application the next day.[26]

At first, as with other attempts to find a way into the war, the Red Cross position seemed unattainable for Hemingway. Three days after he had applied, Pettus responded saying that

> shortly after we issued the call as it came from Washington for volunteers for Red Cross work abroad I received a telegram stating to disregard the call for five Ambulance drivers for Italy. Just what the reason for this was I do not know, but I suppose that they have secured the necessary men for this branch of the service.

He promised to keep Hemingway's application on file and, "if more men are needed as Ambulance Drivers," he wrote, the Red Cross would notify him "if it is found possible to avail ourselves of your services."[27] Even though the initial position was cancelled, Hemingway wrote on March 2 to Marcelline saying that he "was enlisted as an Ambulance driver for the American Ambulance Service in Italy." He told her to "say nought [to] the fambly. They might worry and I probably wont [be] called for some time. Any way it is a big relief to be enlisted in something." He also indicated his disappointment over the withdrawal of the announcement: "I enlisted for immediate service" he explained, "but got gypped on the immediate end of it. You see it is like this there are only five jobs for immediate service and my telegram got in sixth so I and the great Ted [Brumback], who drove on the Aisne for Six months will be next in line." He repeated what Pettus had written as well: "The St. Louis Headquarters said that our enlistments were received in response to our wire they sent blanks, and that they would let us know when they should avail them selves of our service." He emphasized that his sister should avoid spreading the news in general since future positions were still an uncertainty.[28] The Red Cross list of personnel affiliated with the ambulance service confirms the comments by Pettus and Hemingway. Duncan S. Elsworth and Lewis S. May from London enlisted in late February; Thomas Wharton and Bayard Wharton signed up from Philadelphia at the end of that same month; and Wilfred H. Wolfs enrolled out of Newark, New Jersey, and was inducted by April 1.[29] The five men chosen had occupied the only existing vacancies at the time.

While plans for a Red Cross recruitment campaign were under way, other circumstances threatened to disband the operation in Italy in its entirety. As officials were debating the extent to which the success of the Allied cause hinged on the outcome of battles at the Austro-Italian front, militarization of the ambulance units as a result of United States troop commitment seemed likely. Captain Robert Bates wrote of that scenario in one of his reports to Rome:

There has been great discussion of the news that our Government plans to send to Italy thirty officers in command. Mr. Davison, President of the American Red Cross, immediately telegraphed Washington that we place ourselves and our equipment at the entire disposition of the

Government. The Government accepted the generous offer of Mr. Davison and decided to send immediately 100 men to take over our equipment.[30]

Nonetheless, as Thomas Nelson Page wrote in 1920 following his retirement from the American ambassadorship in Rome, "the military authorities in France were not favorable to the proposal" for "they considered" the presence of American troops in France to be "more important."[31] Similarly, by April of 1918, Bates had written that "certain difficulties . . . which were not at first foreseen made [militarization] impossible and we were authorized to continue recruiting in America."[32] Although the cancellation of the ambulance unit takeover by the U.S. army guaranteed the continuation of Red Cross administration, the potential for an American armed force presence in Italy explains why several weeks had passed before Pettus was able to "avail" himself of Hemingway's services.[33]

Even as the threat of militarization had passed, however, regulations stipulated that men older than Hemingway were initially preferred in the recruitment campaign. When Captain George Utassy left the Italian front to return to the United States on a mission to secure enlistees, he issued a press release from the headquarters of the Red Cross Atlantic Division on East Twenty-Third Street in Manhattan. "One hundred Americans are needed at once by the American Red Cross for ambulance service behind the Italian lines," the article announced:

> It is a splendid opportunity for men of independent means, over draft age, who are strong and healthy and able to drive automobiles. Consideration will be given to men 25 years or over, who are exempt for minor defects. All cost of equipment and living expenses abroad will be covered by the American Red Cross, and transportation expenses will be paid, if necessary.[34]

Under those parameters, however, the recruitment drive failed to attract the necessary volunteers. As Pettus explained to Hemingway's father,

> during April Captain Utassy returned from Italy to enlist a unit for ambulance drivers in Italy. At first they endeavored to secure men above the draft age; and then men within draft age over twenty-five who had been discharged for some apparent physical defect. Evidently they did

not secure the requisite number of men and so they decided to take young men between the ages of eighteen and twenty years and three months.[35]

Bates noted likewise. Once Utassy offered younger men the chance to serve, the division was "swamped with applications."[36] When Pettus's branch resumed reviewing candidates, they published another announcement stating that "no more applications will be accepted" because of the large influx of requests for positions along with a backlog of several hundred more.[37] Hemingway and Brumback, in a holding pattern since the end of February, were next in line. The renewed opportunity allowed both of them to be recommended for service in Italy, and they were eventually notified with instructions for completing the enlistment procedure.[38]

The change in Red Cross policy also resulted in a flood of applications from students at colleges and universities. Henry Villard, one of several enlistees from Harvard, was not only the "youngest ambulance driver in Italy," as Nagel explains, but also came to befriend Hemingway later that summer.[39] On April 30, 1918, Villard wrote about the recruitment campaign to his parents:

> Up to last Saturday, the American Red Cross was only taking older men for work in Italy, but on that day, a War Department order came, which authorized a special unit of fellows under draft age, from 18 yrs to 20 and 4 months. Fifty or one hundred,—I don't know which,— are to be taken from Harvard, and as soon as this was known, applications began pouring in.[40]

In addition to Villard, the Red Cross signed up thirty-six freshmen and sophomores from Cambridge for ambulance driving in Italy.[41] Consequently, the service came to include mostly young, highly literate individuals who, like Hemingway, held a keen interest in literary pursuits.

Meanwhile, as Hemingway awaited word from Pettus, the Missouri Home Guard had become an increasingly attractive option for volunteers seeking to serve abroad. On March 23, Hemingway wrote his parents that "the home guard has been formally taken into the National Guard and take the Federal Oath Monday."[42] According to the report of the adjutant general to the governor, the National Guard was "of great advantage" to its members "and to the government because the preliminary training received . . . would prepare them that much earlier for duty in the front lines." Indeed, "hundreds of men passed through the regiment in this way."[43] Lieutenant Colonel H. E. Poor noted likewise, explaining that "during the summer of 1918" a "host of young men" partook in "this method of getting a little military training prior to their induction into service in the National Army."[44] The Second Regiment of the Home Guard was not officially incorporated until May 18, 1918, at which time Ernest was in New York on his way to Italy, but his service record and letter to his parents show that he took the oath all the same. On March 25, 1918, he became a member of Company E in the Seventh Regiment of the National Guard. His honorable discharge was not recorded until August 12, 1918, by which time he was convalescing in the American Red Cross Hospital in Milan after his wounding.[45]

Hemingway's enlistment in the National Guard suggests that he could have become a soldier in the war if he had not opted for the Red Cross. Reynolds implies the same point when he states that "in March, the Home Guard was taken into the National Guard, but by then, Hemingway had volunteered to drive Red Cross ambulances in Italy."[46] Lynn, who is candidly skeptical about the genuineness of Hemingway's attempts to enlist for military service, makes a related comment. "There is no record," he writes,

> of [Hemingway's] having made a formal effort to sign up with the Army, while there is strong reason to believe that he would have been accepted if he had. The Army doctors in Kansas City put no roadblocks in the war path of Harry S. Truman, after all, despite the fact that without his glasses he was helpless. The likelihood, therefore, is that for all his patriotism the prospect of trench warfare put Ernest off.[47]

Lynn offers a reasonable observation, for some Guardsmen undoubtedly skirted regulations to gain their way into combat in France. The fact remains, however, that, Truman's circumvention notwithstanding, foreign service would have still appeared very unlikely for Hemingway. As shown by publicity in the *Kansas City Star,* despite the large turnout of enlistees for the Seventh Regiment in March, "recruiting is still being pushed. It is desired to get 250 more men than the government requires to replace those who will fail on the physical examination."[48] Harvey C.

Clark's *Report of the Adjutant General of Missouri, January 1, 1917-December 31, 1920* confirms this point, noting that the national force ultimately contained "those members of the Home Guard under forty-five years of age who were able to pass the physical examination."[49] Even though Hemingway was allowed to take the federal oath with the Seventh early on in the process of reorganization, regulations stipulated that he would be rejected before its official incorporation into the National Guard in May. Thus, the position with the American Red Cross that became available at the end of April presented him with the best opportunity for participation in the war.

Lynn's other point about trench warfare as undesirable calls attention to a characteristic of ambulance work that was ultimately beneficial to many volunteers intent on writing about the conflict. Malcolm Cowley has explained the "spectatorial" quality of these assignments that still allowed for participation in the excitement overseas.[50] Unlike soldiers, the drivers often witnessed action free from the conditions associated with day-to-day life in the frontlines. Bates, for example, records an instance of sitting on a hill, just out of enemy shell-fire range, where he watched a bombardment as if he were sitting in the bleachers at a football game. It was "fun to watch the earth fly," he wrote afterward.[51] On the other hand, noncombatants still risked exposure to serious danger when they entered the battle zone, a point that is most obvious in the case of Hemingway, whose experience at the front led to his wounding. More often than not, however, the unique perspective of the Red Cross volunteer, as Arlen J. Hansen has noted, allowed for the observation of "grim realities" from a perspective allowing them to "trace the war's ironies" from less dangerous locations behind the lines.[52]

Besides the developments that allowed for an opening with the ambulance service in Italy, several other factors made the Red Cross an attractive option for Hemingway. His family, for instance, placed a high value on the type of humanitarian work accomplished at the front. As Nagel points out, Anson Hemingway founded the Chicago YMCA and, along with his wife Adelaide, actively engaged in community service in Ernest's hometown of Oak Park, Illinois.[53] Morris Buske describes Hemingway's other grandfather, Ernest Hall, as similarly philanthropic.[54] A few weeks after submitting his application to volunteer in Italy, Hemingway wrote Anson and Adelaide saying that "I suppose you are all busy on the Red

Cross work . . . you work harder on those things than I do down here."[55] Both of Hemingway's parents inherited the tradition of aid to those in need and passed it on to their son.

Hemingway was also influenced by family members' involvement in war. Marcelline remembered, for example, that "all of us Hemingways had been brought up on tales of bravery and heroism in the Civil War told to us by Grandfather Hemingway" and his Grand Army of the Republic friends.[56] Anson Hemingway's reputation as one of the "local heroes" from the former era was particularly impressive.[57] Because Anson had become "almost a professional veteran, speaking at Oak Park elementary schools about his war years and enjoying parades," Buske concludes that young Ernest subsequently "gained his lifelong fascination with war" from his paternal grandfather.[58] Ernest Hall, who died before his grandson's sixth birthday, was not as influential, but his involvement in the Civil War was likewise part of the writer's ancestral lore. Hemingway's enlistment in the Red Cross also grew out of such family stories emphasizing his grandfathers' service.

Religious leaders encouraged participation, too. As recalled by Edward Wagenknecht, valedictorian of Ernest's graduating class in 1917, Hemingway "seemed equally enthusiastic about the sermons of the famous Dr. William Barton of the First Congregational Church and the performance of the Chester Wallace Players at the Warrington Theater."[59] Larry Grimes explains that "in many ways the ministry of [Barton] and the religious ethos of Oak Park are one and the same."[60] Ernest had opportunities not only to hear the sermons of the well-known minister, whose sister Clara was instrumental in founding the American Red Cross, but to read about them as well. Appearing regularly in the pages of the local newspaper, Barton's orations, as Reynolds has pointed out, expressed "ideals that many of his younger parishioners would carry into the Great War."[61] Indeed, as the minister characterized the conflict, it offered potential for "a new and universal brotherliness" to follow.[62] One of his discourses, titled "Our Fight for the Heritage of Humanity," supported the United States' involvement in Europe with a scholarly argument concluding that the decision to wage war was not only morally just but also a logically sound resolution.[63]

Hemingway was likewise motivated by his burgeoning sense of adventurism. From an early age, he wrote about his affinity for world travel and exploration, which, as Reynolds has discussed, was influenced by

Theodore Roosevelt's popular exploits: "I desire to do pioneering or exploring work in the 3 last great frontiers in Africa, central south America or the country around and north of Hudson Bay," Ernest wrote.[64] Nagel has pointed out that Hemingway's grandfathers and parents were well-traveled in Europe, especially Paris, and the writer was inspired to accumulate similar experiences abroad.[65] Paul's discussion of Ted Brumback's ambulance-driving activities on the Western front in the summer of 1917 shows the veteran's stories as a major source of encouragement as well. After Brumback joined the staff of the *Kansas City Star,* the newspaper published thrilling accounts of his tour in France, and the friendship that developed between Ted and Ernest offered plenty of chances to talk about the daring work.[66]

Besides the potential for adventure, Ernest was influenced by the emphasis Americans placed on the need for "doing our bit," a pervasive refrain of the period. One patriotic Oak Parker, for example, helped spread a rumor that the community might not live up to expectations for local recruitment drives.[67] Once the gauntlet had been thrown down, the *Oak Leaves* reported numerous ways in which the town had already taken action: "Oak Park and River Forest probably have given more of their men to the military and naval forces since April 6 than any other community in the country, population considered."[68] Another article indicated that "there is possible forgiveness for the bold opponent of the war, but none for the sneak who hopes to hide out during the conflict."[69] After conscription was instituted, the newspaper published lists of "Our Sailors and Soldiers," and, by the time Hemingway had joined up, the message of the era had become clear: shirkers beware. According to an article in the *Kansas City Star* on May 13, 1918, Hemingway had attempted to enlist eleven times before finally gaining admittance into an overseas outfit.[70] It is no surprise that after he was accepted by the Red Cross, Ernest expressed a sense of relief to Brumback by indicating that his wartime obligation would be fulfilled: "Well, I'm no slacker now," Hemingway told him.[71]

Despite the popularity of the Red Cross, public opinion sometimes reflected a stigma associated with noncombatants during the war. As Reynolds has explained, Theodore Roosevelt had a major impact on perceptions of these roles: "Let him, if a man of fighting age, do his utmost to get into the fighting line—Red Cross work, Y.M.C.A. work, driving ambulances, and the like, excellent though it all is, should be left to men not of military age or unfit for military service, and to women."[72] Hemingway initially expressed a similar point of view in his high school prophecy speech delivered in June of 1917. He predicted that female classmates would assume the duties of Red Cross work in the war and men would serve as soldiers.[73] In July of 1917, Dr. E. E. Persons, major in the Medical Corps of the U.S. Army, however, suggested an alternative outlook. He noted that some volunteers

> have chosen the ambulance service after a much closer examination into its requirements than Colonel Roosevelt has apparently made, and with the knowledge that the casualties in this service have thus far been greater than in any of the fighting services except the field artillery and the aeronautic service. All very young men and old men have been deliberately excluded from this service because of the severity of the work, as past experience has shown that the continuous duty—for 48 to 72 hours at a time—to which these men are subjected tests the endurance of the strongest.[74]

On other occasions, even Roosevelt himself expressed enthusiasm about ambulance driving. He wrote an introduction for "With the American Ambulance in France" by J. R. McConnell in which he applauds men who volunteered before the United States declared war "to try to render some assistance to those who are battling for the right."[75] Similarly, he encouraged a group of Californians heading to France with the corps in May of 1917: "I am proud to appeal to you," he told them. "You are going to do something. I am tired of words. I want deeds."[76] As statements by Roosevelt and Persons suggest, Hemingway's enlistment occurred amid a climate of mixed public perception characterizing Red Cross duty as both dangerous and important work but also less vital than the service of combatants. As a result, Hemingway often called attention to the pseudo-military aspects of his experience.

The final sequence of events that precipitated Hemingway's departure for Italy reflects the flurry of activity and excitement surrounding his imminent journey to war. On April 19, 1918, a few weeks before collecting his last paycheck from the *Kansas City Star*, Hemingway wrote to his parents telling them that "I'll hope to see you about the 2nd. I'll let you know when as soon as I find out."[77] On May 2, Pettus sent a telegram to Hemingway in Oak Park, instructing him to "fill out revised form application" and send one copy to St. Louis, a second to J. Leo Skelley, manager of the "Department Recruiting Personnel, Mechanical Division," at the branch office on Fourth Avenue in New York City, and a third duplicate to the Bureau of Personnel in Washington.[78] On May 4, Brumback wrote to Ernest telling him that he was "awfully glad to get your telegram saying that you can go. For a while I was feeling rather blue, as I thought we would both be held up by red tape. How it came through so suddenly is beyond me." Brumback also responded to some of Hemingway's questions. Ernest wondered about the necessary supplies for the trip, the procedure for getting a passport, and whether or not Ted had any information about a sailing date. Brumback had not received any word himself, and he told Hemingway that Pettus "does not seem to be well posted" either. Even so, he advised Ernest about which clothes to pack, suggesting his Guard outfit as "a roust-a-bout uniform for the front" and provided some last-minute news as it came in by telephone: "Just as this letter was being finished Hop [Charles Hopkins] called up and told me he had received a telegram from Roberts," the Washington correspondent for the *Kansas City Star*, "saying the Italian unit will leave *May 15th.*" That evening, Brumback mailed the letter special delivery to Hemingway's parents in Oak Park, where it arrived on Monday, May 6.[79] A week later, on May 12, Ernest was writing a postcard to Anson and Adelaide aboard a train bound for New York City: "We are at Cleveland and having a great trip. It is a fine bunch of fellows. My love to all."[80] Almost three months after he submitted his initial application, Hemingway was finally headed to the front.

Sometime between his departure from Kansas City and the train ride to New York, he managed to squeeze in a fishing trip. What was initially envisioned as a respite from working at the *Kansas City Star* had abruptly turned into a final adventure in the Michigan woods of his youth.[81] Ernest had invited Brumback, but the latter opted to stay with "the folks" until "the last moment," spending his time learning Italian grammar so "I shall be able to order a bottle of Chianti in approved style" and studying Roman history "as a matter of preparedness." Charles Hopkins was invited as well, and he planned on notifying Hemingway whether he could go by May 5.[82] Bill Smith and Carl Edgar, according to James Mellow, were also among those asked to accompany Ernest for the northern excursion.[83]

Marcelline Hemingway later recalled an exciting story about her brother as having received news about the sailing date via "an Indian runner" who relayed the message to his remote fishing spot in Michigan. Upon getting the dispatch, Ernest and his friends apparently started "running pell-mell for the railroad station. Bearded, filthy, they grabbed up their suitcases at the station and made the only train out of there that day by minutes. They arrived in New York just in time to board the ship."[84] The account is a thrilling one, but the story about boarding the ship at the last minute is untrue. On May 7, the day after Brumback's letter arrived stating that their ship would sail in approximately one week, Clarence sent a message to Horton Bay, notifying his son about the news.[85] When Ernest's train arrived at Grand Central Terminal in Manhattan, however, he had roughly ten days to acclimate to his new role as Red Cross volunteer before boarding the steamship that took him overseas.

Hemingway's initiation into the Red Cross in New York coincided with a peak of support for the embattled Italians as they anticipated an increase in action that summer. After Charles E. Hughes, president of the Italy-America Society, petitioned President Woodrow Wilson for a day to demonstrate American encouragement of its ally, his telegram describing what became known as "Italy-America Day" was published in the *New York Times* on May 13, the day after Hemingway disembarked the train from Chicago:

> The Italy-America Society desires to initiate a national celebration on May 24 in honor of the anniversary of the entrance of Italy into the war. We desire that this celebration shall be an expression to the people of Italy by the people of the United States of our friendship and our grateful acknowledgment of the achievements of Italy in carrying out the unswerving purposes of the Allies.[86]

Hughes wrote state governors requesting observance throughout the country, and American citizens were asked to display Italian colors near storefront windows. A slogan was developed: "Wear flowers to signify America's friendship for her Italian allies."[87] Newton Baker, U.S. secretary of war, delivered a speech at the Metropolitan Opera House, and Enrico Caruso, the well-known Italian tenor, famous for a recording of the George M. Cohan song "Over There," performed as part of the celebration. Hemingway's reference to Caruso in the opening pages of *A Farewell to Arms* indicates a mixed response among soldiers debating whether or not the singer "bellows."[88] In May of 1918, however, the vocalist's popularity was central in promoting the American bond with Italy. Hemingway departed from New York prior to Italy-America Day festivities, but announcements for preparations were ongoing throughout his visit.

The Italy-America Day publicity paralleled Red Cross objectives for countering German propaganda abroad. One *New York Times* article indicated that

> insinuations that America is not entering whole-heartedly into the war [are] to be combated by 100,000 letters which will be sent to Italy by American Italians and other Americans on Italy-America Day, and each letter will start a chain system, which, it is believed, will flood that country. The recipients of the letters are being asked in each case to pass them on to their friends, and in this way it is expected that a true picture of America's participation in the war and of its friendly attitude toward Italy will be presented to millions of Italians within a comparatively short time.[89]

As Hemingway was beginning to learn about his role as a volunteer abroad, news reports essentially underscored that mission: to communicate a "friendly attitude" as one measure of American commitment to Italy until military forces could arrive.

Ernest's initiation also coincided with a culmination of support for his organization. New York City Mayor John F. Hylan announced that "Red Cross Week" would begin on May 20. Efforts to back the group were ubiquitous, and the mayor's proclamation proposed among a flurry of other activities an outward display of allegiance through fundraising and volunteerism. "I hereby direct," he wrote,

> that during the week of May 20 to 27 the flag of the American Red Cross shall be displayed upon public buildings in the city, and I call upon all inhabitants of the city appropriately to decorate their buildings and to display therefrom, beside the flag of the United States, the colors of the Red Cross.[90]

Demonstrations of patriotism spurred on financial contributions to replenish the war chest during a second fund drive to raise one hundred million dollars. Theaters hosted celebrity appearances along with "Gala

Events" devised to entertain and solicit donations. Madison Square Garden held boxing exhibitions; the Hotel Astor staged a benefit ball promising that "everybody you ever heard of will be there"; and the week culminated with another concert performance by Enrico Caruso.[91] As a result, volunteers occupied an exclusive spotlight highlighting their service as a key component of the war effort.

Along with several other newly minted recruits, Hemingway participated in the main event, the Red Cross Parade. On May 18, thousands of war workers marched through Manhattan amid crowds of spectators. Hemingway noted the attention he and his organization received when he wrote about the pageant in a letter home: "We paraded 85 blocks down 5th ave today and were reviewed by President Wilson. About #75,000 were in line and we were ye star attraction."[92] The *New York Times* deemed it "the greatest Red Cross demonstration that has ever taken place in the United States."[93] Cities throughout the country held similar events, and all told, approximately five million people had amassed to participate in what newspapers generally referred to as a nationwide "parade of mercy."[94]

News reports likewise praised Red Cross volunteers already serving abroad. A few days before Hemingway's departure, the *New York Times* published a summary of aid over the previous five months, including reference to the "four ambulance sections and seven mobile kitchens giving hot coffee and American jam to the tired soldiers" in Italy. The foreign military had been "very grateful for this small but humane service," and the work was acknowledged as "the creation of good-will between the two countries."[95] Volunteers were commended by high-ranking officials as well. Ambassador Page, King Victor Emmanuel III, Premier Vittorio Orlando, and Pope Benedict XV all issued statements of gratitude.

Considering the prevailing climate of enthusiasm for Red Cross work in Italy, it is not surprising that Hemingway's correspondence from New York often reflected a keen sense of romantic adventure. As in his letters on Guard service, he called attention to the importance of his nonmilitary role by associating it with that of a combatant: "We are treated the same as aviators and while all honorary officers we have non coms in our co. to drill the men," he wrote home.[96] Another comment specified a rank that was not typically assigned to Red Cross workers: "I am corporal of the 1st Squad," he told his parents in a description of the procession down Fifth Avenue.[97] By the end of the event, he had been promoted: "I was made a sergeant in ye squadron and led the 2nd Platoon out In the middle of the avenue all by myself and saluted Ye Great Woodrow."[98] Considering Hemingway's practice with the Home Guard, it is possible that he was made responsible for organizing other Red Cross volunteers for presentation, but his comments on status achieved in New York incorrectly suggest that he was climbing the ranks of a military organization.

Hemingway's letters also emphasized privileges resulting from his newly acquired Red Cross uniform, which resembled the dress of actual soldiers. After donning the garb, he wrote that "all privates and non commissioned officers have to salute us."[99] The experience turned out to be "the biggest bore," he pointed out: "If you go up town at night it is awful because there are thousands of soldiers in town."[100] His letter to Dale Wilson echoes the same sentiment: "Well they have slipped us our uniforms and we are now Honorary 1st Lieuts. Ye G't Hem's'n [Hemingstein] stalked down Broadway and returned 367 salutes night before last. Since then he rides on a bus. It's easier on the right arm."[101] Although he seemed to have become annoyed by the need to return salutes, his descriptions nonetheless call attention to a role of commanding officer with authority over enlisted men in U.S. armed forces. Hemingway's honorary rank as second lieutenant, however, applied only to the Italian army. The uniform was typically not allowed to be worn in America, but he had special permission to do so, considering the events of Red Cross Week. Even then, however, "the required outfit" included a red enamel Geneva cross and bronze "U.S." letters as the "only insignia" authorized for wear while at home; no additional marks of rank were permitted. The privileges according him status similar to military personnel were, more importantly, designed to suggest the appearance of additional Allied troops on the ground in Italy.[102]

Besides describing his soldierly status, Hemingway made an exaggerated claim about his role in the Red Cross parade. On the day of the procession, his letter home somewhat casually announced that, similar to Anson Hemingway, who led Civil War veterans amid memorial celebrations in Oak Park, Ernest would be "at the head of the parade."[103] As reported by the *New York Times* the day after, however, instead of Ernest Hemingway, President Wilson took the lead in what turned out to be an exciting publicity stunt deemed "more dramatic and thrilling than any demonstration witnessed in this city since the war began."[104]

Following Wilson was another noted spectacle: a "human cross" composed of nurses. After these women came an assemblage of dignitaries who were followed by legions of supporters, including French soldiers, various local chapters of Boy Scouts, members of the Red Cross Junior League, and among others, those who made up the Loyal Order of Moose. Ernest marched somewhere in that crowd as well, but his position was no more extraordinary than the vast majority of his fellow participants. Indeed, Hemingway had failed to mention another significant point, which was described as the "greatest procession ever held of women engaged in war work."[105] Instead, he elevated his involvement to suggest a leadership role, and the statement did not go unnoticed in Oak Park. His mother wrote to him: "My! but wouldn't the folks 'back home' like to have seen you leading the parade & saluting 'dear Woodrow'. We all swelled out at the very thought."[106]

Hemingway's letters also show the ways in which he began to conflate notions of love and war. After two days in New York, he wrote his parents that "I've always planned to get married if I could ever get to be an officer, you know."[107] As Nagel has discussed, the statement was part of a joke he played to fool his mother and father into believing he had become engaged to Mae Marsh, the well-known actress who appeared in D. W. Griffith's *Birth of a Nation*.[108] Hemingway had expressed an adolescent crush on Marsh at least as early as March 2, 1918, when he wrote Marcelline from Kansas City commenting on the movie star's most recent release, *Beloved Traitor*. "Any way Kid," he wrote, "that was no idle Jest about the Great Hem_____y being in love. And the one [that] he is in love with is none other than that Mae Marsh, [whom] you and Sam glimpsed. If she would ever become Mrs. HemOOOOOOO__y joy would reign supreme. . . . Maybe she will love me enough some day."[109] In New York, his infatuation over the actress led him to express, as Nagel articulates it, a "naïve interest in the subject of romance and his willingness to invent where it did not exist."[110] Hemingway's parents, however, did not welcome news of the engagement, and it took more than one letter from Ernest to convince them that he had made it up. Both Clarence and Grace tried to point out the consequences of their son's folly, but his mother's letter stands out:

I do trust you will think hard before making such a mistake as to marry at 18, and without any income or visible means of support. I fear you do not realize what a laughing stock you would make of your-self. Marriage is a beautiful and wonderful thing; but it is sacred in proportion to the prayerfulness with which it is entered into. You may come home disfigured and crippled; would this girl love you then? A marriage ceremony should be followed by constant companionship, a little love nest, a bit of heaven roofed over + walled in, for just two loving souls.—Such marriage as you suggest, would be unnatural and apt to bring great sorrow and misunderstanding.[111]

Lynn suggests that Grace's letter angered Ernest because it forced him to confess that his story was a lie. Lynn postulates that Grace's description of marriage, as compared to her own relationship with Hemingway's fa-ther, "must have further enraged him by its almost comic hypocrisy."[112] Whether Hemingway became angry or not as a result is unclear; more importantly, Grace's letter prefigures much about Ernest's love affair with Agnes von Kurowsky that developed in the late summer of 1918, and her description of a meaningful relationship hints at themes on mar-riage that became central to his fiction—as in related passages from "In Another Country," "Now I Lay Me," and A Farewell to Arms.

After less than two weeks in New York, Hemingway's pursuit of ad-venture intensified when he took passage on the steamship Chicago for Bordeaux on May 23.[113] C. E. Frazer Clark, who traveled on the same ship in February of 1917, described the vessel as "a coal-burning, twin-screw, steel-hulled steamer, with a spar deck stem to stern for ocean watching, and three decks below."[114] After setting sail that spring of 1918, Ernest referred to it as "the rottenest tub in the world."[115]

At the time Hemingway boarded the Chicago, the ship had an estab-lished record of dangerous journeys through the feared German subma-rine zone of the Atlantic.[116] By May of 1918, the risk of an encounter with an enemy vessel was somewhat reduced, but some potential for attack remained.[117] As Ted Brumback wrote about his journey with Heming-way, however, "we went over on no American transport convoyed by de-stroyers. The venerable Chicago braved the submarine zone alone."[118] As a result, passengers were required to undergo precautionary measures. Among others, the lifeboat drill was the most prevalent reminder of peril associated with wartime travel.

Such safety measures became not only commonplace but also a popular subject for writers communicating the experience of going to war. Richard

Harding Davis wrote an article on the topic in November of 1915. He describes the type of drill that Hemingway engaged in a few years later:

> Each passenger on the *Chicago* was assigned to a lifeboat. He was advised to find out how from any part of the ship at which he might be caught he could soonest reach it. Women and children were to assemble on the boat deck by the boat to which they were assigned. After they had been lowered to the water the men, who meanwhile were to be segregated on the deck below them, would descend by rope ladders. Entrance to a boat was by ticket only. The tickets were six inches square and bore a number. If you lost your ticket you lost your life. Each of the more imaginative passengers insured his life by fastening the ticket to his clothes with a safety pin.[119]

Bates wrote of a similar introduction to lifeboat drills noting the "free card of admission" that he preserved "with great care!"[120] Clark explains that, during drills, lifeboats were even swung out over the water from davits before passengers could debark back onto the main ship, and upon entering the submarine zone, the emergency crafts were maintained in ready position until the *Chicago* reached safer waters.[121]

Hemingway's letters, along with Brumback's account of the journey published in 1936, indicate that Ernest regarded these threats with little concern; moreover, he seemed to relish the chance for danger. Hemingway wrote to his parents about the news reports before departure: "It may be cheering news to you that the U. Boats have not sunk a ship between the US. and France since the Last of March. They are pretty jolly well bottled up."[122] In a letter written at sea, he included another lighthearted comment: "Well we are approaching our port of deebarkation and are entering the widely known submarine zone so I will get this epistle off so you will besure and get one any way. Very cheerful thought what aint it?"[123] Brumback also recalled that Hemingway was excited at the possibility of sighting an enemy ship. By journey's end, after failing to do so, Ernest apparently "felt he'd been cheated." The lack of a sufficient number of lifeboats did not seem to bother Hemingway either, for when confronted with that fact, he patted his "ancient life preserver" and said, as Brumback wrote, "we've got as good a chance as those in the boats. They might get shelled anyway." Indeed, the lifeboat drills, having become somewhat irksome to many passengers and staff, presented Hemingway with an opportunity for good humor. "The barman had no use for the drills," Brumback mentioned, but Hemingway convinced him nonetheless to pose for a photograph during one such practice session.[124]

Considering that the *Chicago* never encountered an enemy vessel while crossing the Atlantic, Charles Fenton notes that the ship "was in every way a disappointment" for Hemingway. Even so, the voyage allowed Ernest to tighten his bond among the coterie of war personnel heading to the front.[125] As Bates wrote in his diary describing the journey two years prior, a contagious sense of excitement often pervaded the group of volunteers onboard who became united in their shared objective in the conflict overseas. "All of us Ambulance men are animated with the same spirit," he explained. "It is a refreshing and invigorating atmosphere: action and enthusiasm are in the air."[126] Similarly, as Carlos Baker has pointed out, Hemingway wrote in his letters about associates he came to know during his crossing: "Ted [Brumback] and I and Howell Jenkins are paling together and having the grand time," he told his parents.[127] Nagel notes that Ernest also became friends with Bill Horne, a Princeton graduate from Yonkers, New York, and Frederick Spiegel, another Illinois native; he also spent time "with two Polish Lieutenants."[128] An endless poker game and opportunities for shooting craps offered other chances for interacting with various shipmates. "Here you had to be a quick thinker," Brumback recalled, "for you were apt to be 'covered' in French, English, Belgian, Italian, or American money. Hemingway tried it but found that he was behind although he'd won."[129] The friendships Ernest cultivated with Horne and Jenkins lasted throughout his stay in Italy and even after the war.

After the *Chicago* arrived at Bordeaux on June 3,[130] Hemingway and his fellow volunteers spent their day sampling food and drink.[131] Bates described his earlier arrival at the same port:

I stuck my head out of the porthole and a sight truly beautiful met my gaze. We were in a narrow river. So narrow that one could have tossed a stone from the decks to either bank. Sloping gently down to the water were green fields and vineyards, dotted with poplar and willow trees. Further back on the low hills were old chateaux and little red-tiled houses. It seemed one vast park as far as the eye could reach.[132]

One of Hemingway's coworkers, John Bauby, wrote about "thousands of barrels of wine" that were delayed for shipment.[133] While Hemingway's time in the town was brief, the locale made a favorable impression: "Paris is a great city," he mentioned a few days later, "but is not as quaint and interesting as Bordeaux."[134] The young volunteer expressed an initial captivation with European culture, but it would take a few more years and a recommendation from Sherwood Anderson before Paris would claim a central role in his life.

After leaving Bordeaux on a night train, Hemingway's first visit to the French capital led to more preferential treatment bestowed upon Red Cross workers. As Baker has pointed out, the U.S. Army uniforms they wore resulted in "unusual deference" as "French combat officers saluted their wrinkled, ill-fitting uniforms" in light of the recent success achieved by American marines at Belleau Wood.[135] Hemingway acknowledged the exceptional aspects of his journey in a postcard home: "We've been treated like Kings," he wrote.[136] The interior of "Number Four," the Red Cross headquarters at *place de la Concord,* where volunteers were required to register, emphasized the royal treatment. Edward Hungerford describes the location as "a club building—originally a palace with crystal chandeliers and red carpets and high ceilings and all the things that go ordinarily to promote luxury and comfort."[137] The *place de la Concorde* site was not only a significant locale for Red Cross work but later became, along with the nearby Hotel Crillon, center of operations for the American Peace Delegation in 1919.[138] Years after, Hemingway portrayed the hotel in *The Sun Also Rises* as the place that Brett Ashley designates for a meeting with Jake Barnes, an appointment she fails to keep. As an eighteen-year-old volunteer, Ernest noted his impressions of the famed public square and the turmoil of a bygone era in a letter to his parents: "Our hotel is right on the place D'La Concorde where the[y] guillotined Marie Antoinette and Sidney Carton."[139] Hemingway's letter to Clarence and Grace was written on stationary from the Hotel Florida, 12 Boulevard Malesherbes, which is, while not quite "on" the historic location mentioned in the epistle, close enough to identify his lodgings with the more well-known site. Presumably, he stayed at the Florida.[140]

With no other formal duties in Paris, Hemingway spent time visiting the major attractions. He wrote home with news of his itinerary:

This afternoon Ted and Jenks (who you met at the train Dad) went all through the Hotel Des Invalides. Napoleans Tomb. They have a wonderful exhibit of captured enemy artillery and air planes there. It covers several acres. We have been all over the city in the ancient two cylinder busses that pass for taxis. You can ride for an hour for about 1 Franc. Have seen all the sights—the Champs Elysee, Tuilleries, Louve Invalides Arc D'Triomphe etc.

Experiences such as these marked the origin of the writer's trademark pursuit of travel. "If the war ever ends," Hemingway wrote from Paris, "I intend to bum all through this country."[141] He had been on the continent for less than three days and already expressed plans for a more extensive tour.

The German shelling of the city with the long-range artillery, known as Big Bertha, did not seem to dampen Hemingway's spirits either.[142] Brumback recalled that Ernest was eager to hire a taxi and hunt down shell craters even though the proposition made Ted "nervous." The older volunteer suggested they "better use a little discretion," but Hemingway's penchant for thrill seeking trumped Brumback's sense of caution; the two managed to track down a shell burst that damaged the façade of the Hotel Madeleine. Ted's account indicates that Ernest's exploits were influenced by journalistic aspirations. "Hemingway was as excited as if he'd been sent on special assignment to cover the biggest story of the year," he remembered. While he could not recall if Hemingway ever composed a story about the "taxi adventure," Brumback said that this "sort of subject was right up his alley."[143] Indeed, Ernest's description of the bombardment in his letter home suggests a reporter's sensibility:

The people accept the shells as a matter of course and hardly show any interest in their arrival. We heard our first shell arrive soon after Breakfast. Nothing but a dull boom (like blasting at Summitt[)]. We had no means of knowing where it hit but it was a long way away.

There were several more during the day but no one evinced any alarm or even interest. However about 4 oclock Booom came one that seemed about 100 hundred yards away. We looked to see where it had fallen but an English artillery officer told us it alighted at least a mile away.[144]

Even though Hemingway never captured this experience in journalism or fiction, his epistolary description prefigures dispatches he later wrote as a foreign correspondent and indicates an initial stage of development as a writer dealing with the effects of war.

Besides the introduction to combat artillery and its impact on an urban environment, Paris afforded Hemingway an opportunity to enhance his nondescript Red Cross uniform. Before leaving the city, he wrote home about the Sam Browne belt he purchased, an addition to his garb that made him "look like the proverbial million dollars."[145] The accoutrement was just as extravagant as his letter indicated, for the leather band worn with a Red Cross uniform was not only superfluous but also somewhat misleading. The shoulder strap was originally designed to stabilize scabbard and pistol holsters attached to the waist belt, and the accessory ultimately came to be associated with the trappings of a military officer. Since Hemingway was not required to carry either sword or pistol, and he was not a commissioned officer in an armed force, the addition proved solely ornamental and might have allowed him to be more readily mistaken for a soldier. Such belts were banned in the United States in 1917, and the decoration was criticized by some as an unnecessary "mark of privilege" that led to the segregation of enlisted men from their superiors.[146] They "serve no useful purpose," one article indicated, "but set off the uniform of an officer."[147] In Paris, the ban no longer applied, and Ernest was free to don the accessory as he pleased.

Hemingway was not alone among Red Cross workers who added such ornaments to their standard-issue uniforms. An article in the monthly newspaper published by Section One of the ambulance service notes other embellishments: "Regardless of consequences," the piece states,

> this paper comes out flat-footedly against the wearing of spurs by Red Cross officers. English officers returning from Rome recently brought rumors that beautiful, clanking spurs were seen on an American Red Cross lieutenant who probably had never straddled a horse without rockers on it. *Come Stà* didn't believe it. Then we went to Rome ourselves. And we saw the same thing. We blushed and appeared not to see. After that we examined every Red Cross officer's heels before we saluted. Then we came back to camp and penned this. P.S. This is a serious editorial.[148]

Although Sam Browne belts were more commonplace than spurs, the enhancements were still conspicuous among seasoned Red Cross workers suspicious of colleagues' attempts to overdo their appearance. Hemingway's purchase of the accessory, moreover, indicates a romantic point of view associating his uniform with that of a dashing officer.

After departing Paris on an overnight train that arrived in Milan on Friday, June 7, Hemingway's first day in Italy included exposure to the brutal reality of war. When an explosion occurred in a storage area at the Sutter and Thevenot munitions factory outside of Bollate, fourteen kilometers northwest of Milan, Hemingway and his colleagues were conveyed to the site to help.[149] As Luca Gandolfi has discussed, after extinguishing fires, they collected dead bodies and other remains that littered the countryside. Although one news report on the memorial service told of "twenty-one coffins containing entire bodies and ten coffins containing the fragments of other victims," the blast had claimed thirty-five lives.[150] As the incident comprised Hemingway's initiation into the horrors of war, it is noteworthy that the experience occurred not on a battlefield but at a civilian factory employing female workers in the manufacture of munitions. Since the disaster took the lives of all those involved, Hemingway did not witness pain and suffering typically associated with transporting and caring for wounded. Indeed, his initial Red Cross duty was conducted in a relatively calm countryside instead of the chaos of the front most ambulance drivers experienced while hauling casualties. Other aspects of the incident were troubling, however, and had a long-lasting effect on him. Because the explosion resulted in the scattering of human body parts, the experience was particularly gruesome. He also expressed his disturbance over the fact that all of the casualties were women.

Hemingway later recalled aspects of the experience at Bollate in *Death in the Afternoon*.[151] Ernest's poignant reflection on the episode, which he titled "A Natural History of the Dead," initially appeared at the end of chapter 12:

> We drove to the scene of the disaster in trucks along poplar-shaded roads, bordered with ditches containing much minute animal life, which I could not clearly observe because of the great clouds of dust raised by the trucks. Arriving where the munition plant had been,

some of us were put to patrolling about those large stocks of munitions which for some reason had not exploded, while others were put
at extinguishing a fire which had gotten into the grass of an adjacent
field, which task being concluded, we were ordered to search the immediate vicinity and surrounding fields for bodies. We found and carried to an improvised mortuary a good number of these and, I must
admit, frankly, the shock it was to find that these dead were women
rather than men.[152]

Although Hemingway later described the munitions plant episode from
the perspective of a mature writer, he wrote about the rite of passage in
the spring of 1918 with youthful exuberance. In a postcard to colleagues
at the *Kansas City Star*, he stated: "Having a wonderful time!!! Had my
baptism of fire my first day here, when an entire munition plant exploded. We carried them in like at the General Hospital, Kansas City. I
go to the front tomorrow. Oh, Boy!!! I'm glad I'm in it."[153] Still a novice
in war, Hemingway had not expressed any outright cynicism after the
ghastly conditions in Bollate.

Before leaving Milan, he received a specific assignment with the ambulance service. The week before he arrived, Captain Utassy and the
Harvard volunteers were entertained by Major Guy Lowell and Captain
Bates at a dinner in honor of new drivers before they left for their sections around the first of June. After the initial contingent of recruits
were distributed among the first three ambulance units, Bates returned
to Red Cross headquarters at Vicenza and left Meade Detweiler in
charge to receive Hemingway's group. Designated to replace the last of
the drivers whose enlistments were about to expire on June 10, Ernest
and some of his friends were assigned to Schio.[154] He wrote a postcard
to his father from Milan on June 9 indicating his mailing address: "Section 4. Italian ambulance Croce Rosa Americana. Milano. Italy."[155] After nearly a month-long journey, he had finally secured a position near
the frontlines of the Great War. His tenure in active service was already
more than half over.

Three   **Active Duty**

After Ernest Hemingway left New York in the spring of 1918, he told his parents that his period of active duty would begin "from the day we start driving" and "probably carry us pretty well into the winter."[1] Instead, his term as an ambulance driver lasted for only fifteen days. When he joined the canteen service immediately following, his work continued for another two weeks before he was wounded.[2] In many ways, the locales near Schio and the Piave River where he operated during this "shortlived tour," as Michael Reynolds has explained, "bore no resemblance to the front at which Frederic [Henry] had served for two years as an ambulance driver in the Italian army."[3] Nevertheless, the existing records add not only important details of Hemingway's biography but also show that he incorporated substantial material from his experience into *A Farewell to Arms* and his other writing about the Great War. Indeed, many aspects of the fictional settings and themes originated with his time in the ambulance and canteen units that lasted for roughly one month during the late spring and early summer of 1918.

By June of that year, the Red Cross service was approaching the peak of its effectiveness in the field. Earlier that spring the corps had included "135 ambulance drivers," as James Nagel has pointed out.[4] By the time of Hemingway's arrival, the outfit increased to 148 men, with six more scheduled to arrive in July.[5] Indeed, Robert W. Bates noted that the recruitment campaign conducted during April by George Utassy had been so successful that they even "had men to spare."[6] The new volunteers were divided among four sections, and there was a fifth in the formative stages but not yet fully deployed. Distributed directly behind the front, the units were headquartered in locations that stretched from the mountainous area in the west to the lowlands of the Piave River, which becomes increasingly marshy in the coastal region of the Veneto.

Hemingway's section at Schio was situated in a picturesque locale some twenty-six kilometers northwest of Vicenza in the Leogra Valley at the base of the Little Dolomites. James Mellow indicates that the town was "about four miles from the Austrian lines."[7] Even so, it was the farthest from the Piave, where the most intense action developed during June and July. With thirty-six drivers, Section Four was also the largest group among the five units.[8] According to Bates, they aided the "5th Army Corps of the 1st Army."[9] The town, known for textile production, provided accommodations in a wool factory with access to another building for a kitchen. The drivers had ample parking nearby for their vehicles: seventeen Fiat and six Ford ambulances, two trucks, a staff car, and a motorcycle.[10]

The other divisions were located east of Schio: Section One was attached to the Ninth Army Corps at Bassano near Monte Grappa; Section Two operated with the Thirteenth Army Corps from Roncade, a town north of Venice; and Section Three served the Twenty-Third Army Corps in the same region from Casale Sul Sile.[11] After members of the fifth unit picked up their newly manufactured ambulances from Varese on July 4, the "Yankee Doodle Section," as they referred to themselves, entered the field the following week and worked from Fanzolo between the Bassano and Roncade posts.[12]

Hemingway arrived three days after Captain Bates issued his latest memo dealing with a lingering controversy over "the matter of censorship." Bates had asked the heads of each unit to "please explain" for "the benefit of the new men" the "trouble we have had in the past and warn them against any improper remarks." After receiving a report from the General Intendenza stating that another missive was "held up by the censor," the captain announced that the government had agreed to send "the objectionable letter" to Red Cross administrators "so that we are able to fasten the blame on an individual man." Bates also explained that "we are requested by the Supreme Command to notify them of whatever action we take." The latest memo, he noted, had been distributed "as a warning to the new men who may not realize the seriousness of the censorship situation." The "old men," he mentioned, "have been sufficiently warned."[13]

Indeed, John Dos Passos was a central figure in the controversy, and despite his claim that he had met Hemingway in 1918, the "censorship situation" actually led the experienced driver away from the front as Ernest journeyed closer to the action.[14] While Hemingway was aboard the *Chi-*

cago anticipating heading "right out to the lines" to "take the place of the gang whose time is up," Dos Passos was in Lucca, Italy, some three hundred kilometers south of the battle zone.[15] On June 1, he wrote that the

> day before yesterday I was just sitting down to sketch the Bassano mountains when news came that Utany's [Utassy's] Millions were on hand and that we were to go into Vicenza that afternoon. We were joyful at the idea of going and the general staff was joyous at the idea of getting rid of us—so the incident was closed.[16]

Even so, after Dos Passos arrived in Rome a few days later, he wrote that he was still "under the ridiculous accusation of being *proGerman*, . . . but I think we are managing to prove our innocence to Red Cross officials."[17] Bates implied that he, at least, would not be easily swayed, for he believed that Dos Passos had "endangered the cordial relations between us and the Italians" despite "repeated warnings." Regarding the "group of Pacifists" from Section One to which Dos Passos allegedly belonged, the captain suggested, moreover, that "we need not give them further employment."[18] Dos Passos's letter to Rumsey Marvin implies that officials had followed Bates's recommendation: "My term in the Red Cross in Italy has expired," he wrote, "I am going to France to see what else I can get to do."[19] Even after leaving Rome by the end of June, he was still embroiled in the affair: "At present I'm in Paris fussing and squabbling and trying to clear myself of charges—a hell of a nasty business," he explained in another letter to Marvin.[20] Despite his efforts, however, Dos Passos was not allowed to reenlist. In fact, out of the volunteers who originally made up the first three sections from France, only nineteen were permitted to sign up again. Since Section Four came to include at least a dozen of the drivers who did stay on, many of Hemingway's fellow servicemen were pioneers from the Western front, but Dos Passos was not among them.[21]

On June 9, Hemingway was still in Milan, where he wrote to his father telling him that "we go to the front tomorrow."[22] Before proceeding to Schio, he checked in with Captain Bates at the Palazzo Pigatti headquarters in Vicenza.[23] Ernest was registered according to the date of his initial service helping with the explosion aftermath in Bollate on June 7.[24] In a 1923 letter to Bill Horne, Hemingway remembered the "hot day in June" when his group first reported to their supervisor, recalling in particular "what a shit Capt. Bates was."[25] Even so, Bates noted that he had welcomed the new recruits with enthusiasm. Not only had he been in the midst of disagreements with many of the veteran drivers whose enlistments were about to expire, but the corps was also on the brink of its "first real activity" since arriving the previous December.[26] Bates indicated that he was excited to engage the work of new, even inexperienced, volunteers and that the men were arriving in "the nick of time."[27]

The most influential figure in the service during the summer and fall of 1918, Bates not only held a prominent role in shaping the nature of the outfit, but the story of his initial involvement also suggests key aspects that resonate with themes Hemingway later dealt with in his writing. Before heading the units in Italy, Ernest's commanding officer had acquired a reputation for exemplary service on the Western front.[28] When the war broke out in August of 1914, he had been living in Boston working with his uncle at the Bates-Mitchell Piano Company after having graduated from Harvard three years prior. Like many others, he anticipated "the greatest conflict the world has ever seen" and one that would "probably be the last."[29] On May 8, 1915, after a German submarine torpedoed the *Lusitania,* he recorded the event in his diary: "It is a terrible thing," he wrote, "and makes my blood boil."[30] In February of 1916, after one of his frequent dinners at the Harvard Club, he spent the evening reading Leslie Buswell's *With the American Ambulance Field Service in France.* "It was the letters of an ambulance driver," he noted in his journal, "and gave me exactly the information I have wanted."[31] A few months later, Bates submitted an application to serve in Richard Norton's corps and sailed for Europe at the end of April.

His first tour of duty with Section Seven in France coincided with some of the most intense combat in World War I and made for a particularly daunting trial by fire for the "gentlemen volunteer."[32] In a diary entry describing his work at the Battle of Verdun, he explained the conditions:

> The infirmary was the cellar of a house; it was crowded to overflowing; there were so many stretchers on the floor that it was almost impossible to enter the room, and the atmosphere was fetid. We had to lay our poor fellows outside in the rain. The doctors wanted us to keep them in the machine until they could take them but we could not; we had to go back for more. And then there was the fight for stretchers.

We had to make them dump wounded men off stretchers and give them to us; it was fight, fight, fight, and then off in a rush.[33]

In another passage, he referred to the hauling of the wounded: "The suffering of those poor devils was frightful as we pounded and banged over the bumpy road. I could hardly keep my balance, and as we struck an extra hard bump, they all cried out in chorus." Instances of battle fatigue and hysteria were common: "This last trip to Balycourt" he wrote, "one of the men was out of his head. He was on a top stretcher and tried to pull the man across the way off his stretcher, so I had to ride inside and hold him. It was like being shut up in a cage with wild animals." He told about another soldier who was "crazy, curled up at one end of the stretcher, peeking out from under his blanket and then pulling it over his head." A German that he met underwent suffering that was more "mental than physical" as well. Bates suggested that despite having been taken captive, the prisoner was better off for having escaped the trenches. The man agreed and announced "that he was through with the war."[34] Upon completing this intense period of service, Bates copied out excerpts from his diary in letters home to friends and family, adding that his days in the battle zone "came the nearest to hell of any that I ever hope to go thru. . . . Thank God there is only one Verdun." He even wondered if he had been a "fool" to have gone to Europe in the first place.[35]

After experiencing the action for himself, Bates began to mistrust other accounts of the situation at the front. He read about battles in newspapers and magazines but found that stories did not match up with events as he observed them. Some descriptions, moreover, seemed utterly inadequate when compared to the actual circumstances of combat. He noted one news report, for example, that summarized a night of horror by referring only to a "violent bombardment on the right bank of the Meuse."[36] Bates even came to ridicule Buswell's *With the American Ambulance Field Service in France,* the volume that inspired him to volunteer in the first place: "It beats any funny book I ever read," he wrote, "and I've been shouting extracts to an amused audience in nearby tents."[37] Also wary of his own descriptions sent to friends and family, Bates sometimes added comments so as not to appear overly valorous: "I suppose that my letters sound pretty strong but I do hope I haven't given you any 'I'm a noble little hero' stuff. There is nothing of the hero stuff about it," he explained.[38]

When Bates returned to Europe in the summer of 1917 for a second tour, his prior experience earned him a position as chief of Section Sixty-Three. Although the unit never offered a chance to aid soldiers amid intense action like he underwent at Verdun, his leadership role ultimately led him to the position as head of Hemingway's outfit. After Sixty-Three was disbanded during militarization, Major C. G. Osborne, director of transportation in Paris, offered Bates a job directing the drivers on the Austro-Italian front. Trying to enlist as a soldier with the Foreign Legion at the time, Bates initially thought about passing up the opportunity: "There is a strong desire in the heart of every man who has been over here as long as I," he wrote, "to wear the 'regular' uniform, to be one of the crowd, a fetish or no, I have it as badly as anyone." The prospect of foreign armed service, however, finally lost its appeal: "To throw away a big chance for service in the R. C.," he explained, "to take a small job in the regular army just for the sake of satisfying this desire seemed weak-minded." When Osborne told Robert Perkins, commissioner of the American Red Cross in Rome, that Bates had decided to accept the position, Perkins agreed that he was "just the man for Italy."[39]

Bates was a strict disciplinarian who valued his role supervising the drivers and managing the vehicles. Among other duties, he often reconnoitered the front in preparation for major offensives and made frequent visits to the sections overseeing the conduct of his volunteers. Not long after he signed on, Bates gave each group a "little talk" about "what would be required of them under the organization of which I was now head."[40] In one diary entry, he recalled that his tactics, especially in curtailing expense accounts, led him to become "extremely unpopular with both officers and men."[41] In addition to his persistent demands regarding the censorship issue, which led him to ban Dos Passos from reenlistment, Bates reminded volunteers to abstain from drinking, avoid infection from venereal disease, and refrain from joy rides in the ambulances.[42] He instructed them on matters of "courtesy toward the Italian people" as well, noting that

> it is not exaggerated to raise one's hat if in civilian clothes or salute if in uniform, when asking a direction or acknowledging a courtesy from a stranger.
>
> On the contrary, failure to do so indicates to the foreigner lack of breeding and to other Americans, ignorance.[43]

He recommended another policy suggesting that

> the men salute 1, on first meeting their officers outside in the morning; 2, when they meet them outside of the encampment; 3, and on any other occasions when their own judgment tells them it is appropriate. According to regulations saluting is not required when driving a car.[44]

Bates also requested that persons in charge of each section submit summaries of weekly activities to Vicenza, and when they neglected to do so, he reminded them of their noncompliance. The captain himself sent monthly, and sometimes weekly, reports to the headquarters in Rome.

Not long before Hemingway's group had arrived, Bates wrote to his family that he had become disheartened by the many duties he shouldered and had felt isolated among the men. He even entertained the possibility of "quitting" and renewing his attempt to enter a military outfit: "I am so weary of honors that I never sought, of work that I never bargained for, and of responsibilities that have been thrust on me, that I would welcome a relief," he told them.[45] Nevertheless, the captain remained loyal through the armistice in November. Indeed, the arrival of the new recruits in June played no small part in revitalizing his commitment, and the action that ensued during the coming months led to his most significant contributions while serving in Italy.

While Captain Bates directed the drivers from Vicenza, Major Guy Lowell served as the supervisor in Rome and had a significant influence on Hemingway's unit as well.[46] As director of the Department of Military Affairs, Lowell headed up the entire branch of Red Cross activity that not only included the ambulance and canteen operations but also accounted for various hospital work along with distributions of gifts to soldiers. During his frequent visits to Vicenza, Lowell often accompanied Bates on trips to the battle zone for meetings with local officials in addition to checking on each of the sections. Lowell was also responsible for documenting the activities of his department in monthly reports, and his descriptions of the work at the front relied heavily on accounts submitted to him by Bates.

Lowell not only served as an important figure in the Red Cross, but he also had an established reputation as a prominent architect.[47] Prior to the war, he had lived in Italy to pursue his studies, and he renewed that interest during visits to the battle zone in 1918. After compiling a series of photographs for a book on villas built in the manner of influential Renaissance designer Andrea Palladio, the major noted that working around Vicenza offered a particularly rich opportunity for research. "By the perversity of the gods, and principally of the great god Mars," he wrote,

> there was a veritable court of Italian attendants, officers, soldiers, and servants, hospitably provided by the Italian Army to make easy the work of a small band of Americans who had come to express to the fighting soldiers of Italy, through the American Red Cross, America's friendliness and desire to help. So I came strongly under the spell of the great architect [Palladio] and in my leisure moments had an unequalled chance to study his works and his influence,— the more so because we seemed to have gone back to the life of his times. The darkened streets at night, the picturesque uniforms, the capes and the swords, the nearby fighting, the daily trips to the country through the broad farms and fertile vineyards which were still worked with primitive tools, all formed pictures that gradually blotted out the memories of New York skylines and animated electric signs, and enabled me to form a clearer idea of what Italian life had been during the great years of the Renaissance. [48]

Known for his design of the Boston Museum of Fine Arts, Lowell's latest project led him to visit well over a hundred buildings in the vicinity of the front. When he published *More Small Italian Villas and Farmhouses* in 1920, the volume included a preface acknowledging his debt to colleagues he served with during the war.[49] Several of his pictures show fellow personnel and vehicles at work, and a few include captions that explicitly refer to the Red Cross. One description, for instance, mentions Section One headquarters at Bassano.[50] Indeed, the major's interest in local building design was an integral component of his service.

In addition to Bates and Lowell, those who managed the section were also notable figures during Hemingway's tour. The *Chef* and *Sous-chef*, named for titles borrowed from France, served as immediate supervisors in the field. Hemingway's fondness for the leaders of Section Four, both pioneers from the Western front, led him to invite them to visit his home in Oak Park. Ernest wrote to his parents about the possibility when the men returned to the United States in August:

Ed Welch who was Sous Chef, a in Englesi, Second Lieut, a second in command of our section is leaving for home next week. He lives in Roge[r]s Park and will come out to see you folks as soon as he gets home. He is a peach of a fellow and will tell you all about me and our bunch. He is a Catholic so dont pull any boners.

Charles Griffin a chef, or head of the section, is also going back to the States. He lives in N.J. but may come to Chicago to see you folks. He and Eddie are both fine fellows.[51]

As managers of the unit, Welch and Griffin supervised the assignment of ambulances to various posts behind the lines, inspected travel routes, and communicated with superiors and military personnel regarding the drivers in their charge.

Hemingway also had opportunities to mingle with local personnel assigned to his group. As Bates had indicated, the government initially "started off the first Section with 23 Italian mechanics, orderlies etc. attached."[52] Although the captain ultimately reduced the number of these workers to nine per unit, the volunteers nonetheless relied on men from the military for vehicle maintenance and repair, and Hemingway would have been aware of their integral role with the service.[53]

Captain Felice Cacciapuoti had a more significant presence among his countrymen. As the English-speaking liaison officer responsible for coordinating affairs between the Red Cross and armed forces, he operated from the Vicenza headquarters. Although Bates recorded that he sometimes had difficulty motivating Cacciapuoti to perform his duties, section newspapers indicate that Felice got along well with the volunteers. The members of Section One, for example, credited him as inspiring the name change for the periodical they created. After they were unable to understand why copies of *Avanti* failed to arrive at their intended destinations, the editors consulted the captain. "He solved the riddle at once," they announced. In providing Cacciapuoti's explanation, the men humorously noted Felice's use of expressions that veteran drivers were accustomed to in France:

"Alors." said he. "Perhaps the Avanti is being confused with a former journal of the Italian socialists, also called the Avanti. It was suppressed at the beginning of the war. Perhaps it would be well to find another name for our paper. N'est-ce pas?"

Other Italian mentors and friends of the Section agreed with Captain Cacciapuoti and urged a new name. Personally, we never thought much of the old name anyhow . . . so from now on it's *Come Stà*.[54]

Section Four was largely established through the coordinating efforts of the Italian officer as well since he was instrumental in attaching the drivers to the army and arranging for their lodging at the wool factory in town.[55]

Stories of soldiers who fought in the vicinity were also commonplace, especially tales of the Arditi, elite combatants known for their extraordinary bravery in battle. As Bates wrote, these units carried with them a bravado that resulted not only in admiration but also contempt. He described one incident when the Arditi "waylaid us as only these troops, encouraged in their natural lawlessness, could do. They threatened the drivers with their knives until they were taken on."[56] Angelo Pirocchi provides another anecdote about a company chaplain who failed to provide the soldiers with pasta instead of rice. As a result, the men emptied the contents of their mess tins on a field where they forced the priest to remove his clothes and sit in the pile of discarded food. "As proof of his Christian charity," Pirocchi writes, "the chaplain never revealed the names of his tormentors."[57] In "Al Receives Another Letter," Hemingway's Ring Lardner parody published in the June edition of *Ciao*, the Section Four newspaper, Ernest joked about the Arditi: "They are the real rough guys, and if you don't let them ridexon [sic] your ambulance they stick a knife through you. Loots of the fellows have had that done to them."[58] Indeed, Hemingway was particularly impressed with tales of the hardened fighting men that he had heard about early on in his tour.[59]

Although confrontations with Arditi were not the norm, typical duties expected of drivers were still potentially dangerous. An account by Section One Chef Lieutenant Gale Hunter describes activities common to all the units: "We are now serving 7 postes," Hunter wrote. "Drivers and cars remain at poste on 3 day shifts. . . . Beside the regular poste work, there was an average of 9 cars out on call per day."[60] Major Lowell explains the "three kinds" of "services rendered" while "at poste": "First, transporting wounded from the first line to the smistamento or sanita distributing stations; secondly, carrying them from the sanita stations to the field hospitals; and thirdly, evacuating them from the field hospitals to the smistamenti (distributing stations)."[61] When the men were not on duty near the trenches, they resided at section headquarters awaiting their turn in the rotation during which time they were said to be "*en repos*," another term borrowed from the French service. After three months, volunteers were permitted a two-week "permission," which allowed them to depart from the front as long as they informed superiors as to their whereabouts. Upon their return, they resumed their assignments for another ninety days.

As a common "volunteer," Hemingway shared the same status as most of his fellow drivers at Schio, which was that of an honorary second lieutenant in the Italian army with no specific classification as an officer in the Red Cross. He joked about his rank in "Al Receives Another Letter":

> Well Al I am now and officer and if you would meet me you would have to salute me. What I am is a provisional acting second lieutenant without a commission but the trouble is that all the other fellows are too. There aint no privates in our army Al and the Captain is called a chef. But he dindt look to me as tho he could cook a dam bit.[62]

Hemingway's letters from New York emphasized his nominal title as granting him authority over enlistees in the United States military, but in Schio he recognized the position as commonplace. Bates described the situation as it allowed ambulance drivers special privileges with the army while working in the combat zone: "The men on poste dine with the officers," he noted in a letter to H. Nelson Gay, and "they are lodged as officers" as well.[63] Hemingway would have received board with soldiers if he ever operated in the field. Otherwise, he messed with his fellow Red Cross workers at the quarters in Schio.

Although all volunteers were shown special deference by the army, a limited number of men were assigned ranks that were recognized only within the Red Cross. Those who assisted with the supervision of sections were designated as second lieutenants. Volunteers who led the units or headed a canteen station became first lieutenants. More prominent titles were given those who held greater responsibilities, such as Captain Bates. Directors who managed each of the five departments earned higher classifications, as in the case of Major Lowell. Indeed, the entire commission was supervised by a colonel, Robert P. Perkins. Those who achieved officer status in the Red Cross, moreover, were granted the rank of honorary first lieutenant in the military.[64] During his stay at Schio, Hemingway had not attained any special distinction in the organization.

In terms of the unofficial pecking order that developed, Hemingway was an eighteen-year-old novice among other inexperienced peers and seasoned drivers from France. Those in leadership positions attempted to encourage good will among the volunteers of varying ages and levels of experience. As one announcement indicated: "We want to thank the A. R. C. officials for sending us such a crowd of good fellows, and with our old men as a nucleus, this section's star of supremacy will be understanding between the men and the officials and we are pulling together for the good of America and the A. R. C. in Italy."[65] Years later, Emmet Shaw, one of the "old men," contemptuously recalled Ernest standing out among the crowd. Hemingway "wanted action," Shaw explained. "He wanted to 'participate in the struggle.' He thought we were a bunch of do-nothings. On our part we thought he was an impulsively presumptuous child come to endanger our nice life at Schio."[66] As Brumback's recollections about the journey to Europe similarly attest, Ernest's enthusiasm to enter the fray was a distinguishing feature that was not as common among more experienced men.[67] In the case of Shaw, it even led to some ill will.

Although Hemingway was eager to enter the action, his assignment as an ambulance driver is best characterized as being *en repos*. Accordingly, Section Four headquarters earned its nickname "the Schio Country Club" not "because of its stark accommodations and pervasive smell of sheep," as Kenneth Lynn suggests, but for the general leisure afforded the volunteers who resided there.[68] Shaw, for example, recalled that "many of us veteran drivers had already served with the French on the Western front. We felt that at Schio we were doing good work and we hoped that we would be able to continue it. Of course we also liked to relax. We liked to swim. We liked to sun bathe."[69] Days consisted of baseball games and dips in a nearby creek, and nights included meals of spaghetti and beans, "rotten" wine, outings at a local eatery called the Due Spadi, or gambling on the second floor of the wool factory.[70] As Shaw's comments suggest, several of the experienced volunteers were content with the status quo.

Section Four was also somewhat infamous among administrators for their objectionable behavior during downtime. Some of the drivers inadvertently called attention to themselves in March when Bates received a telegram from Lieutenant Griffin in Milan requesting the captain's assistance. Afterward, Bates noted that "it was necessary to release 4 men of that Section; one for unpatriotic utterances and 3 for a disposition to question orders."[71] Lowell also became concerned over "the conduct of ambulance men in Milan." On April 27, he wrote to Bates referring to a related series of "altogether unfortunate incidents."[72] Bates distributed yet another memo on May 7, noting "five separate cases of drunkenness" among volunteers "away from their sections."[73] As a result, officials implemented strict prohibitions restricting drivers from taking trips to Milan while *en repos* "unless furnished with a written authority."[74] When Hemingway's group arrived, Bates wrote that "I thought it advisable" to assign "all of the new men whom I could not place elsewhere" in Schio "rather than leave them in Milano and surrounding cities, as we did with Section 4 while the men were waiting for their cars." Bates hoped they would be "out of temptation" there, but descriptions in the section newspaper alluding to their carousing suggest otherwise.[75] Articles often relied on jokes about antics resulting from consumption of wine, Pernod, and other libations.[76] Hemingway recalled a similar detail to James Gamble a few months after the war, asking him if he ever tried "the beer at the little Birraria down near the rail way station at Schio."[77] Since the town was in a remote location, however, it was less likely that behavior of men *en repos* could be noticed by "other nationalities than our own," which Lowell had feared, as their conduct had already become a "subject of complaint" among local authorities.[78]

The arrival of the men in Schio also created something of a stir among Italian women. After Section Four left Milan for the front on April 8, they received "an enthusiastic reception" in the town, but at least one of the residents was "discontented," as Bates noted. The "proprietor" of a factory complained "that he is losing 500 lire a day, because the girls crowd to the windows to look at the Americans." As a result, the employer "closed the interior court to ambulance men."[79] Even so, the contents of *Ciao* indicate that the attraction between drivers and the female workers continued. One poem notes that some of the volunteers looked forward to the end of the girls' work day and the potential for a chance meeting:

The whistle blows the knell of parting day
The factory girls run quickly home with glee
(Save one, who stops with Johnnie by the way)
And leave the court to darkness and to me.[80]

Another article describes one of the drivers "lounging in the court by the gurgling, rippling fountain whose waters flow, clear as coffee from the mountains near-by, and watching the girls in the factory play."[81] Indeed, the allure of foreign romance captured the imagination of many Red Cross personnel.

As their contributions to *Ciao* indicate, the men also devoted much of their idle time to producing the section newspaper.[82] "The origin" of the title, editor Lawrence Fisher explained, "is the Italian word *Schiavo* which means slave or servant. The Venetians contracted this to *Ciao*, and as this it has come into universal use in Italy as a word of greeting or good cheer."[83] Not surprisingly, many of the volunteers adopted the popular expression denoting both hello and goodbye, and the use of the word as a title aptly suggests the dichotomy of meanings evident in submissions that show patriotism in contrast to more cynical views. One article, for example, underlines the Red Cross message that prevailed during Hemingway's stay in New York. The piece explains that, based on the connections between the United States and Christopher Columbus, Giovanni da Verrazano, and Amerigo Vespucci, "rightly every Italian has a sense of proprietorship in America and all things American."[84] Another article, "And Yet More Driving Power," criticizes the dissemination of idealistic notions through a sardonic account of Section Four: "One day last November a group of Very Wise Men sat long in council. It wasn't Guns that the Italians had lacked; it wasn't Men; it was Propaganda. Thus was sown the Acorn from which Section IV has blossomed."[85] Indeed, as indicated in the pages of their periodical, several volunteers at Schio were less than optimistic about the usefulness of their mission.

Many of the contributions to *Ciao* likewise reflect the tendency to treat grave aspects of the experience with wry wit. Serving as a bulletin board of sorts modeled on high school and college newspapers, the broadsheet included various articles, poems, diary entries, advertisements, and general announcements that frequently relied on puns to obscure the reality of war beneath a humorous façade. In suggesting a clearinghouse for "all the hysterics" of Section Four on the masthead, for example, the editors evoke a state of mind that was not a joke for many soldiers. Ambulance drivers rarely experienced the terror that combatants underwent in the trenches, but they were familiar with the condition nonetheless. The allusion in the banner underscores the type of irony expressed by many whose perspectives had been altered observing the atrocities of war.

The humorous mission expressed in *Ciao* also developed from a rivalry between the sections.[86] In January of 1918, the editors of *Avanti* explained the inspiration behind their initial number: "The idea of a section newspaper is not original. Norton-Harjes Section Number 63 published one before this ambulance unit was even dreamed of."[87] Indeed, *Soixante Trois*, created in the summer of 1917 by the section that Bates led in France claimed to be the "first American newspaper printed at the front."[88] The editors of *Avanti* noted that "we believe we are the pioneers in Italy, however, and we take a certain satisfaction in that fact."[89] After Section One changed the title to *Come Stà* in March of 1918, the men of Section Four printed the first edition of *Ciao* in April.

Hemingway's group acknowledged that their monthly was "not the first American newspaper in Italy, but it will in time undoubtedly be the best." To that end, the editors enthusiastically encouraged submissions: "We know that it will if you all *Write*. Don't shirk your share. Lets go at this as Russell does his wine." Consequently, the June number included an appeal to the recent arrivals: "We hope the new men will contribute largely to *Ciao*," the editors announced, "we know that there is talent among them. *Ciao* is the Section's paper, and not the sheet of one or a few individuals. Make a name for yourself by writing for *Ciao*."[90] Hemingway's "Al Receives Another Letter" appeared in the same issue.[91] The competition that developed among the sections not only allowed him the opportunity to show the skills he acquired with the *Kansas City Star* but also earned him some standing among those trying to promote camaraderie in his unit.

Hemingway, however, was not the first to contribute a Ring Lardner parody to the section newspapers. "His Letter Home" by "Your pal Rip" appeared in the August 12, 1917, issue of *Soixante Trois*. The February edition of *Avanti* contained "Beg Pardon, Ring!," and the April number of *Come Stà* included yet another imitation called "Al on Permission." As Fenton observes, Hemingway's article reveals his growing skill as a writer and his "precocious mastery of this new milieu," but the piece, as compared to those written by drivers from France, also underscores his position as a novice among men with more experience of war.[92]

"Beg Pardon, Ring!" by "yoor fd. Cy," for example, was written by a volunteer who jokes about the conditions upon arriving in Italy after serving in France. He writes about his new environment consisting of mountain warfare, roads obstructed with snow and ice, and frozen soldiers:

Most of our fellers Freeze to Death trying to Drive up the Montins but it dont bother me Much. The rodes is Terribul, Al, all ice and Snow and Narrow and everything, nothing but Rocks on 1 side and holes Milluns of miles deap on the Other and runaway Cameos running away all over. The Rode aint so bad but they aint much Room to back up when you has to Dodge a shell.

Gen. Sherman said war is hell, but hell is Hot and its Cold down hear so he was talking threw his Hat. thats One on the gen.[93]

"Beg Pardon, Ring!" highlights the experience of those who arrived at the snow-covered front when most of the fighting had ceased after the onset of winter. Hemingway's experience, however, would be limited to observations of the conflict during the summer and fall. Even so, he could have learned about the earlier conditions from his colleagues.

"Al on Permission" provides jokes about the freedoms drivers enjoyed on their vacations, circumstances that not only became a source of embarrassment for administrators, as evidenced by the problems with men in Milan, but also yielded opportunities for sensational storytelling about exploits away from the front. Writing from "somwher in Italy," the author of "Al on Permission" opens with a joke about being out of the action: "Well Al, they aint much to rite you about the Wars down hear because i been Awai for 2 wks. And they aint been no Wars." The writer goes on to describe his various off-duty escapades:

You See, i been on Permishun to roam and Flourance and napuls an Pompay and the Is. a capree and lots of places what aint showed on any Map. A Permishun is what the red+ gives you to get sum Rest and Edjukashun so we can Enetertain italian soldatii when were settin in Dugouts. Lots of Rest cums in Bottles and moast of the Edjukashun is brewnets. Youd hardly know me Al, i got so Wild since i cum to War I gess its smell of italian Powder that makes me Wild.

After mentioning a trip to the "Pope's house" in Rome, the article continues to say that

1 of our fellers met a Lady who told him she was an U. S. A. like him and was a Countez and that she vood like to be a Mother to him and Protect him frum the Perils of the Strange Toan. and this feller he was

yung and innuset and from a place called Flatbush so he thot it was ok but we got back in time to Save him and then we went to napuls.[94]

Written not long after some of the drivers enjoyed their breaks in March, the parody shows that volunteers often had high expectations for romantic adventures during excursions behind the lines.

The section newspapers indicate that Hemingway was not alone in his appreciation of storytelling and literary pursuits. Since the "cycle that led from campus to ambulance," as Fenton has discussed,[95] resulted in a highly literate group, it is no surprise that the broadsheets also contained allusions to James Russell Lowell, Henry Wadsworth Longfellow, Oliver Wendell Holmes, William Cullen Bryant, Thomas Gray, and John Keats. Other volunteers, moreover, also wanted to become or already had experience as professional writers. James Baker is listed among the "Who's Who in Section One" as desiring "to beat Ring Lardner out of his job."[96] F. J. Nash, an editor of *Come Stà,* had written that "most of us are hardened in newspaperdom and we no longer pity our readers; we punish them if need be, we inform them if we can, and amuse perhaps."[97] Gouverneur Morris, listed as a "cub reporter" for *Avanti,* was an author of some renown. He had even promised to write the story of the ambulance drivers upon his return to America.[98] John Dos Passos, whose name appears several times in the periodicals, never contributed articles of his own, but *One Man's Initiation* and *Three Soldiers* were significant literary works that originated with his service in the war.

Although Schio offered plenty of leisure time, reports indicate that the chances for actually hauling wounded in June of 1918 had been very limited.[99] Bates's report for that month documents an increase of overall driving, but Hemingway's group remained relatively inactive; he wrote that the work of "all but the 4th Section has been very great."[100] When the numbers were tallied for casualties transported during that period, Section Four statistics appeared at the bottom of the list. The unit's 1,020 total cases carried over 140 trips suggest a relatively slight workload as compared to Section One, which hauled 4,549 injured soldiers during 406 trips.[101] With light activity and a pool of eighteen pairs of drivers operating in shifts lasting two or three days, it is unlikely that Hemingway would have been called upon to sit behind the steering wheel of an ambulance other than to pose for a photograph.[102]

The start of the Austrian offensive on June 15 did not result in much activity for Section Four either. The massive bombardment that ranged across the entirety of the Italian front signaled the opening of a confrontation that was anticipated since Caporetto. In the mountain sector, the battle had been decided by the end of the second day. The enemy made initial gains, but the Allied forces pushed back in a series of counter offensives that served as the hallmark of General Armando Diaz's winning strategy over the Austrians. By June 17, the major fighting had essentially ceased in the region near Schio, and ambulance work remained relatively quiet.[103]

The other units, however, experienced intense activity. Bates visited Section One in Bassano on the first day of the battle and noted that the men had been "working hard" with "all the machines on the road" and "various posts filled with wounded waiting for their return." One vehicle had even been "cut off by the enemy." Initially, "nothing was known of the whereabouts, either of the car or its two drivers," Bates indicated, but on the morning of June 16, they finally returned and told of being detained after a munition dump had been struck by a shell. The blast initiated a series of continual explosions forcing the volunteers to remain in their makeshift "*abri*" (shelter) for hours. Stories about episodes such as these began circulating around the sections.[104]

When Bates arrived at Roncade on June 17, he found that Section Two had been operating under the most intense conditions. In addition to their "twenty-four hours of exceedingly stiff work," he reported the loss of three vehicles to the Austrians as well as other cars that had been "laid-up" as a result of collisions while hauling wounded. As with the Battle of Caporetto, rumors of enemy infiltration and fear of retreat had spread. Drivers were required to transport their baggage to Vicenza since "they might have to get out on short notice."[105] Indeed, "there was an element of uncertainty which gave a thrill that I never felt in France," Bates wrote in his diary. "Perhaps it was because I was too ignorant of the situation" on the Western front, he suggested, "and perhaps it was because I did not have sufficient confidence in the Italians. In as much as they had confidence in themselves this is not surprising."[106] The activity that emerged in the early stages of the Battle of the Piave dramatically increased tensions for armed forces and Red Cross workers alike.

Although the volunteers reportedly performed in an exemplary fashion, drivers were nonetheless overwhelmed by the sudden increase in work: "They have been doing almost without sleep and look tired out,"

Bates reported.[107] As a result, the captain chose to supplement the staff and vehicles of his active sections with resources from the one place that did not require them: Hemingway's Section Four. "At one time we had thirty-eight cars and forty-nine men working in Section 2 alone," Bates indicated.[108] Acquiring close to double the amount of personnel and vehicles typically allotted to a unit, Section Two absorbed more than half of the ambulances from Schio along with nine of the volunteers.

The editors of *Ciao* published an article about the loan of personnel entitled "Our Part in the Big Drive." Referring to themselves as the "Shock Unit of the American Ambulance in Italy," they noted that "the section has sent men and cars wherever the action has been hottest and its members have been in every big attack."[109] While some of Ernest's friends were selected to help out in the affected areas, Hemingway remained behind. The circumstances of the offensive underscore the frustration he expressed in his comment related to Ted Brumback: "I'm fed up. There's nothing here but scenery and too damn much of that."[110] He also announced his intention to leave the unit: "I'm going to get out of the ambulance section and see if I can't find out where the war is," he told Brumback.[111]

Hemingway's article in *Ciao* jokes about the lack of action that inspired him to seek out an alternative. He wrote about employing the harsh tactics used by Arditi forces in order to commandeer a vehicle:

> And I am going to buy a knife Al because that looks like the only way that you can get to ride on one of these ambulnces anyway. Well Al they say I am going to be seventh on cal tomorrow and so I want to get ready because you know me Al always right on the spot all the time so I am not going to take off me clothes tonight.[112]

Indeed, much of Hemingway's humor in the Lardner parody grows out of this inactivity: "I would tell you about our hardships Al but we mustnt reveal no military secrets even to those nearest and dearest to us." Other than his remarks about "the Battle of Paris" and "the Battle of Milan," Ernest had little to tell about the supposed "hardships." Instead of writing about ambulance driving near the trenches, he refers to the accommodations, gambling aboard the *Chicago,* and the general sense of camaraderie, which were his main experiences at the time.[113]

On June 24, two weeks after he was assigned to Schio, he was offered a chance to get into the action.[114] Bates received a telegram from B. Harvey

Carroll, the American consul in Venice, requesting personnel to staff a series of emergency canteens along the front as a response to the offensive. He immediately dispatched ten men and a camion under the charge of John S. Vanderveer. The volunteers were transported to Mestre, the supply hub for workers at the lines, and they received assignments the following day. Hemingway and George Clapp Noyes, one of the recently arrived Harvard undergraduates, were dropped off in Fornaci, seven kilometers from the Piave.[115] Of the four emergency posts established that day, the Fornaci location was closest to the trenches. Ernest had finally achieved a front-row seat in the Italian theater of war.

As with the ambulance sections, the canteens were established by veteran drivers from the Western front.[116] In late February of 1918, Lieutenant Edward Michael McKey, inspired by the success of similar work in France, initiated the service to comfort soldiers with hot coffee and jam for bread. In early March, his "Cucina No. 1" entered the field near the Asiago Plateau and served roughly eight hundred men per day. By the beginning of June, five posts operated mostly in the mountain region, serving upwards of two thousand men daily. Plans were underway to establish additional operations in the lowlands. Officials noted the work as crucial to the mission in Italy, and volunteers who managed the kitchens were usually promoted to lieutenants. Bates, who directed the service until James Gamble took over on June 2,[117] wrote that he envisioned it as "destined to be the most important R.C. work at the front."[118] Indeed, when Hemingway volunteered, he joined a select group who occupied a privileged position for boosting morale by working directly among the soldiers fighting in the trenches.

Unlike canteens located behind the lines, the unit Hemingway joined reached forward areas using kitchens mounted on wheels. At first, McKey planned to situate equipment at sites where personnel could supply passing troops with hot food and drink after which they were expected to move the device nearer the trenches to offer relief during breaks in the fighting. The operation had therefore come to be called the "rolling kitchens" service. Captain Bates reported early on that the original idea had to be altered: "Due to the heavy construction of the present kitchens which weigh 3,000 pounds each," he wrote, "it has been found impracticable to move them up to the trenches at night as was originally planned." Bates suggested adapting a "stationary stove" that included a "lightly constructed apparatus similar to the New York street sweepers' movable cans which would carry a couple of hundred litres of coffee in thermos marmites."[119] The service at the time of Hemingway's enlistment, however, included mostly stationary canteens that served soldiers marching to and from the lines by day after which the volunteer in charge had to find other means for transporting provisions to the trenches at night.

Many of the fixed locations evolved into elaborate houses and offered a variety of comforts. McKey describes one such operation in his weekly report:

> The kitchen is run in this fashion. I am given a log house at one station and a shed was built at the side for the kitchen. The house is on the second line. In the morning we make 300 liters of coffee, strain it and sweeten it; then cover the machine. If it is necessary we make more later. All day long we serve coffee and also all night long, and the boys are happy.
>
> At four o'clock I commence the service of the marmalade and I have the cans opened and the contents placed on the plates on the bar: then we allow about 25 in at a time. Each man brings his own bread and we spread it quite thickly with the marmalade; then give each man a cup of hot coffee very sweet. After they have finished they pass out and I give them either 2 Cigarettes or ½ a Toscano. It is quite all right, I assure you, and every one is happy.[120]

Once a system had been established, the service provided additional luxuries. Besides coffee, jam, cigars, and cigarettes, the operators distributed chocolate and other "sweet things," which McKey indicated as the top priority among soldiers.[121] Sources of entertainment were added as well. Bates reported that "in every crowd of a hundred . . . who stop at [McKey's] kitchen for coffee, there are at least twenty-five who play some instrument."[122] As a result, mandolins and guitars were provided so men could perform for those waiting in line. Phonographs followed soon after, and McKey requested "records of all the patriotic airs of Italy" for broadcast along roads that led to the trenches.[123] Nationalistic literature was likewise distributed, and plans were developed for installing "cinematographs" by which men could view patriotic films.[124] In June, Coles Seeley, whom Hemingway later met in the hospital in Milan, volunteered to operate a camion rigged for movie projection at the kitchen posts, but the plan was stalled when he was wounded while "attempting to unscrew a shell head" for a souvenir.[125]

The formal openings of new kitchens sometimes resulted in elaborate celebrations. Gamble's kitchen, which officially opened on May 19, was one of the most well-attended. Bates reported the event:

> One hundred and fifty men from each Brigade had been notified and there were many high officers present, including three Generals. Each General made a speech, and at the end of the ceremony a private soldier thanked the American Red Cross in broken English for himself and his comrades for the work which they are doing. All the officers, both American and Italian, were then entertained by Lieutenant Gamble near the barracks, while the soldiers passed through the Kitchen and received coffee, jam, marmalade and sweet chocolate. The permanent Kitchen which has been built for Lieutenant Gamble is beautifully constructed on a terrace built out from the side of a hill, supported by a rough stone wall. Mr. Gamble occupies a small room next to the General's and is a guest at the General's mess.[126]

Similar to receptions held in Milan before the introduction of new ambulance sections, the festivities at new canteen locations served as opportunities to underscore relations between Italians and their U.S. allies through pomp and ceremony. Indeed, the significant turnout of local officials demonstrated that these kitchens were highly appreciated by the military. One general requested McKey for permanent assignment to his division. Army officers made use of the "rest-rooms" that adjoined the kitchens for conference space.[127] As Bates observed, "the scope of this service is almost unlimited and is a success from every angle."[128]

Major Lowell identified the rolling kitchen operators as key in accomplishing the main Red Cross objective. In his final summary of that work, he described their character and mission:

> It was necessary that these officers in order effectively to fulfill their duties should be men who could readily establish cordial relations with Italian officers. At the same time it was essential that they should know how to impress soldiers of the ranks with sincerity and friendliness of the message which they had been delegated to transmit. The chief aim of the service was to make clear to the Italian soldiers that

the American people were grateful to them for the services which they had rendered to the cause of civilization during the long years in which Italy was engaged in the war, and that in addition to sending over troops to fight for the same cause, the Americans desired in every tangible way possible to express their appreciation.

Consequently these lieutenants had to be men who liked and were capable of understanding men of all kinds and of getting on well with men of another race. A further essential qualification was executive capacity and business ability as each canteen served many hundreds of men daily and dispensed large quantities of supplies. Courage and coolness under fire may also be mentioned as an attribute that these canteen officers were called upon to frequently display.[129]

As Lowell indicated, those stationed at the front served as American representatives in a way that surpassed the role of ambulance drivers in terms of boosting morale. Those who staffed the rolling kitchens serving hundreds of soldiers each day had the potential for more substantial contact with the foreign military than did many of their fellow workers. Soldiers considered their visits as opportunities to experience United States culture as well. The *Corriere della Sera* mentioned that Italians fondly referred to the kitchens as "American Bars," and the statement "let us go to visit America" became a common refrain whenever the Stars and Stripes was hoisted in their vicinity.[130]

Gamble and McKey achieved great success in the service as a result of the rapport they established among soldiers, and their work paved the way for Hemingway's job. Bates wrote, for example, that Gamble "has a personality which is liked by the Italians, and he realizes and appreciates not only the practical but the moral objects which we hope to obtain through our contact with the Italian Army."[131] McKey was also said to be "loved and respected" by those whom he served.[132] Hemingway would have been held to similar standards. His assignment brought him to forward areas extremely close to the battlefield where, in contrast to an ambulance driver *en repos*, he was expected to serve passing troops on their way to and from the combat zone, carry food to the lines, and propagandize among the combatants. Indeed, the last objective was an essential function that allowed for direct contact with military personnel. Brumback's accounts and the letters Ernest wrote home suggest that he was well qualified for his new role.

Other aspects of Hemingway's service differed, however, from those of typical canteens established in the early days of the operation. Perhaps the most important distinguishing feature of Hemingway's work is evident in his association with the emergency "*posti di conforto*" (canteen posts). Unlike standard kitchens, these temporary posts were created in response to a heightened need for aid during the offensive. Although Hemingway had been assigned by Bates, he came under the authority of those who initiated the emergency service: American Consul B. Harvey Carroll and Venice District Delegate Moses S. Slaughter. After the offensive had subsided, several of the emergency posts continued to operate, including the one Hemingway staffed until his wounding. The management of those sites was subsequently transferred to Gamble, who is usually identified as Hemingway's supervisor while in the service.[133] By that time, however, Ernest was recovering in the Milan hospital and never returned to active duty.[134] Since the work of rolling kitchens and emergency canteens overlapped during the offensive, Gamble would have been involved in both operations. Nonetheless, Hemingway's initial assignment under Carroll and Slaughter is evident in reports and reveals a fuller picture of the period that Ernest served in the battle zone.

Hemingway's Fornaci site was located in the vicinity where McKey had planned to establish a rolling kitchen a few weeks prior.[135] On June 9, McKey moved "Cucina No. 1" to Pralongo, the crossroads located between Fornaci and Fossalta di Piave.[136] Three kilometers from the Piave River, Pralongo was also four kilometers east of the area where Hemingway had been assigned. McKey's goal, according to Gamble's report, had been to work "more in accordance with the original plans of the service, i.e., to drag the Kitchen itself by means of mules along the road back of the trenches." A letter from McKey to Gamble elaborates on this point: "In a few days it will all be up and running. I shall start before the house is quite complete as they are anxious for me to get underway."[137] McKey's death, however, "came before he had an opportunity to work out his idea."[138] On June 16, he was killed by an Austrian shell. The next day, Cucina No. 1 was "completely wrecked" by enemy fire as well.[139]

The Fornaci site did not offer an established canteen station either, and Hemingway most likely did not manage one.[140] Slaughter's report notes that the "posto" had been moved from Meolo to Fornaci but does not indicate transfer of equipment furnished there or at any of the emergency locations established on June 25.[141] In contrast, other such reports document supplies received or moved in the field. Since temporary *posti di conforto* were somewhat hastily organized, Hemingway's canteen would have consisted of a rudimentary base without the benefit of a "rest room."

Moreover, he had difficulty obtaining resources.[142] After the first few posts were established a few days before June 24, supplies were slow in arriving, and some requests had been left unfilled even at the end of July.[143] As a result, volunteers found it necessary to purchase goods from "*sussistenza*" (supply merchants) catering to local military divisions until rations began to trickle in on July 1.[144] The only extant letter from Hemingway during this period also suggests that he operated in a limited capacity lacking a fully provisioned canteen station: "What I am supposed to be doing," he wrote, "is running a posto Di ricovero. That is I dispense chocolate and cigarettes to the wounded and the soldiers in the front line."[145] The lack of supplies also explains why Hemingway referred to only "six days" that he spent "up in the Front line trenches" before his wounding on July 8, even though the Red Cross reported his arrival in Fornaci on June 25.[146]

Documentation by Bates, Slaughter, and Gamble yields other important details about Hemingway's rank while serving at the front. During his two weeks in the battle zone, Ernest maintained the same status he was assigned in New York and Schio: honorary second lieutenant in the Italian Army with no additional distinction in the Red Cross. Although men who headed kitchen operations were often promoted to first lieutenant, Hemingway's assignment as a temporary worker differed. Several of those who volunteered during the offensive eventually returned to the ambulance sections once the increased need had subsided, and they maintained their status as general volunteers. Hemingway had not received an upgrade during his period of active duty either.[147]

Even so, he had ample opportunity to observe battle conditions while serving near the trenches. When he arrived at the most active region of combat along that front, the Austrians had already been defeated in the Battle of the Piave, and the Italians were in the midst of launching their counterattack.[148] A week prior, the Austrians succeeded in traversing the river and advancing through the town of Fossalta di Piave almost to the crossroads at Pralongo. After heavy rain caused severe flooding that destroyed bridges and crippled the conveyance of troops and equipment as well as pinning down forces already on the left bank, the Italians succeeded in halting the attack. On June 22, the Austrians began a disastrous retreat.[149]

Once Hemingway reached the area, the Italians had advanced to resume positions at the Piave. Evidence of the battle remained, however, and carnage was widespread.[150] Bates referred to the region in his diary, saying that "it was interesting to go over roads which had witnessed a rout or an advance but a few hours before, dead men in the ditches and muddy farm-yards, the houses in ruins and the roads covered with abandoned equipment."[151] He described another nearby location:

> The Austrians had been driven back the day before and we went out to the advance post which had been in enemy hands since the beginning of the attack. They were cleaning out dead Austrians from the rooms of our little farm house and sprinkling lime. The Austrians lay by the windows, little piles of empty cartridges beside them, and our truck was carrying lime while one of the ambulances collected bodies. It was an ugly sight; many of them had been dead for days.[152]

Hemingway would have observed similar conditions while traveling from his post at Fornaci through the crossroads at Pralongo past the previously overrun town of Fossalta di Piave and on to the trenches near the river.

Scouring through the aftermath of the battle, he collected a vast amount of souvenirs and wrote about all the "junk" in a letter home:

> Austrian carbines and ammunition, German and Austrian medals, officers automatic pistols, Boche helmets[,] about a dozen Bayonets, star shell pistols and knives[,] and almost everything you can think of. The only limit to the amount of souvenirs I could have is what I could carry for there were so many dead Austrians and prisoners the ground was almost black with them.[153]

On the same day Hemingway was wounded, Bates wrote about the situation as well:

> I have never in my life seen such souvenirs as the soldiers and our boys have brought in during this attack, and if I had not long ago got over

the souvenir-hunting stage, I could have had a trunkful. As it is I have brought back junk every time I have driven in to Vicenza, and given it to our visitors.[154]

A popular pastime, especially for initiates, souvenir collecting was particularly fruitful after the June offensive.

Most importantly, Hemingway's service allowed him access to front-line trenches during the heat of battle. Reports on McKey's stint in the same area are helpful in approximating the type of activity Hemingway was engaged in that led directly to his wounding.[155] As quoted in one account, McKey explained that

> I am lunching and dining at the Divisione where they are most kind and give me a horse and cart each day to go to my work. You can imagine I make no demands or requests except those entirely necessary for my work, and in fact have really had to ask for nothing as everything has been done for me. There is wonderful work there and I see a great opportunity. I think, however, there is danger of perhaps losing the outfit with a shell. The street is shelled constantly and during the time, about an hour, in which we were in the line some fifty shells came over, striking in or near the street. I have, however, found several spots into which I can crawl and be quite safe.[156]

Instead of traveling on horseback, Hemingway rode to the trenches via bicycle. As he described it, "each aft and morning I load up a haversack and take my tin lid and gas mask and beat it up to the trenches."[157] Although both Hemingway and McKey were struck by enemy shell bursts, Hemingway, of course, lived to write about the explosion that ended his active duty.

Four Hero of the Piave

On July 8, 1918, in the frontlines beyond Fossalta di Piave, Ernest Hemingway was wounded by fragments from a mortar shell explosion. Shortly thereafter, he received additional injuries from machine-gun fire and apparently carried to safety a soldier hurt from the same blast. Once at a dressing station behind the trenches, he obtained medical attention and was taken to a field hospital in Treviso where he remained for five days. He was subsequently transported by ambulance to the railway station at Mestre and by train to Milan where he checked in at the American Red Cross Hospital, his primary residence in Italy for the next six months.[1] Although scholars have referred to Guy Lowell's *Report of the Department of Military Affairs January to July, 1918* as the official document recording the episode,[2] administrators filed five additional reports containing descriptions of the incident and related circumstances. In conjunction with letters and other related accounts, these materials provide the full story of the events as they unfolded during Hemingway's convalescence in the summer and fall. His later writing incorporates much that he learned about heroism and personal sacrifice as a result of the baptism by fire that rendered him out of commission for the remainder of the war.

In the days leading up to Hemingway's wounding, the ambulance corps as a whole began to receive recognition for duties performed during the recent offensive. On June 22, 1918, Major Guy Lowell sent a telegram to Captain Robert Bates offering his "hearty congratulations" for the "heroic work" of the drivers even before the fighting had ceased. Their conduct during the battle, he noted, was "real poetry."[3] In his description of activities for that month, Bates reported that the work of the new members was particularly impressive: "Although the vast majority of them have had no previous ambulance training," he remarked, they "behaved admirably . . . showing a great spirit of sacrifice."[4] Their contributions were also acknowledged by the Italian government. Bates explained that local authorities were "delighted and told me they marveled at the enthusiasm of these young boys. . . . It is certainly a satisfaction that we can at last show the work we are capable of and that it is met with such appreciation."[5] The Italian press issued laudatory comments as well. After the *Corriere della Sera* referred to the volunteers in an article on the recent campaign, Bates indicated with pride that "this is the first time to our knowledge that any American Ambulance work has ever been noted in the account of a battle."[6] As the soldiers fought for long-awaited victories against the enemy, Red Cross workers were achieving success in their mission to boost morale among the troops.

Many of the volunteers were singled out in Red Cross reports documenting their "instances of individual bravery" and "narrow escapes from death."[7] By early July, Bates indicated that six men had already "been cited in the order of the day and awarded the Italian War Cross," a commendation often bestowed by the military on those who participated in action.[8] Even more, "as a result of the activity during the month of June, and particularly of that during the first few days of July," Section Three alone received "twenty-one individual citations entitling the recipients to wear the *Croce al Merito di Guerra*."[9] One of those honorees, George Clapp Noyes, had been assigned to the emergency canteen post at Fornaci along with Hemingway.[10]

Red Cross administrators also reported citations for distinguished service during combat.[11] Section Two *Chef* Lieutenant James P. Gillespie noted that Goldthwaite H. Dorr was on duty at the start of the offensive when his post was hit by a shell "which demolished part of the house and completely covered his ambulance."[12] Dorr returned to headquarters to obtain another vehicle after which he drove back to the field "in order that he might continue his work of pity."[13] Afterward, he received a Silver Medal of Valor, the second-highest award given by the military. Walter J. Feder and Robert C. Corey were honored likewise.[14] On June 17, they

> went to a front post where fighting was very fierce and were stopped by a colonel, who told them it was impossible to proceed. At this very moment the colonel was struck and seriously injured by a piece of shell. They carried him immediately to a surgical station; on their return they were stopped at a bridge by military police, who said it was fatal to go farther; but taking advantage of a moment's inattention on the part of the guards, they went on in spite of his warning, and succeeded in carrying a great number of wounded from this area.[15]

Lowell described similar acts of bravery performed by Frederick J. Agate and John W. Miller. On June 23, Agate and Miller "advanced under enemy fire to a house to rescue a wounded soldier, in spite of being advised to retire by the medical officer who had been forced out of the position."[16] The *Washington Post* explained that when the men arrived at

> a crossroad they found it covered with barbed wire obstacles and two machine guns in place. With the help of the machine gun operators, they tore down and opened the barbed wire and advanced 300 meters farther, and reached a house where the wounded were being cared for while bullets of the two armies were raining all around them. Having loaded their ambulance with wounded, they returned to the stations where the injured received first-aid treatment.[17]

Both men, as Lowell noted, were "recommended for decorations" and received the Silver Medal not long after.[18] Among others named for their "display of devotion and valor," Lieutenant Gillespie and *Sous-chef* Alfred E. Collinson also received commendations for their leadership during the battle.[19]

As the first fatality among American Red Cross workers in Italy, Lieutenant Edward Michael McKey, who was killed on the second day of action, received the highest praise.[20] In one report, Captain James Gamble explained that "there is probably no one whose death would have meant a greater loss to the Kitchen Service than Lieut. McKey." Referring to his "unselfish and courageous nature combined with excellent judgment," Gamble added that "I, personally, miss more than I can express his very splendid advice and the constant inspiration caused by his unswerving sense of duty and ideals."[21] When administrators gathered in Rome for a meeting held four days after McKey was killed, Colonel Robert E. Perkins, overseer for the entire operation in Italy, "ordered that a record appear expressing the high esteem and affection in which Lieutenant McKey had been held by the members of the Commission" as a mark of their "heartfelt gratitude." Consequently, the minutes included a two-page biography with special mention of the canteen operator's accomplishments. Administrators noted in particular "his patriotic purpose to serve his country and his great love of Italy" as well as "the devotion, intelligence and zeal with which he rendered that service."[22] The *Red Cross Bulletin* in Italy published a full-page spread called "With the Rolling Canteens" as a "small tribute."[23] The *New York Times* reported the incident on the front page, and the *Washington Post* ran a story on him as well.[24]

Military authorities also spoke highly of McKey. One lieutenant spent time talking with him as the men traveled to the front together prior to the battle in June. The soldier reported afterward that "I don't remember any conversation so interesting" and mentioned McKey's ideas on the role of his organization in Italy:

> "I never carried a weapon," [McKey] said, "and I think that is the spirit of the Red Cross. We have lost some of the spirit that inspired the Red Cross in its inception. We look too much to ranks, make too much of military organization. The Red Cross was born as a protest against war and its brutalities. Our task is to wipe away the blood of the wounded and to spread the spirit of fellowship. The true symbol of the Red Cross is not the Sam Browne Belt, but the rope of the Cappucine. Yes, that should be our uniform. We should all have the same spirit as those men who in the Middle Ages went out to preach to the poor."[25]

Captain Alfredo Colabattisti, the officer in charge of the field battery in the vicinity of McKey's post, noted his colleague's last words uttered just before the explosion that ended his life: "How splendidly the Italians are fighting!" McKey told him.[26] Captain Felice Cacciapuoti, the liaison officer for the Red Cross in Vicenza, spoke for many of his fellow soldiers when he said that "Lieutenant McKey is mourned by all and has left behind him a legacy of great affection. I who knew him can sincerely say that he had the love and enthusiasm of an apostle for his work."[27] Within a month of his death, as Lowell reported, the military "awarded to the memory" of the fallen volunteer a Silver Medal of Valor in honor of his sacrifice.[28]

Bates was particularly affected by McKey's death. In a letter to Lowell during the heat of battle in mid-June, he mentioned that "it was a great shock" when he learned that his comrade had been killed.[29] After searching through piles of corpses to recover the body, Bates wrote about the improvised funeral service that he helped arrange even as the fighting still raged nearby:

> I had managed to get a coffin made out of some old boards and again
> I had to help put him in the coffin. It spoiled the whole thing for me,

and in spite of the flowers with which we covered him and which hid the rough boards the whole experience was crude and ugly for me. We put him in a little ambulance and four of us walked beside it. About 40 old territorials marched behind as a guard of honor, and two or three of our staff cars brought up the rear. A battery of big guns deafened us during the brief ceremony at the grave.[30]

Even after witnessing countless casualties in the midst of hauling wounded during two tours on the Western front, Bates indicated that McKey's death had a profound impact:

> Poor fellow; he was about as good a friend as I have made here and there was nothing of him left. He was always spick and span, fresh gloves in his hand, a little swagger stick, and a smart uniform. I have never before realized what gross clay we are when the spirit of life has left us. I have often thought how unpleasant it would be to have ones friends see one disfigured in death. Now I know that it makes no difference; there was nothing of McKey in that lifeless clod.[31]

Indeed, along with recognizing his contributions, McKey's peers showed sincere admiration and sorrow for their fallen colleague.

As administrators paid tribute to many of the volunteers for their actions in June, Hemingway was working amid the fighting that resumed in the same region where McKey had been killed. Evidence of the incident still remained in the area. Bates and Gillespie tried to recover McKey's demolished equipment, but they "found the supplies buried in the ruins and the Kitchen so badly damaged that in the present condition of the roads it is impossible to remove it."[32] As Lowell noted, "on the first of July the Italian army started a counteroffensive on the lower Piave," and work in that region continued to be dangerous.[33]

After the daring exploits accomplished in recent weeks, Bates circulated a memo warning volunteers to avoid unnecessary risk taking as the fighting intensified:

> It is a strict rule of the American Red Cross that no member of that organization shall deliberately put himself in the way of danger, excepting in the performance of his duty. This refers to sight-seeing ex-

peditions to the first line trenches, to flights in aeroplanes and to any other action which has in it an element of danger due to our proximity to the front.[34]

He also reminded them of their mission as humanitarian aid workers, noting that they were "forbidden to fire off field artillery or in any other way to perform an act of aggression which is not compatible with their character as Red Cross workers."[35] After losing his close friend and reporting the narrow escapes among many of the new recruits, Bates not only endeavored to avoid future casualties but also made efforts to see that his volunteers adhered to the rules of the Geneva Convention.

As heavy fighting continued, workers were encouraged to participate with Italians in celebrations observing Independence Day. In honoring "our national fete," as Bates reported, the headquarters in Vicenza hosted "various officials" during festivities that included a large gathering with a performance by a local band and public addresses by local and American administrators.[36] Lowell stood on the balcony of a Palazzo where he spoke to a group that gathered in the street, and Bates went on a "speech-making tour" of his own.[37] Later that evening, the captain joined Section Four for "a special Fourth of July dinner" after which the drivers "were entertained at the Officers' Club in the main square of Schio" by civic and military leaders. Another "crowd of about two thousand" gathered in the town square where a group of "school children sang the Star Spangled Banner and the Italian anthem."[38] The holiday served as an opportune occasion to underscore solidarity between the Red Cross and their beleaguered ally.

At the lower Piave, work for the canteen operators increased after delayed shipments began to arrive on July 1, and volunteers were also instructed "to make the Fourth of July a specially memorable occasion."[39] Hemingway spent the evening with Bill Horne and Warren Pease, who were manning a post at nearby San Pietro Novello.[40] The following day, Pease gave up on the assignment and was replaced by Section Four driver William D. Moore Jr.[41] Although some of the temporary volunteers returned to their sections, Hemingway decided to see his work through.[42] He wrote to high-school classmate Ruth Morrison telling her that "I sure have a good time but miss there being no Americans" and reflected on how far he had come since the year before:

It all seems about a million miles away and to think that this time last year we had just finished graduating. If anybody had told me when I was reading that damn fool prophecy last year that a year from date I would be sitting out in front of a dug out in a nice trench 20 yards from the Piave River and 40 yards from the Austrian lines listening to the little ones whimper way up in the air and the big ones go scheeeeeeeeek Boom and every once in a while a machine gun go tick a tack a tock I would have said, "Take another sip." That is some complicated sentence but it all goes to show what a bum prophet I was.[43]

In his class speech delivered in June of 1917, Ernest portrayed himself as a radio operator reporting "the news as it comes from the front." One of the "bulletins" predicted that some of his classmates would serve as "Red Cross nurses" and be "recommended for the cross of exceptional bravery."[44] After he was wounded at the Piave, supervisors sent dispatches referring to Hemingway's work conducted among the trenches instead.

Initial reports were based on limited information, but overall they indicated that Hemingway was not badly hurt. Although most accounts record the incident as it occurred "around midnight, on or about 8 July 1918," Bates did not contact Hemingway until July 11.[45] On the eighth, the captain wrote home to his family saying that he was "beginning to take things easy" and seemed "to have run out of news."[46] Three days later, he sent a letter of consolation to the injured man in his charge. "Dear Hemingway," he wrote,

I have learned with regret of your accident, and am very much relieved at the report which Captain Gamble has brought in. He assures me that your wounds are not serious and that you will soon recover. I went out to the Piave today with Major Lowell, and we tried to find the hospital that you were in, but having no exact information as to just where it was, we were unable to find it. You will receive good care in Milano, and I trust that before long you will be back again at the front.[47]

He signed the note and sent it to "Mr. E. M. Hemingway" at the "American Red Cross Hospital" at "4 Passagio Centrale" in Milan.[48] Meanwhile, administrators in Rome conducted two orders of business during their staff meeting held the same day. The secretary recorded that "a telegram from Major Lowell was read as to the injury to E. M. Hemingway and that such injury was not serious." After that, the officials "authorized to have rations for five hundred ambulance men continued," and the meeting was adjourned.[49] Around the same time, Lowell filed the first official report on the incident in his summary of activities of the Department of Military Affairs for the month of June. He noted only that "Mr. Hemingway, while discharging his duties, was wounded by a trench bomb."[50]

Notifications were also sent to Hemingway's family and published in newspapers. On July 13, the Red Cross office in Kansas City received a telegram from Rome that was forwarded through Washington D. C. and picked up by Ernest's aunt Arabella, wife of Alfred Tyler Hemingway.[51] The brief message arrived in time to be included in the 6:30 edition of the *Kansas City Star*. "E. M. Hemingway Wounded" appeared with an illustration of the former cub reporter and referred to him as "the first casualty to any of the *Star*'s 132 former employees now fighting with the Allies." The "meager details" told that Ernest was "temporarily doing canteen work, wounded, not dangerously," and a similar write-up appeared on the following day.[52] Arabella sent the cable along with a clipping of the *Star* to Hemingway's parents in Oak Park two days after she heard the news.[53] Meanwhile, Hemingway's father received a wire from Washington on July 13 as well.[54] Three days later, he got another cable from Ernest: "Wounded in legs by trench mortar; not serious; will receive valor medal; will walk in about ten days."[55] The *Chicago Evening Post* ran a story mentioning the incident that same day, and on July 17, the *Kansas City Times* printed another report saying that "Army headquarters" recommended Hemingway for "the Italian Cross for Valor for bravery in action" after he had supposedly brought "several wounded Italian soldiers into a dressing station."[56]

William Castle of the Washington Bureau of the American Red Cross wrote to Clarence with an update on July 20. He passed along word that many of the ambulance drivers were decorated after the recent victory and mentioned a cable indicating that

> your son was wounded while distributing relief to the soldiers in the trenches, and that he is progressing and will recover. He was wounded by a bomb from trench mortar and received 237 separate wounds in his leg. All but ten of these wounds are superficial.[57]

Clarence responded to say that "I assure you we are proud . . . and shall ever pray that he may recover and do more good work to help you as you have seen he is brave and fearless in his service."[58] On the same day Castle's letter arrived, the *Oak Leaves*, Hemingway's hometown newspaper, printed a photograph of Ernest from his high school yearbook along with a brief account of his recent exploits at the Piave.[59] A picture of Anson Hemingway in his Civil War uniform appeared on the page after the story about "his grandson."[60]

In the weeks that followed, the Hemingway family received more substantial news. Ted Brumback wrote a letter addressed to Hemingway's father on July 14, stating that "I have just come from seeing Ernest at the American Red Cross Hospital here. He is fast on the road to recovery and will be out a whole man once again."[61] Brumback told Dr. Hemingway that "some two hundred pieces of shell were lodged in him" but "none of them were above the hip joint" and "only a few of these pieces was large enough to cut deep; the most serious of these being two in the knee and two in the right foot." Describing the "circumstances of the case," Ted added that

> an enormous trench mortar lit within a few feet of Ernest while he was giving out chocolate. The concussion of the explosion knocked him unconscious and buried him with earth. There was an Italian between Ernest and the shell. He was instantly killed while another, standing a few feet away, had both his legs blown off. A third Italian was badly wounded and this one Ernest, after he had regained consciousness, picked up on his back and carried to the first aid dug-out. He says he does not remember how he got there nor that he had carried a man until the next day when an Italian officer told him all about it and said that it had been voted upon to give him a valor medal for the act.[62]

Brumback explained that Ernest "has not written himself because one or two of the splinters lodged in his fingers." The wounded volunteer added a postscript nonetheless, saying that "I am all O. K." and "not near so much of a hell roarer as Brummy makes me out."[63] Hemingway's father had copies made of the "fine letter" bringing "first news from Ernest direct" and distributed them among friends and family.[64] Although Brumback's letter did not mention anything about machine-gun fire, his account provided new details about aiding a wounded man and explained that soldiers had elected to recommend Ernest for the Silver Medal immediately following the incident. The *Oak Leaves* published Brumback's account in full on August 10.[65]

On his nineteenth birthday, Hemingway wrote his first letter home since his hospitalization. He told his parents that "I hope that the cable didn't worry you very much but Capt. Bates thought it was best that you hear from me first rather than the newspapers."[66] Surprisingly, considering McKey's recent death, Hemingway announced that "I'm the first American wounded in Italy and I suppose the papers say something about it."[67] He was also receiving a lot of attention from the nurses who had only a few patients to deal with at the "peach of a hospital" where he resided in Milan. The surgeon decided to "wait for the wound" in "his right knee to become healed cleanly before operating," he explained. Besides the shell fragments, Ernest indicated that he was struck by additional projectiles, noting that the doctor "will also remove a bullet from my right foot at the same time" of the operation on the knee. Otherwise, "all the other bullets and pieces of shell have been removed," he added, and "there will be no permanent effects from any of the wounds as there are no bones shattered." Hemingway indicated that he hoped to be driving an ambulance in the mountains by "the latter part of August," and he anticipated being home by Christmas. At the end of the letter, he sketched a picture of "me drawn from life" showing his bandaged leg with a note indicating "227 wounds" written in the center. He drew a speech balloon coming out of the stick figure's mouth: "gimme a drink!" it said.[68]

A few days after Hemingway's birthday, Captain Bates filed "Ambulance Report No. 9," the first Red Cross document to describe the incident at any length. In summarizing the work of the emergency canteen posts, Bates explained that

> in addition to serving coffee, cigarettes, chocolate, etc. at the points set directly back of the line, the men carried supplies into the front line trenches. During such a trip, E. M. Hemingway of Section 4 was wounded by the explosion of a shell which landed about three feet from him, killing a soldier who stood between him and the point of explosion, and wounding others. Due to the soldier who lost his life and who protected Hemingway somewhat from the explosion, and due also to the fact that the eclats [shell-casing fragments] had not yet obtained their full range, Hemingway was only wounded in the legs. He sustained ten fairly serious wounds and two hundred and twenty-seven punctures. He is now in the American Hospital at

Milan and has yet to undergo an operation to remove shrapnel from his knee.[69]

Although Bates referred to "ten fairly serious wounds" as more substantial than he originally indicated in his initial letter on July 11, he characterized the 227 "punctures" as minor, and he explained that the injuries were confined to Hemingway's legs. As the first sentence of the description shows, the captain underscored that the incident occurred in the course of typical duties expected of all "the men" who "carried supplies into the front line trenches." Additionally, he associated Hemingway with Section Four, a detail that calls attention to the fact that Ernest was not transferred permanently out of his ambulance unit upon being assigned to the *posti di conforto*. More remarkably, however, Bates did not say anything about Hemingway aiding another wounded man and actually referred to a soldier who shielded him from the explosion instead. In employing the word *protected*, Bates implies that the Italian might have deliberately sacrificed himself in order to save Ernest. The report mentioned nothing about forthcoming citations for Hemingway either.

On July 30, Gamble filed "Cucina Report No. 6: June," his first description of the canteen service after having succeeded Bates as director on June 2.[70] Although Gamble did not provide a description of Hemingway in his summary, he attached a dispatch from Moses S. Slaughter "showing the very splendid work which was done by him and Consul [B. Harvey] Carroll" during the Austrian offensive.[71] Slaughter's "Report on emergency *posti di conforto*," dated July 26, 1918, contains a brief account of the incident: "In the discharge of his duties, carrying food to the men in the trenches, Mr. Hemingway was wounded by a trench bomb and is now in the hospital at Milano."[72] Similar to Bates's report, Slaughter indicates that Hemingway was injured in the course of performing work expected of him, and there is no mention of carrying a soldier to safety amid machine-gun fire or a recommendation for an award.

Contrary to initial Red Cross reports, letters by Hemingway written around the same time indicate that he received high praise. In early August, he told his parents that

there was a big parade last Sunday and they took me out with my legs strapped to a board.

With a body guard of about six Italian officers I sat on the plaza and

reviewed the troops. The crowd cheered me for about ten solid minutes and I had to take off my cap and bow about 50 times. They threw
flowers all over me and every body wanted to shake my hand and the
girls all wanted my name so they could write to me. The master journalist was known to the crowd as the American Hero of the Piave. I'm
nothing but a second Lieut. or Soto Tenente but all the Captains saluted me first. Oh it was very thrilling. I tried to act very dignified but
felt very embarrassed.[73]

A few days later, Hemingway wrote to his sister about the "scars" he received as "marks of valour which be many and various" and repeated
the designation he mentioned to his parents, telling Marcelline that he
was "now known as The Heero of the Peehave."[74] A month later, the *Oak
Leaves* reported that "Lieut. Ernest Hemingway, Ambulance Service, is
packing enough thrills away into his old kit bag to last any ordinary soldier a lifetime." The article stated that "King Victor has personally decorated him" and provided an embellished version of the account that he
had recently sent to his parents:

Strapped to a board, his body riddled with wounds where two hundred pieces of shell had found lodging, he was carried out on the pi-
azza of the Red Cross hospital at Milan the other day and given an ova-
tion worthy of an Admiral Dewey or a General Pershing. Italian girls
pelted him with flowers and high Italian officers stood at salute while
crowds acclaimed him as the "American hero of the Piave."[75]

Outside of the Red Cross record, Hemingway apparently received significant recognition by the Italian people for his deeds in the trenches.

On August 5, 1918, Lowell published another account on Hemingway
in the *Red Cross Bulletin* in Italy. The announcement was the first description by an administrator referring to a heroic act by Ernest in addition to
"distributing relief to soldiers in the trenches." Lowell wrote that "volunteer F. M. [*sic*] Hemingway of Kansas City, an Ambulance Driver of Section No. 4 . . . has been commended for the way in which he conducted
himself, having carried a wounded Italian some distance to succor after
having been wounded himself."[76] Although the *Bulletin* provided only a
brief mention, it nonetheless seems to verify the stories about Hemingway's self-sacrifice.

Lowell's subsequent report on activities for July contains another description of the incident that is more detailed than the brief mention in his summary of work for June:

> On July 12th Lieut. E. M. Hemingway who was lent to this service temporarily by Ambulance Section Four and who was working at Fornaci, back of the Piave, was wounded by a trench mortar projector [sic]. He was in the first line trenches at the time distributing supplies to the soldiers as he had been every night while he was connected with the canteen service. Lieut. Hemingway was taken to the American Red Cross Hospital in Milan where he is still.[77]

Similar to Bates and Slaughter, Lowell stresses that Hemingway was performing duties in keeping with his assignment and even points out that he was engaged in his work "every night" while affiliated with the *posti di conforto*. The incorrect date he provides is a relatively minor error, but more surprisingly, after publishing his announcement in the *Red Cross Bulletin,* Lowell did not mention that Hemingway carried the Italian soldier "to succor." He said nothing about a proposal for a military citation either. Lowell's reference to Hemingway as a "lieutenant," on the other hand, is the first indication that Ernest received a mark of distinction among his peers.

Lowell refers to Hemingway again in an overview of the first six months of work conducted by his department. Most of the information presented in monthly reports has been abridged, and the statement on Hemingway's wounding is a brief rewording of the earlier description issued by Bates in "Ambulance Report No. 9." Once more, the heroic story about aiding a soldier has been omitted:

> The men serving these canteens not only distributed coffee, cigarettes and chocolate at the canteen bases, but also carried supplies into the frontline trenches. During such a trip, E. M. Hemingway was wounded by the explosion of a shell which landed about three feet from him, killing a soldier who stood between him and the point of explosion, and wounding others.[78]

Elsewhere in the report, Ernest's name does not appear in the appendix indicating those "decorated by the Italian Government" either.[79] Lowell did, however, include Hemingway among the "names of the lieutenants in charge of the canteens at the end of July," designating him along with Samuel Sturgeon as assigned to Post 14 even though Ernest was convalescing in Milan by that time.[80] Hemingway sent a copy of this report to his parents with a handwritten note on the front cover indicating the paltry coverage he had received: "Official Red Cross Bulletin only allowed to print cold facts—that's why there is no story," he told them.[81]

On August 18, Hemingway wrote his own detailed account of the incident.[82] He addressed the epistle to his "folks" including "Grandma and Grandpa and Aunt Grace" and referred to it as "the longest letter I've ever written to anybody." After his limited experience in combat, he wrote from the point of view of an expert: "I wouldn't say it was hell," he explained, "because that's been a bit overworked since Gen. Sherman's time, but there have been about 8 times when I would have welcomed Hell. Just on a chance that it couldn't come up to the phase of war I was experiencing." He described the trenches "during an attack" and noted that "shells aren't bad except direct hits. You just take chances on the fragments of the bursts. But when there is a direct hit your pals get spattered all over you. Spattered is literal." Unlike the types of "hardships" he had jokingly referred to in the June edition of *Ciao,* he discussed actual risks at the front: "Well I can now hold up my hand and say I've been shelled by high explosive, shrapnel and gas. Shot at by trench mortars, snipers and machine guns. And as an added attraction an aeroplane machine gunning the lines." Although he "never had a hand grenade thrown at" him, a "rifle grenade struck rather close."

After noting that he had a reputation for leading a "charmed life" while at the front, he described his wounding. He was "struck by a trench mortar and a machine gun bullet while advancing toward the rear" he explained:

> The 227 wounds I got from the trench mortar didn't hurt a bit at the time, only my feet felt like I had rubber boots full of water on. Hot water. And my kneecap was acting queer. The machine gun bullet just felt like a sharp smack on my leg with an icy snow ball. However it spilled me. But I got up again and got my wounded into the dug out. I kind of collapsed at the dug out.

Although it is unclear why he mentioned only one "bullet," he referred to his legs as "a mess" due to fragments from the shell explosion and added that the soldiers "couldn't figure out how I had walked 150 yards with a load with both knees shot through and my right shoe punctured two big places. Also over 200 flesh wounds." Hemingway told the amazed "Captain who was a great pal of mine" that "in America they all do it!"[83]

After passing out for "a couple of minutes," he "came to" and was carried on a stretcher "three kilometers back to a dressing station." The stretcher bearers dropped to the ground "because the road was having the 'entrails' shelled out of it. Whenever a big one would come, Wheeeee whoosh—Boom—they'd lay me down and get flat. My wounds were now hurting like 227 little devils were driving nails into the raw." At this point, he told of another selfless act on his part:

> The dressing station had been evacuated during the attack so I lay for two hours in a stable, with the roof shot off, waiting for an ambulance. When it came I ordered it down the road to get the soldiers that had been wounded first. It came back with a load and then they lifted me in.

He rode in the "Italian ambulance" for "a couple of Kilomets" until "they unloaded me at the dressing station where I had a lot of pals among the medical officers." He received his first medical treatment there: a "shot of morphine" and "an anti tetanus injection" after which personnel "shaved my legs and took out about twenty 8 shell fragments." Subsequently, "they did a fine job of bandaging" and "would have kissed me but I kidded them along. Then I stayed 5 days in a field hospital and was then evacuated to the Base Hospital," the American Red Cross facility in Milan.[84]

Hemingway explained that he had also undergone an operation on August 10. "The Italian surgeon did a peach of a job on my right knee joint and right foot," he told his family, and "the wounds all healed up clean and there was no infection." The doctor had stabilized "his right leg in a plaster splint" and Ernest had saved some of the shrapnel extracts for "snappy souvenirs." The cast would be removed in a week after which time he would be allowed on crutches. "I'll have to learn to walk again," he said, but the medical staff assured him that he would do so "as well as ever."[85]

Considering all the details that came to light by August, it is surprising that Red Cross reports did not emphasize the incident. After examining Lowell's January-to-July report, Robert W. Lewis has also wondered why "Hemingway's wounding and his alleged carrying of a wounded comrade to safety" was not "played up" since the story appears to have exemplified the very reason Red Cross workers were serving in Italy.[86] Even more, while convalescing in Milan, Hemingway had, according to Carlos Baker,

> enjoyed the brotherly admiration of his comrades-in-arms, and gloried in his consciousness of having behaved well throughout his ordeal by fire and the long recuperation. Day after hot day in August, he sat or lay in his bed like a king on a throne, holding court and greeting all comers. Red Cross captains came to sit at his feet and listen to his monologues: Meade Detweiler, the Milan representative; Bob Bates, the inspector of ambulances; and Jim Gamble, the inspector of rolling canteens.[87]

Indeed, if officials were in awe of Hemingway as a result of his conduct in the trenches and thereafter, the omission of his story from the official record is even more puzzling.

Other descriptions of Hemingway by those who knew him, however, suggest that he was not venerated by all of his supervisors for heroism accomplished during the offensive. Agnes von Kurowsky recorded in her diary while working at the hospital in Milan that "everybody seems to be down on him for some reason, and he gets raked over the coals right & left. Some of the heads have an idea he is very wild and he is—in some respects."[88] Henry Villard, a fellow patient and otherwise enthusiastic admirer of Hemingway, acknowledged that Ernest could sometimes be "imperious if not downright irascible."[89] Bates would have agreed. When he became aware of Baker's account of Hemingway "holding court" from his "throne" in the hospital, the captain attached to his copy of "Ambulance Report No. 9" a note stating that the description, "except for the visit, was a complete lie, since I not only did not admire him but knew him to be an incomparable braggart and liar!"[90] Hemingway's statements about his status as the "first American wounded in Italy" as well as his recognition as the "Hero of the Piave," moreover, suggest a disregard for McKey, who earned the highest of accolades among his colleagues and was the only Red Cross worker Bates named as a close friend.[91]

Bates had other reasons to downplay Hemingway's story. Not long after the captain wrote his report at the end of July, Ernest made comments that suggested a violation of the notice that his supervisor issued during the June offensive. On July 29, Hemingway wrote to his mother that "while the master woodsman was putting in his week in the trenches he managed to strike several slight blows towards discouraging the Austrians."[92] Another message to Marcelline a little over a week later mentioned that he would soon tell her about "the many Austrians that have fallen at my [brawny] feet."[93] Similarly, Charles Fenton has written about "the legend which developed in Section IV" whereby "Hemingway was said to have been wounded a moment after he had seized an Italian rifle and began firing toward the Austrian lines."[94] Indeed, many of Ernest's letters over the course of his term with the Red Cross suggest, as Lewis has surmised, that he "wished to be perceived as an authentic combatant."[95] Although instances of Hemingway actually shooting at the enemy have never been verified, rumors indicating as much suggest noncompliance with Bates's order as well as a potential scandal for administrators in charge of workers providing humanitarian aid. Bates had previously intercepted letters by John Dos Passos and barred him from reenlistment as a result of his insubordination. Red Cross documents do not state that Hemingway was reprimanded for flouting regulations per se, but officials nonetheless failed to elaborate upon his story, and as a result, his extraordinary actions were not emphasized as exemplary within the organization.

Lowell's final summary downplays the incident even more. The "Report of the Department of Military Affairs January, 1918, to February, 1919" fails to even mention Hemingway's name in the passage referring to his injury:

> Courage and coolness under fire may also be mentioned as an attribute that these canteen officers were called upon to frequently display. One of these lieutenants was killed by an Austrian shell and another wounded in a front line trench while distributing supplies to soldiers by the explosion of a shell which landed about three feet from him.[96]

Although Lowell specifically elaborates upon courageous acts by McKey and other volunteers elsewhere in the account, Hemingway's episode was not highlighted in the final overview either.

Even though the reports never emphasized him as a hero, they do show that Hemingway was promoted to first lieutenant. As an officer in the Red Cross, he would have held the same rank, albeit honorary, in the Italian military. On August 18, however, Hemingway had yet to hear news of the upgrade. The postscript he wrote that day mentioned a letter he had received that was "addressed to Private Ernest H—." He clarified that "what I am is S. Ten. or Soto Tenenente Ernest Hemingway. That is my rank in the Italian Amy and it means 2nd Lieut. I hope to be a Tenente or 1st Lieut. soon."[97] Despite Lowell's report for July indicating that Ernest was promoted about a month after his injury, it was not until September that Hemingway wrote home to share the news with his family:

Oh, yes! I have been commissioned a 1st Lieutenant and now wear the two gold stripes on each of my sleeves. It was a surprise to me as I hadn't expected anything of the sort. So now you can address my mail either 1st Lieut. or Tenente as I hold the rank in both the A.R.C and Italian army.[98]

Several days later, he wrote to Marcelline likewise telling her that he was "wounded in the first lines and promoted for merit."[99]

Although Red Cross reports failed to mention that the Italian army planned to decorate him, Ernest's letters suggest otherwise. In early September, he wrote home to say that "my silver medaglia valore is on the way," and he had been "proposed for the war cross before I was wounded because of general foolish conduct in the trenches I guess."[100] In early November, he said that he was "wearing the ribbons of two medals" and mentioned that his "chief" had visited to say that the "Silver Medal wound had all gone through and would arrive in about three days." He told of an additional "Croix D'Guerre" that he "picked up this final offensive" and noted that "the cross and citation are out at the section now and I'll have 'em in a couple of days." He also referred to the "Distinctive Service Medal Ribbon," which was "green white and Red" and "pretty good looking." Indeed, Hemingway wrote that he was "getting quite a railway track" on his new uniform, but "it is kind of embarrassing because I have more than a lot of officers that have been in three and four years."[101] The well-known portrait taken of Hemingway in formal attire shows him wearing lieutenant stripes on his sleeves and ribbons over the left breast pocket of his uniform.[102]

Unlike several other volunteers who had been personally decorated by King Victor Emmanuel at the end of July, Ernest waited much longer to receive his medals. At the end of November, Captain Cacciapuoti informed him that the recommendation for the Silver Medal had not yet gone through:

> A proposition for a medal of valour to be awarded you has been presented some time ago to the War Office. This procedure will take sometime, but I trust that you will receive your medal before leaving Italy. As soon as anything will be heard of, we will immediately let you know.[103]

It was not until almost a year after his wounding on July 2, 1919, that he was notified about the exact wording of the proclamation,[104] and the official decree was not mailed until April 4, 1922.[105] Although Hemingway referred to three decorations in his letters, the citation he received stated that he had been given two awards, "the War Cross of Merit from the headquarters of the V Army Corps" and "the Silver Medal of Military Valor."[106] The formal explanation for the latter indicated two separate acts of heroism:

> Ernest Miller Hemingway of Illinois Park (Chicago) Lieutenant of the American Red Cross.——Officer of the American Red Cross, responsible for carrying sundries (articles of comfort) to the Italian troops engaged in combat, gave proof of courage and self-sacrifice. Gravely wounded by numerous pieces of shrapnel from an enemy shell, with an admirable spirit of brotherhood, before taking care of himself, he rendered generous assistance to the Italian soldiers more seriously wounded by the same explosion and did not allow himself to be carried elsewhere until after they had been evacuated.[107]

Overall, the June offensive resulted in a particularly high number of citations, but Hemingway's honors nonetheless placed him in an elite group. Out of the roughly three hundred personnel affiliated with the ambulance sections, only ten men received the Silver Medal. Approximately sixty received the War Cross.[108] In the context of all the volunteers serving at the front, Hemingway's decorations were exceptional among his peers. Moreover, although he was not the first American wounded in Italy, his circumstances were unique. During the Battle of the Piave, he was the only Red Cross worker to be injured in the trenches and survive his baptism by fire.

Hemingway "matured quickly" during his convalescence.[109] Among his mentors, he had "great old gab fests" during frequent visits from "a peach of a Catholic missionary Priest from India."[110] According to Agnes, he was also "devoted to" Italian Captain Enrico Serena, whom she had been dating prior to her romance with Ernest. "They tell each other all their secrets," she wrote.[111] Hemingway's conversations with British infantry officer Eric "Chink" Dorman-Smith often fixated on, according to Baker, "subjects of war and death, the behavior of men under fire, and the enthralling topic of personal courage."[112] Dorman-Smith told Hemingway about the quotation from Shakespeare's *The Second Part of Henry the Fourth:* "By my troth, I care not; a man can die but once; we owe God a death . . . and let it go which way it will, he that dies this year is quit for the next."[113] One of Ernest's letters from that fall expressed a similar sentiment: "Dying is a very simple thing," he told his father, "I've looked at death, and really I know. If I should have died it would h[a]ve been very easy for me. Quite the easiest thing I ever did." He included another statement diminishing his personal sacrifice: "There are no heroes in this war," he remarked, "we all offer our bodies and only a few are chosen, but it shouldn't reflect any special credit on those that are chosen." After sharing his latest impressions, Ernest asked his parents if he still sounded like "the crazy wild kid you sent out to learn about the world a year ago."[114] He also began to express uneasiness about some of the things he had previously written related to his wounding. Once he learned that newspapers were quoting liberally from his letters, he told his sister that "somebody has a lot of gall publishing them and it will look like I'm trying to pull hero stuff."[115]

Hemingway also expressed his continued commitment to the Allied Cause throughout his remaining time in Italy. A month after his operation, he told his father that "I would like to go back to the ambulance but I wont be much use driving for about Six months. I will probably take command of some 1st line post up in the mountains."[116] At the end of August, Bates distributed a memo quoting from a directive issued by President Wilson encouraging noncombatants to stay with their assignments even though the draft age had been lowered. Administrators feared that the change would inspire men to abandon the Red Cross for a chance at military service. Wilson had announced that

> as the American Red Cross is such an important auxiliary to our armed forces, I hope that every man connected with the work either at home or abroad will have a full appreciation of its importance and will if possible continue to render service unless and until specifically called to other and clearly more important duty.[117]

Accordingly, Hemingway told his father that "all of us Red X men here were ordered not to register. It would be foolish for us to come home because the Red X is a necessary organization and they would just have to get more men from the states to keep it going." He was also apt to point out the significance of the work despite Wilson's emphasis on "more important" service: "The ambulance is no slackers job," Hemingway wrote, "we lost one man killed and one wounded in the last two weeks."[118] Indeed, his awareness of the recent casualties did not lead him to shy away from the action either.

By the end of October, an opportunity to get involved once again came when the final major offensive was launched. Since the U.S. Army ambulance corps began to operate in the region, the number of personnel remaining in Hemingway's organization decreased significantly. The volunteers from Harvard were shipped home on September 21 so they could resume their studies for the fall semester. Several others left to join various branches of foreign military service. With only sixty-seven men still serving at the front, drivers were in high demand to aid in the final push against the Austrians when intense fighting broke out on October 24. Bates toured the sections and shifted personnel and vehicles to locales where they were most needed. Nearly all of the workers from Hemingway's unit at Schio were in Bassano to help bring wounded down from Mount Grappa. Bates reported that he found "terrible conditions" there. Despite the efforts of the volunteers, there were "at least a hundred and fifty" injured soldiers "lying at the dressing station without a single conveyance to carry them down." Many of them had to "lay in the mud outside of the post" until additional resources could be spared from other sectors.[119]

After a few days of intense action, the Battle of Vittoria Veneto, as it came to be called, resulted in a major victory for the Allied Cause. Early in the morning of October 30, several of the drivers from Section Five put together a convoy to join the throng preparing to cross the Piave as Italian troops advanced into territory that had been occupied by the enemy ever since the retreat from Caporetto. The Red Cross workers spent hours sitting in a traffic jam that kept them waiting until nine o'clock at night before they could move forward. Bates finally gave up on the venture and decided to go over on foot the next morning. The "conditions lasted for three entire days and nights," he wrote, and "added tremendously to the confusion" as soldiers and combatants alike attempted to forge ahead. Bates observed that "civilians were already returning to their homes carrying house-hold furniture on their backs or pushing it along in wheel-barrows over the almost impassable roads."[120] As the ambulance units advanced with the military, the drivers had to deal with makeshift accommodations. Many of them resorted to camping in open fields or sleeping in their vehicles. Finally, on November 3, heads of state signed an armistice. Hostilities were scheduled to cease at three in the afternoon the next day. Bates spent November 4 touring the headquarters of each section to check on remaining personnel and vehicles. He passed through "villages decorated with flags" and was "greeted with cheers by the townspeople." While driving through Schio, the clock struck the appointed hour, and "the church bells were ringing and there was great rejoicing."[121] The war had officially ended on the Italian front.

At the start of the offensive, Hemingway had recuperated enough to be able to visit his colleagues, but he still required the use of a cane. "I now have a bum leg and foot," he wrote, "and there isnt an army in the world that would take me. But I can be of service over here [a]nd I will stay here just as long as I can hobble and there is a war to hobble to."[122] On the eve of the battle, he caught up with his fellow ambulance drivers at Bassano. Hemingway experienced none of the excitement, however, since he returned to Milan the next day after onset of hepatitis. He wrote about the end of the war from his hospital bed, telling his parents that he "worked hard day and night where the worst mountain fighting was and then came down with jaundice." Even so, he had "the satisfaction of being in the offensive any way."[123] After peace had been declared throughout Europe, he sent another letter stating that "its all over!" Apparently, he had come "very close to the big adventure in this last offensive" and was glad to "end it with such a victory!" Now that hostilities had ceased, he planned to begin "the war to make the world Safe for Ernie Hemingway" by figuring out a way to earn a living.[124]

Even though he attempted to help out in the final battle, most of Hemingway's remaining months in Italy were spent enjoying opportunities for leisure. His time in Milan included frequent gatherings with nurses he befriended, American aviators, and several of his colleagues who came in and out of the hospital because of various ailments: Coles Seeley, Henry Villard, Bill Horne, and John Miller were among them. A trip with Miller to Stresa in September offered fishing on Lago Maggiore, drinks and billiards at the Grand Hotel, special attention shown by the prominent Bellia family, and conversations with Count Emanuele Greppi, who, as Ernest wrote, "has had love affairs with all the historical women of the last century it seems and yarned at length about all of them."[125] Another prospect for travel with Italian officer Nick Neroni promised "two weeks shooting and trout fishing in the province of Abruzzi."[126] Instead of going with Neroni, Hemingway made another visit to the defunct combat zone in December and observed remnants of the final offensive during a tour "all up over the old battle field." He "walked across the suspension bridge and saw the old Austrian front line trenches and the mined houses of Nervessa [sic] by moonlight and searchlight." It was "a great trip," he told his parents.[127] After a sojourn to Taormina later that month, Hemingway divulged to Dorman-Smith that he "had seen nothing of Sicily except from a bedroom window because his hostess in the first small hotel he stopped in had hidden his clothes and kept him to herself for a week." The story, as Baker has explained, seemed to have grown from Hemingway's "love of yarning."[128] Related tales among ambulance drivers no doubt influenced him as well. After the jaunt in December, Hemingway considered yet another opportunity for adventure with Gamble, who had offered to cover expenses while the two lived together for a year abroad.[129]

Despite the chance to loaf around Europe, Hemingway's romance with Agnes von Kurowsky led him to consider other options. On the same day he wrote home about his promotion and forthcoming citations, Agnes gave the "Kid," as she called him, her ring as a token of affection. In October, after being transferred from her nursing assignment in Milan to Florence, she began to sign her letters to Ernest as "Mrs. Kid" and mentioned that "I sometimes wish we could marry over here."[130]

Ernest made a few references to "the girl" in letters to his parents, but he shared more revealing information to his sister:

> I don't know what I've written you about my girl but really, Kid Ivory I love her very much. Also she loves me. In fact I love her more than anything or anybody in the world or the world its-self. And Kid I've got a lot clearer look a[t] the world and things than when I was at home. Really Ivory you wouldn't know me. I mean to look at or to talk to. You know those pictures we took at home before I left? Well showing them to Ag the other day she didn't recognize me in them. So that shows I've changed some.[131]

Hemingway's enthusiasm for his relationship, unlike the Mae Marsh episode in New York, included serious plans to earn a living with the goal of supporting a family.[132]

Letters from Agnes and Brumback suggest that Hemingway initially tried to find gainful employment by seeking additional work with the Red Cross. Agnes wrote to Ernest on November 3 asking him to "tell me something about that Publicity Dept. job. Will you be in Rome all the time, or traveling around through Italy?"[133] Ted informed Hemingway's parents that Ernest had intended to remain abroad through the following summer: "I think his plan is to enter the Red Cross civilian relief, work down somewhere in Southern Italy," he told them.[134] Instead of staying on in Europe, however, Ernest had been convinced by Agnes to pursue a more productive career in the States, where he could find a job and "bring home the proverbial" bacon.[135]

Two days after hostilities ceased, Bates filed his last report on the ambulance and canteen operations. After accounting for activity during the Battle of Vittorio Veneto, he declared the dissolution of all units except for Section One, the first "to come down over the road from France." Hemingway's group at Schio was scheduled to leave by November 20 at the latest. "Our work," Bates wrote, "is practically at an end." The captain concluded with a final assessment of their overall effectiveness:

> There have been periods of inactivity and there have been times when we have all of us questioned our usefulness. The writer feels, however, in looking back over the past ten months since he has had charge of this service that there can be no question regarding the

good work which we have done. In our opinion the work done during the Austrian offensive and the Italian counteroffensive in June alone justified the service, and had we done no other work but this, we would feel the service has been worth while.[136]

Hemingway's date of release from the Red Cross was recorded as November 16.[137] His "official discharge papers" were signed by Commissioner Robert Perkins in Rome on December 31, certifying that "Lieut. Hemingway has served in the capacity of ambulance driver in a faithful and efficient manner, and is hereby given an honorable discharge from the service of the American Red Cross."[138] He continued to receive therapy treatments for his leg through December, and on January 4, he boarded the *Giuseppe Verdi* for the voyage home.

As soon as the ship pulled in to port, Hemingway began to receive attention as a hero. The day after he arrived in lower Manhattan, a journalist from the *New York Sun* ran a story on his homecoming called "Has 227 Wounds, but Is Looking for Job."[139] The article referred to Ernest as "the first wounded American from the Italian front" with "probably more scars than any other man in or out of uniform, who defied the shrapnel of the Central Powers." His injuries "might have been much less," the reporter noted, "if he had not been constructed by nature on generous proportions, being more than six feet tall and of ample beam." The account added that Hemingway "believes he will be qualified to take a job on any New York newspaper that wants a man that is not afraid of work and wounds." Three days later, the *Oak Leaves* printed a notice stating that the "first American to be wounded in Italy" is "convalescent" and "expected home" soon.[140]

Roselle Dean's article in the *Oak Parker* appeared the following week. "First Lieutenant Hemingway Comes Back Riddled with Bullets and Decorated with Two Medals" took up two-thirds of the page and was accompanied by a handsome photograph of Hemingway dressed in his tailored uniform adorned with Sam Browne belt. After his "opportunity came to get into the Italian Ambulance service," Dean explained that he

landed in the Trentino mountains of Italy and was in the big Austrian offensive along the Piave River. He moved later to Fossalta and became attached to an Italian infantry regiment there, remaining from the middle of June until he was wounded on the 8th of July. In the fight at Fossalta he was wounded three times when he went with a motor truck into the front lines to distribute cigarettes and block chocolate to the soldiers.

Even though "Lieutenant Hemingway scoffs at being referred to as a 'hero,'" his "valor" was much to be admired, she added. The "soldier" was otherwise reticent about his experience, but "his medals and Italian newspapers tell the rest." Nowhere in the account did she explicitly mention that Hemingway served as a volunteer for the Red Cross.[141]

Hemingway's exploits earned him invitations to speak at various meetings around Oak Park.[142] According to Frederick Ebersold, who reported the event for the student newspaper, Hemingway made a visit to his former high school at the end of the first week of February and lectured to the Hanna Club about his "adventures as a war correspondent and ambulance worker in Italy."[143] Ebersold explained that although Hemingway was "too modest to tell much about himself," he shared stories about the Arditi and told "a little about" his wounding. Regarding the trial by fire, Ernest recalled to the audience that

> it was night and the star shells were continually lighting up the place. I happened to look over the top, and just then there was a bright light and I felt as if I were falling through the air. I thought I was dead, but I soon came to and found the observation post was strewn all over the ground.[144]

Ebersold filled in the rest of the details, noting that Hemingway "rescued the Italian by carrying him back to the trench hospital after Ernie, himself, had been wounded two hundred and thirty-some times." When the meeting ended, Hemingway led everyone outside where he fired off a star shell "to the satisfaction of all."[145]

Despite the praise, Hemingway's letters suggest conflicted attitudes toward the accolades bestowed upon him. A week after he arrived in Oak Park, he wrote to Horne telling him that he was "sick of this country" and annoyed by "people that want to be vicariously horrified" by "second hand thrills."[146] In early March, he sent a missive to Gamble saying that "I'm patriotic and willing to die for this great and glorious nation. But I hate like the deuce to live in it." He had become "so damned homesick for Italy" and noted with dissatisfaction that "they've tried to make a hero out of me here. But you know and I know that all the real heroes are dead." Although he included himself among "the male youth" from his town who had experienced serious action, he acknowledged that others were more qualified to lecture on the subject: "I've been doing the honors," he told Gamble, "but Al [Winslow] gets home next week and he brought down several boche and left an arm in a German Field Dressing station so I have announced my retirement from the public eye on his arrival."[147] Indeed, Hemingway was trying out the voice of the seasoned veteran, but he also expressed that he was reluctant to take on the role.

A few weeks later, he spoke about his exploits to the entire student body of his high school. On the morning of the event, the *Trapeze* printed "Learn This for Assembly," a brief announcement providing words "to be sung to the tune of the Oak Park song":

Hemingway, we hail you the victor,
Hemingway, ever winning the game,
Hemingway, you've carried the colors
For our land you've won fame.
Hemingway, we hail you the leader,
Your deeds—every one shows your valor.
Hemingway, Hemingway, you've won
—Hemingway![148]

After he gave his speech, the student newspaper ran another story summarizing the main points of his lecture. According to Edwin Wells, Hemingway was "late of the Italian Ambulance Service of the American Red Cross and then of the Italian Army."[149] Wells's reference to military service was "not exactly a lie," as Michael Reynolds has explained, "but it was difficult to explain why."[150] The talk included sensational accounts of the Arditi, one of whom "had been shot in the chest but had plugged the holes with cigarettes and gone on fighting." Hemingway likewise referred to a popular song among the shock troops that "would have meant three months in jail" if sung by "any other body of men." He sang it "in Italian and then translated it" for the audience. In addition to tales of martial exploits, he provided another description of his near-death experience. Elaborating on the anecdote he used in his account to the Hannah Club, he explained that it seemed as if I was moving off somewhere in a sort of red din. I said to myself, 'Gee! Stein, you're dead' and then I began to feel myself pulling back to earth. Then I woke up. The sand bags had caved in on my legs and at first I felt disappointed that I had not been wounded.

Additional details referred to the circumstances thereafter. One of the soldiers with him had started crying, and Hemingway "told him to shut up" because the "Austrians seemed determined to wipe out this one outpost." When Ernest picked up the injured man to carry him back to the trenches, he noticed his own knee cap "felt warm and sticky, so I knew I'd been touched." After summarizing Hemingway's "modest story," Wells described the veteran's decorations, the souvenirs he brought home, and his "punctured trousers."[151]

Although accounts of Hemingway's wounding were in high demand in Oak Park upon his return, his exploits were not included in the volumes published by Red Cross officials the following year. Henry Davison, former chairman of the War Council, referred to the ambulance and rolling kitchen operations in his chapter on "The Story in Italy," but other than a brief mention noting that some of the "Italian Divisions" said that McKey "was the entire American Army," he avoided references to individual volunteers.[152] At the same time, Charles Bakewell, past administrator in the Department of Public Information in Rome, produced an entire volume on the commission in Italy. Although he noted that "as far as it is possible to do so, names will be omitted altogether," Bakewell also made an exception for McKey and devoted part of a chapter to the canteen operator's contributions and the story of his death.[153] Otherwise, he anonymously alluded to the men who performed "many deeds of individual daring" during the June offensive, providing details from Red Cross documents that indicate the actions of Goldthwaite Dorr, Robert Corey, Walter Feder, Frederick Agate, and John Miller.[154] Among the "narrow escapes from death," he referred only to "one man who was wounded and that slightly, and one had to spend some time in the hospital as a result of a gas attack."[155] In one of the appendices, Bakewell listed Hemingway with the members of Section Four and added an asterisk next to his name denoting that he received a Silver Medal, but his War Cross was not mentioned. Neither was he referred to under the heading for those who served with "the Rolling Kitchen Service."[156] Indeed, the final official chronicles had little to say about Hemingway as a hero.

Five *Dopo la Guerra*

As the war came to a close, the men who formed the ambulance units moved on to other endeavors. After Richard Norton had a falling-out with U.S. officials during militarization on the Western front, he took an assignment with the French government to investigate rumors of German espionage. In December of 1917, he returned to his home in London and died of meningitis the following August. Robert W. Bates was on leave from Vicenza at the time and assisted as a pallbearer at the funeral. A. Piatt Andrew and several of his drivers converted the American Field Service into a charitable organization supporting students from the United States studying in France. In 1921, Andrew was elected to the House of Representatives by the people of the Sixth Congressional District in Massachusetts and held his seat for seven consecutive terms. Herman Harjes served in the American Expeditionary Force under General John Pershing and was wounded in August of 1918. He was discharged as a lieutenant colonel in May of 1919 and returned to his position as Senior Partner of Morgan, Harjes & Co. in Paris.[1]

After peace was declared in Italy, the Red Cross commission was demobilized by March of 1919. Colonel Robert P. Perkins, formerly president of the Bigelow-Hartford Carpet Company and a director in the National Park Bank, took up residence once again in New York City and resumed his activities among various social clubs in Manhattan. Friends of his claimed that "he sapped his strength during the war," and Perkins died after a long illness in April of 1924.[2] Major Guy Lowell went to Brookline, Massachusetts, where he continued as an architect until his death on February 5, 1927. A week later, officials paid tribute to his "supreme and final achievement" at the dedication ceremony for the New York County Court House.[3] In October of 1918, Captain Bates declined an offer from Perkins to stay on as an administrator. Instead, he went to Paris and married Juliette Marchand, a French nurse who cared for him after his appendectomy at the American Hospital in Neuilly. Bates returned to Boston and later moved to California where he took up farming.[4] Before heading the canteen units, Captain James Gamble had studied at the Pennsylvania Academy of Fine Arts. After the armistice, he remained abroad for several months until he went home to Philadelphia and resumed painting.[5] In late January of 1919, Lieutenant Ernest Hemingway returned to Oak Park, Illinois, and embarked on his career as a professional writer. His adventure abroad had a profound impact on his work, and he drew from each phase of his experience for a substantial amount of material over the course of his entire career.

Hemingway never published a fictional account that closely follows his journey to war, but his writing incorporates many related aspects, albeit from a different point of view. One of the most obvious parallels is apparent in portrayals that depict the youthfulness of participants at the front. The injured narrator of "In Another Country," for example, frequently refers to himself and the wounded soldiers with whom he associates as "boys."[6] In A Farewell to Arms, Catherine Barkley mentions her deceased fiancé as "a boy" killed at the Battle of the Somme.[7] When Frederic Henry is convalescing in Milan, he describes three of his fellow patients likewise, referring to a "thin boy," a "nice boy," and a "fine boy" (107–08). Even though Henry appears somewhat older and more experienced, he also thinks of himself in youthful terms, as when he leaves the action on the battlefront to enjoy his idyll with Catherine in Switzerland: "I had the feeling of a boy who thinks of what is happening at a certain hour at the schoolhouse from which he has played truant" (245). Colonel Cantwell, in Across the River and Into the Trees, frequently describes his younger self as a "boy" when recalling his World War I adventures, and Hemingway remembered himself likewise, as evident in his comments in the introduction to Men at War suggesting that he was "a boy" who "was very ignorant" in 1918.[8] As James Steinke has observed on "In Another Country," the fictional stories indicating youthful idealism are not "fictionalized personal history,"[9] but they demonstrate the influence of a key feature of Ernest's departure for war considering that numerous volunteers were inspired to join because of their naïveté.

A fragment from Hemingway's unpublished account of a journey analogous to his own, significantly titled "Along with Youth a Novel," not only focuses on many of the participants as young men but also contains, as Michael Reynolds has pointed out, descriptions of apprehension over impending involvement in the battle zone.[10] Although aspects of the volunteers' voyage aboard an ocean liner to Bordeaux are very near Hemingway's trip on the *Chicago*, the mood is strikingly different from the writer's in 1918.[11] Instead of characterizing the episode as a lighthearted adventure, Hemingway's fictional narrative renders the events with muted undertones that create an ominous atmosphere. The lifeboats, for example, serve as a setting for the ignominious sexual diversions of Gaby, "the only girl" among the passengers, as well as the site of a late-night conversation between two young men on their way to different battlefronts: Nick, who "won't be in France" but expresses a desire to fight there nonetheless, and Leon Chocianowicz, who will serve on the Western front (137, 141). While Chocianowicz tells Nick that "we don't have to think about being scared. . . . We're not that kind," it is clear that his partner is nonetheless nervous about what lies ahead (142). The lifeboats that are "swung out ready to be lowered" increase the level of anxiety: "It scared Nick to look down at the water as he climbed out on the davits" (138, 141). Indeed, the conversation about expectations for war amid the potential for enemy attack during the crossing is laden with angst over the uncertainty of conditions at the front.

"Along with Youth a Novel" is an incomplete experiment for writing about the journey to war, but another one of Hemingway's earliest accounts handles the same theme with more complexity. "Chapter I," a short piece that he twice published as the introductory story in a series of sketches before including it as an inter-chapter of *In Our Time*, provides a brief but effective description of soldiers headed to battle in France.[12] In a letter to Ezra Pound describing the subject and design for the sequence of short pieces, Hemingway wrote that "the war starts clear and noble just like it did, Mons, etc."[13] Accordingly, "Chapter I" ironically emphasizes the combination of anxiety and intoxication as a prelude to combat. The sketch begins by pointing out that "everybody was drunk. The whole battery was drunk going along the road in the dark. We were going to the Champagne."[14] Besides the inebriated soldiers, the narrator mentions a nervous adjutant who orders him to extinguish the fire in his mobile kitchen: "You must put it out. It is dangerous. It will be observed," he is told, even though the group is still some "fifty kilometers from the front" (65). Considering the drunken antics of the men and the absurdity of the adjutant's concern, the speaker remarks that "it was funny going along that road" (65).

On the other hand, the sketch implies that these events are extremely grave. The irony is achieved through the narrator's comment indicating his temporal distance from the events described: "That was when I was a kitchen corporal," he states at last (65). From a perspective grounded in the aftermath of combat at the Champagne, a "notoriously bloody" battlefield, as Milton A. Cohen explains, the narrator's account of drunkenness as a prerequisite for courage implies a tragic outcome for the soldiers who seem unprepared to face fighting in the trenches.[15] The "highly stylized" prose, as Cohen describes it, shows a particularly sophisticated approach to portraying prewar innocence from the perspective of a mature, unobtrusive point of view.[16]

Another fictional account suggests the experience of going to war as "the thing left out."[17] Hemingway's "Soldier's Home," a story that focuses on the aftermath, begins with a brief introduction alluding to the protagonist's enlistment. The three-sentence opening omits overt discussion of the fervent publicity and hawkish enthusiasm that were widespread during Hemingway's enrollment:

> Krebs went to the war from a Methodist college in Kansas. There is a picture which shows him among his fraternity brothers, all of them wearing exactly the same height and style collar. He enlisted in the Marines in 1917 and did not return to the United States until the second division returned from the Rhine in the summer of 1919.[18]

The remarks serve as a classic example of the author's trademark "iceberg" theory put into practice, evoking the idealism that inspired Krebs and his fellow undergraduates from a postwar point of view.[19]

Furthermore, Hemingway's fictional references to military uniforms contrast with the enthusiastic letters he wrote describing similar garb donned in Kansas City and New York. In "A Way You'll Never Be," for example, Nick Adams is sarcastic about his attire:[20]

> "The uniform is not very correct," Nick told them. "But it gives you the idea. There will be several millions of Americans here shortly."
>
> "Do you think they will send Americans down here?" asked the adjutant.
>
> "Oh, absolutely. Americans twice as large as myself, healthy, with clean hearts, sleep at night, never been wounded, never been blown

up, never had their heads caved in, never been scared, don't drink, faithful to the girls they left behind them, many of them never had crabs, wonderful chaps. You'll see."[21]

Indeed, Nick's ironic remarks echo information that only fully came to light after the war. In *The Story of the American Red Cross in Italy*, a book Hemingway owned, Charles Bakewell explained that "the maximum number of American troops in Italy, all told, including twelve hundred ambulance men, was in round numbers only six thousand."[22] Although that number might not appear to be insubstantial, the practical assistance provided by United States soldiers in combat was actually close to nil. Reporting on Red Cross work at the Tagliamento River during the final confrontations in the fall of 1918, Bakewell noted that "this was the first and only battle in which Americans were engaged on the Italian front, and our losses were: one killed, and seven wounded."[23] In light of those statistics, Nick's profound cynicism regarding the promise suggested by his uniform in "A Way You'll Never Be" is not surprising.

A Farewell to Arms deals with military apparel as well. While traveling aboard a train dressed in mufti, for example, Frederic Henry notes that "in civilian clothes I felt a masquerader. I had been in uniform a long time and I missed the feeling of being held by your clothes." He goes on to mention that "some aviators in the compartment" were "very scornful of a civilian my age" (243). Henry's comment calls attention to those who value the outfit as evidence of the wearer's sharing of the burden during wartime. While others who advocated that principle previously ignited a passionate response from Henry, such criticisms no longer have the same effect: "I did not feel insulted," he states. "In the old days I would have insulted them and picked a fight. They got off at Gallarate and I was glad to be alone" (243). At this point in Henry's story, the lack of uniform underscores his conflicted feelings about having deserted, which is not something he cares to announce.

In a related passage, Frederic visits an "armorer's shop" in Milan where, in contrast to Hemingway's similar experience in Paris, he procures a gun instead of a Sam Browne belt (148). Henry alludes to the pointlessness of the officer's shoulder strap when the seller of military supplies makes a brief sales pitch for "used swords very cheap" (149). Instead of explicitly declining the offer, Henry simply states that "I'm going to the front," implying that he has no use for an archaic weapon in modern combat (149). After buying a firearm instead, he notes that the "pistol felt heavy on the belt," another detail that suggests he is wearing only a standard holster without the benefit of the additional accessory intended to aid in distributing the weight of a side arm (149). Indeed, the fictional protagonist's realistic point of view contrasts with the romanticism exhibited by young Hemingway when he wrote about the shoulder strap as highly desirable.

Hemingway incorporated details related to "the Paris part" of his adventure into "A Way You'll Never Be" (311). The references appear within a jumble of memories recalled by the main character while in the battle zone. In one section of the story, which is rendered in third-person point-of-view limited to Nick Adams, Hemingway blends allusions to the French capital amid notions of combat. Thoughts of "Sacré Coeur, blown white, like a soap bubble," the taxi Nick exited "when it got steep going up the hill," and song lyrics from performers known for their connections to Paris, all rush into the character's mind while he tries to focus solely on the reality of war (310).[24] The reflections cause him to "get so damned mixed up" that he has trouble keeping "it all straight so he would know just where he was" (311). The complex stream-of-consciousness passage illustrates Nick's mental instability as he has a difficult time sorting out reality from the figments of his imagination, what Joseph Flora refers to as a sort of "Eliotic nightmare."[25] The ideas related to Parisian tourist attractions mixed in with recollections of the horrors of battle create a surreal and disturbing portrait of the incongruities that abounded in wartime Europe.

Hemingway's experience with the munitions factory explosion outside of Milan resonates with his fiction as well. In addition to "A Natural History of the Dead," the Bollate incident suggests a parallel with the fishing idyll in *The Sun Also Rises*. H. R. Stoneback has argued that, during the rendered action of the novel, Jake and Bill fish not the Irati River but the Fabrica instead. Stoneback notes that Hemingway omits mention of nearby ruins that once housed an armament manufacturing facility that inspired the naming of the Fabrica River.[26] Considering the author's initiation into extreme violence at a similar factory, it is not surprising that he depicts a protagonist who struggles to find solace while resting in a locale not unlike where Ernest first experienced the brutality of war. The detail underscores Jake's ability to maintain his composure even amid an obvious reminder of his troubled past.

The disintegration of the victims at Bollate, moreover, prefigures Hemingway's prominent themes regarding characters who, as he writes in *A Farewell to Arms*, struggle to become "strong at the broken places" (249). As he wrote in *Death in the Afternoon*,

> we agreed too that the picking up of the fragments had been an extra-
> ordinary business; it being amazing that the human body should be
> blown into pieces which exploded along no anatomical lines, but
> rather divided as capriciously as the fragmentation in the burst of a
> high explosive shell.[27]

Robert E. Gajdusek has suggested that "the writer, the artist, was initially created on those fields," calling attention to the breaking apart of bodies as related to themes that became not only significant in Hemingway's fiction but also a main feature of the modernist movement of the 1920s.[28]

Much of Ernest's active duty experience along with the circumstances of various members of the Red Cross also provided source material for his writing. Not long after he returned home, Hemingway made several attempts to produce fiction based on his service. One story, written "sometime in the winter of 1919–1920," as Paul Smith explains, drew on his time at Schio.[29] "The Visiting Team" depicts two recruits from Harvard and their initiation into a section of ambulance drivers.[30] After an evening of practical jokes that make light of battle conditions, the volunteers are called into action. The most experienced of the group, Red Smith, returns from the trenches after being severely wounded himself. His final words, "only the good die young," as Reynolds discusses, show that he "jokes his way right into the grave."[31] As its title suggests, the tale emphasizes that some participants in the conflict were the same age or not much older than athletes who compete in sporting events in high school or college. Although "The Visiting Team" criticizes the "classical analogy" pairing war and games, as Peter Stine describes the comparison, Hemingway's early attempt at incorporating the type of irony expressed by his fellow volunteers falls flat, and the work was never published.[32]

Two other pieces from this period are similarly problematic. One story about "a Red Cross officer" suggests an early attempt at satirizing the leaders of the corps. A dishonest administrator named "Brackell," as Paul Smith explains, "goes from post to post each day and tells the Italian commanders it is his birthday. He reaps the benefits of wine, capes, and pistols as presents, until he is finally caught out. The sketch ends with a glimpse of him, a short, swarthy fellow, 'with a wicked eye.'"[33] Another unfinished work from 1920 is set twelve kilometers behind Fossalta di Piave in the same vicinity as the Section Two headquarters. In one draft of "How Death Sought Out the Town Major of Roncade," Hemingway depicts a vengeful Ardito named Sarsi who murders Vergara, a corrupt and cowardly official given to drinking and womanizing. Vergara is particularly afraid of the sound of artillery as the enemy threatens to advance. Although this early work prefigures subsequent fiction that deals candidly with similar anxieties, in this story, as Michael Stewart explains, it is "presented by the young Hemingway in a manner far from the modernistic style of implication and understatement he would come to perfect only a few years after."[34] Indeed, although he had chosen to write about issues that were closely related to his time in Italy, his work had yet to demonstrate techniques that later allowed him to capture the profound complexities of his subject.

Hemingway's writing reached a turning point in 1922, however, when he published "A Veteran Visits Old Front, Wishes He Had Stayed Away."[35] Although in some ways the nonfiction article "gave the impression that he had spent years in the war," as Reynolds notes, the main idea of the piece deals with Ernest's longing for the days spent at Schio and the area around Fossalta di Piave.[36] The lengthy description of the mill town where Section Four was headquartered, for example, is imbued with nostalgia:

> Schio was one of the finest places on earth. It was a little town in the Trentino under the shoulder of the Alps, and it contained all the good cheer, amusement and relaxation a man could desire. When we used to be in billets there, everyone was perfectly contented and we were always talking about what a wonderful place Schio would be to come and live after the war. I particularly recall a first-class hotel called the Due Spadi, where the food was superb and we used to call the factory where we were billeted the "Schio Country Club." (177)

In 1922, however, the town "seemed to have shrunk." The mountains looked "dull," the entrance to the old factory that lodged the volunteers had been "bricked up," and the stream where the men "used to swim" had become polluted by "black muck." Overwhelmed by disappointment,

Hemingway wrote that he decided against seeking out the "garden in Schio" where the volunteers "used to drink beer on hot nights with a bombing moon," using a phrase lifted straight out of a facetious "weather report" printed in *Ciao* and adding that "maybe there never was a garden" in the first place.[37] He even questions whether or not there was "any war" (177).

His description of Fossalta includes similar reminiscences, explaining that the "wrecked town" near the old "sunken road" had been replaced by "a new, smug, hideous collection of plaster houses, painted bright blues, reds and yellows." Hemingway preferred the "devastated town," which "always had a dignity as though it had died for something. It had died for something and something better was to come" (179). Although "A Veteran Visits" romanticizes aspects of his period of active duty, the piece significantly introduces his sense of disillusionment over the outcome of the war. Moreover, as William Adair has explained, many of the "situations and images" from the article came to "appear in his fiction throughout his career."[38] Indeed, Hemingway's early essay demonstrates the realizations that eventually led him to depict aspects of his tour in fiction that is profoundly tragic in tone.

One of Hemingway's earliest published poems points in that direction as well. "Riparto d'Assalto" deals with the devastating consequences for many of the Arditi units he admired during the summer of 1918. He depicts the soldiers as they "drummed their boots on the camion floor" while riding to the front: "Sergeants stiff, / Corporals sore. / Lieutenants thought of a Mestre whore."[39] While Ernest and his fellow canteen workers rode in a truck on their way to staff the emergency *posto di conforto* stations, the soldiers he describes were taking a "sullen ride" into battle at "Asalone" [*sic*]. As Verna Kale notes, "it helps to know" that the "attack division" of the "elite shock troops" that Hemingway refers to in his title "are the ones who arrive first" in combat.[40] Indeed, on June 24, 1918, the Arditi were engaged in a particularly brutal assault on Mt. Asolone. One Italian lieutenant wrote that "we are in front of new barbed-wire fences and, moreover, exposed to a hellish machine-gun fire. . . . In addition, enemy artillery shells the crest, hitting friend and foe, trying to keep the position. Our losses are impressive."[41] Although the soldiers "did manage to take the mountain," as Angelo Pirocchi explains, the victory came at a great sacrifice.[42] "Riparto d'Assalto" ends likewise by abruptly stating that "the truck-load died," communicating the sudden deaths that occurred for many of those engaged in the conflict.

One of Hemingway's sketches from the early twenties combines aspects of his experience in the frontlines and stories about volunteers away from the action. Ultimately published in *In Our Time* (1925) as "Chapter VII," the vignette originally called "chapter 8" from *in our time* (1924) describes a bombardment that was "knocking the trench to pieces at Fossalta."[43] The narrator tells about one soldier who "lay very flat and sweated and prayed oh jesus christ get me out of here." The unnamed combatant, he goes on to say, promises to "tell every one in the world" that Christ is "the only one that matters," but "the next night back at Mestre he did not tell the girl he went upstairs with at the Villa Rossa about Jesus." Although the narrator includes himself in the action after the "shelling moved further up the line" by stating that "we went to work" to repair the fortifications, the closing line indicates an omniscient point of view: "And he never told anybody," the speaker explains (16). This "shifting" perspective, as Cohen points out, is somewhat "ambiguous, with problems Hemingway did not fully resolve."[44] Nevertheless, the chapter serves "to nail down the shallowness of trench-borne religiosity," as Cohen puts it.[45] Indeed, the sketch shows how Hemingway incorporated behavior that his fellow volunteers celebrated while *en repos* into a fictional portrayal that juxtaposes these forms of pleasure seeking with the "no atheists in foxholes" concept.

Hemingway relied on his canteen duty once again in "Now I Lay Me," but his depiction of fear is much more subtle than in earlier works.[46] As an American in Italy, Nick Adams has adopted the cause of the foreign army, but the exact nature of his role is vague.[47] Having been wounded prior to the events of the story, Nick recalls "that summer" when he had difficulty sleeping while lying on "blankets spread over straw" in a room somewhere "seven kilometers behind the lines."[48] While he tries to occupy his mind with nonwarlike thoughts and images, he is unable to ignore the pervasive sounds of silkworms eating mulberry leaves. The noises from the local insects, as Carlos Baker has pointed out, were inspired by similar conditions that existed at Bill Horne's canteen post in San Pietro Novello, which Ernest visited while stationed in Fornaci.[49] Since Nick has already been wounded, however, his proximity to the front proves extremely unsettling, and the narrative indicates that he is particularly susceptible to night terrors. The nocturnal sounds suggest an ominous tone: "There were the noises of night seven kilometers behind the lines outside but they were different from the small noises inside the room in the dark," he remembers (279). Hemingway's use of the retrospective first person allows Nick to communicate limited information about his actual function with the military, but his acknowledgement of the disturbing details related to the setting indirectly conveys his anxiety over being within earshot of the combat zone.

A Farewell to Arms relies substantially on Hemingway's period of active duty, especially in Book I. Many of the passages describing Frederic Henry's actions, for example, suggest Ernest's fellow workers. Henry refers to his role in overseeing "the business of removing wounded and sick from the dressing stations, hauling them back from the mountains to the clearing station and then distributing them to the hospitals named on their papers" (16). Also responsible for dealing with preparations for an approaching battle, he mentions that

> the offensive was going to start again I heard. The division for which we worked were to attack at a place up the river and the major told me that I would see about the posts for during the attack. The attack would cross the river up above the narrow gorge and spread up the hillside. The posts for the cars would have to be as near the river as they could get and keep covered. (17)

Likewise, Henry notes that "I found a place where the cars would be sheltered after they passed that last bad-looking bit and could wait for the wounded." He seems assured that the vehicles "would be all right with their good metal-to-metal brakes and anyway, coming down, they would not be loaded" (24). Similarly, he describes duties while he "was away for two days at the posts," stating that "I came back the next afternoon from our first mountain post and stopped the car at the *smistamento* where the wounded and sick were sorted by their papers" (28, 33). Upon his return from reconnoitering the front, he explains that he made out a "report" as well (36).

Much of Henry's account of the prelude to the Tenth Battle of the Isonzo, as Reynolds has demonstrated, shows precise correlation with military histories written after the war, but the passages dealing with ambulance-driving duties incorporate the responsibilities held by Hemingway's superiors during the Battle of the Piave. Indeed, Henry's wide range of tasks indicates activities conducted by personnel at various levels in the Red Cross chain of command. Although Frederic is an American lieutenant in the Italian army, the portrayal shows parallels with the roles of Major Lowell, Captain Bates, Lieutenant Griffin, and Second Lieutenant Welch.[50] The first-person account of Henry's functions amid the bustling activity along the front demonstrates his noncombatant role in conjunction with his officer status in the foreign army while underscoring a sense of expertise in a job that he has, unlike Ernest, performed since the "late summer of" 1915 when Italy first entered the war (3).

Henry's circumstances prior to the outbreak of hostilities suggest additional correlations with the work of Major Lowell. Similar to the Red Cross worker, Frederic also spent time studying architecture before he signed up with the army.[51] Unlike Lowell, however, whose preface to *More Small Italian Villas* shows an unadulterated sense of romanticism associated with his occupation, Henry, as Robert Lewis has noted, implies that the subject "seems to be of little significance to him."[52] Indeed, even though the lieutenant twice mentions that he had "wanted to be an architect," Frederic displays no passion for the field of study that seemed to lead him to Italy in the first place (242, 280). His indifference suggests that, along with his loss of Catherine, their child, and his position in the army, his interest in the vocation he pursued prior to his enlistment has become another "casualty" of the war.

As a result of his long involvement in the conflict, Henry expresses a great deal of cynicism over his job, a facet of his characterization that correlates with attitudes expressed by many of Ernest's seasoned colleagues. When Henry returns to the combat zone after his extended leave, for example, he surmises that "it evidently made no difference whether I was there to look after things or not. I had imagined" he states, that the "smooth functioning" of the service "depended to a considerable extent on myself" (16). Later in the novel, he is forced to desert after members of the Italian army attempt to execute him amid the retreat from Caporetto. Although Captain Bates never "adopted the arid cynicism of Hemingway's Frederic Henry," as Stephen Bates has noted, his record nonetheless indicates that he not only became disillusioned as a result of his work in the trenches but also considered quitting his job as director.[53]

Similarly, Henry describes his role as less important than that of the fighting men, noting the "false feeling of soldiering" it gave him and explaining that his position is "not really the army. It's only the ambulance" (17, 18). He finds it difficult to take rules and regulations seriously, noting

that the "Italian salute" was impossible to perform "without embarrassment" (23). In another episode, when Helen Ferguson bids the lieutenant good night after announcing that she has "some letters" to write,
Henry jokingly cautions her against including "anything that will bother
the censor." She responds with ironic banter: "I only write about what
a beautiful place we live in and how brave the Italians are." Henry coun-
ters with yet another wry remark: "That way you'll be decorated" (25).
Indeed, the lieutenant's viewpoints, like those of volunteers who scoffed
at Red Cross objectives, show a similar pessimistic outlook on the nature
of his work.

As with most of Hemingway's time spent in the ambulance corps *en
repos*, much of *A Farewell to Arms* depicts action that, as James Nagel explains, also occurs "away from the front."[54] The dining scene in chapter
2, for example, provides details not unlike the exploits of Section Four as
described in *Ciao*. Similarly, Henry describes "that night in the mess after
the spaghetti course," the free-flowing "wine from the grass-covered gal-
lon flask," and the bawdy jokes intended to embarrass the army chaplain
(6, 7–9). After another meal among the soldiers, Frederic and Rinaldi try
to seduce the "beautiful English girls" employed at the nearby hospital
where Henry first meets Catherine (12).

Articles by seasoned drivers in section newspapers such as "Al on Permission" also suggest a source for Henry's extended vacation during the
winter of 1916–1917.[55] Similar to the stories in the broadsheets, *A Farewell
to Arms* alludes to Henry's "beautiful adventures" in "Milano, Firenze,
Roma," and "Napoli" (11). More than gratuitous accounts of drinking
and sexual conquest, however, Henry's off-duty habits add a crucial component to his journey toward a serious relationship with Catherine. After
he tells the priest that he had failed to spend his leave in the Abruzzi,
"the high clean place of honor and dignity and good manners," as Stoneback characterizes this "sacred landscape," Henry attempts to explain
his initial propensity for self-indulgence:[56] "I tried to tell about the night
and the difference between the night and the day and how the night was
better unless the day was very clean and cold and I could not tell it; as
I cannot tell it now. But if you have had it you know" (13). The details
of Frederic's early pleasure-seeking stage serve to set up the irony that
becomes clear when Catherine dies during childbirth. Indeed, Henry's
telling of the story is, in many ways, an attempt to come to terms with
the profound sense of loss he has experienced by the end of the novel.[57]

The sequence of events leading up to Frederic's wounding, moreover, parallels the circumstances of the author's canteen service. When Henry checks on his men as they wait for the attack, for example, he notes that he "gave them each a package of cigarettes" (47). Afterward, he tries to find out when "the field kitchen would be along" and explains that he "would get them as soon as the food came" (48). Not long after that, he manages to find some macaroni and cheese, returning with it to the dugout where the drivers wait. As the Italians discuss their cynicism, Henry encourages them to stay involved: "It would not finish it if one side stopped fighting," he tells them. "It would only be worse if we stopped fighting" (49). Moments before his near-death experience, Henry sets the scene in general: "They were all eating, holding their chins close over the basin, tipping their heads back, sucking in the ends. I took another mouthful and some cheese and a rinse of wine. Something landed outside that shook the earth" (54). Indeed, all of these details resemble what Hemingway experienced in the *posti di conforto* before sustaining his own injury. In the novel, however, Henry is in command of the Italians with whom he waits in the dugout, and the meal he shares serves as a sign of solidarity despite his superiority in rank.

The passages that depict Henry's interactions with foreign servicemen also benefit from Hemingway's work with the Italians. The drivers who operate under Frederic, for example, are similar to men who were assigned to Section Four. In the novel, the local personnel express their objections over the continuation of hostilities: "They were all mechanics," Henry says, "and hated the war" (48). The discussion before the offensive centers on the ways the conflict has affected those who rank low in the social hierarchy: "There is a class that controls a country that is stupid and does not realize anything and never can. That is why we have this war," one of them states (51).[58] Even so, Hemingway depicts the camaraderie between the Italians and his American protagonist. When Henry returns with the food, he jokes with them after listening in on their subversive ideas: "Here, you patriots," he says (53). Henry's relationship with Rinaldi shows a more developed bond, and the roles are reversed. The medical officer refers to his American friend as "little puppy" and "baby" (27, 40). Similar to the interactions between Captain Felice Cacciapuoti and the Red Cross volunteers, Rinaldi expresses his fondness through lighthearted humor that indicates the Italian officer as something of a caretaker to his foreign "brother" (171).[59]

Hemingway provides few descriptions of the hauling of wounded in his fiction, but Frederic Henry's trip as an injured passenger benefited from the author's tour as well:

> As the ambulance climbed along the road, it was slow in the traffic, sometimes it stopped, sometimes it backed on a turn, then finally it climbed quite fast. I felt something dripping. At first it dropped slowly and regularly, then it pattered into a stream. I shouted to the driver. He stopped the car and looked in through the hole behind his seat.
> "What is it?"
> "The man on the stretcher over me has a hemorrhage."
> "We're not far from the top. I wouldn't be able to get the stretcher out alone." He started the car. (61)

Hemingway, of course, had firsthand knowledge of a similar ride, and the account suggests a common experience among volunteers who, as Charles Fenton has noted, "expressed again and again their horror when at the end of a long drive, under shelling, they discovered they had been driving not an ambulance but a hearse."[60] Hemingway renders his related scene with exceptional skill:

> The stream kept on. In the dark I could not see where it came from the canvas overhead. I tried to move sideways so that it did not fall on me. Where it had run down under my shirt it was warm and sticky. I was cold and my leg hurt so that it made me sick. After a while the stream from the stretcher above lessened and started to drip again and I heard and felt the canvas above move as the man on the stretcher settled more comfortably.
> "How is he?" the Englishman called back. "We're almost up."
> "He's dead I think," I said.
> The drops fell very slowly, as they fall from an icicle after the sun has gone. It was cold in the car in the night as the road climbed. At the post on the top they took the stretcher out and put another in and we went on. (61)

Whether Hemingway had a related experience, heard of a similar episode from his fellow drivers, or invented the scenario, his description shows a particularly impressive piece of writing that captures not only the futility

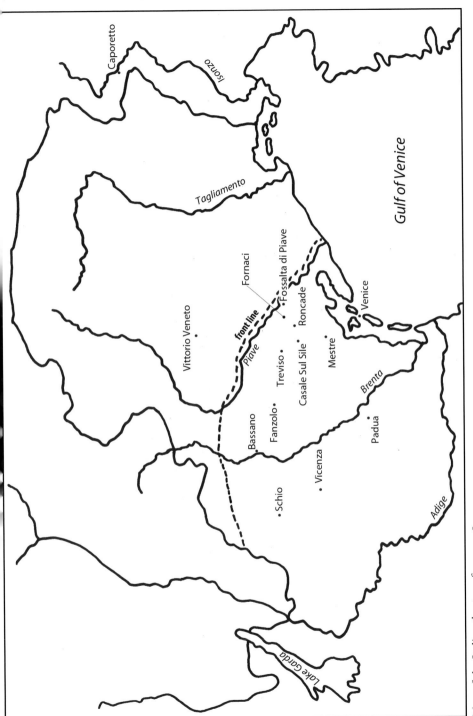

Map of the Italian theater of war, 1918.

August 22 '18

More has happened in the last 6 months since my entry of Feb 8, than perhaps has ever happened to me in a like space of time, so much that I shall not attempt even to summarize it. My diary is a barometer not of the weather, but of the work I have to do. When the most is happening and when as a result there is the most to "chronicle," I have no time to put it

down + conversely, when time hangs heavy on my hands I write copious by! This is unfortunate, from all points of views! We froze during the winter, thawed out in the spring, have sweltered all summer + have we left our diana palace of the Pozzo Rosso moved to the office, a magnificent palazzo on the Via San Marco where we are truly lodged like kings. Our little circle has grown + will continue to grow. The old days with a table for 4, Caccia Gusti, near Preston and I, (Utan having returned to America in February) are now no more. Today we have 14, including 4 ladies (4 including my stenographer) Miss Lewis (my stenographer) Miss Corey (? the station rest-house) & the misses Innocente & Casella, hen helpers. I have tried to preserve some record of my work & daily life in my official reports of which I have preserved copies & in letters home. Some & any

these, written on the machine, I have copies of what I did with them & the reports; & occasional newspaper clippings. I have a poor substitute for a daily journal. To go back to the early days; for a while in fact for some months, I was the only Capt. at Vicenza, consequently was head of the G.H.Q. Ser. that time I got a Post & do Florence. represented the U.S. on official occasions, dined with Generals, & distributed

This and facing page: Excerpt from a diary entry by Robert W. Bates, August 22, 1918 (Robert W. Bates Papers).

Drivers of Red Cross Section One in Milan, December 1917 (Library of Congress).

American Red Cross officers in Bassano del Grappa. From left to right: Captain George Utassy, Quartermaster General; Major Guy Lowell, Director of the Department of Military Affairs; Colonel Robert Perkins, Commissioner; and Captain Robert Bates, Director of Ambulance and Rolling Kitchen Services (Robert W. Bates Papers).

AVANTI

—— Jan 1 1918 ——

PUBLISHED BY SECTION ONE A. R. C. ON THE ITALIAN FRONT

To the First Section

By Gouverneur Morris

(Editor's Note – Mr. Morris accompanied the section from Marseilles to the Italian front. He came at the invitation of the American Red Cross as a guest of the organization. He has been far more than a guest, however. He has been one of the most active members of the section. What annoyances and hardships we have encountered, he has shared with us and helped us to overcome. The section will not feel that a guest has departed when he leaves shortly. It will feel that it has lost one of its most valued members).

I have been ordered by the Associate Editors to write two or three hundred excrutiatingly funny words for the first number of the first American paper to be published in Italy. But I shall do no such thing.

Upon the thought that I shall soon be a man without a Section there is no fun left in me.

No father can spend Christmas away from his babies without solemn thoughts; nor can any comrade, no matter how good his reansons, leave his comrades to a life of genuine self denial and danger, without the feeling that he is in some sense their deserter.

We have had some devilish hard times together: we have had to put up with aesthetic deprivations for which there seemed to be no reason founded on common sense; and too often when we have been ready we have been kept waiting until endurance crumbled, and the cold got into our bones, and the pale lights of some of the vilest cafés in all Europe have looked like Heaven to us.

Nevertheless, the Hike to Italy has been a great Hike. And sometimes with Homeric laughter we have shaken from the damps and the iciness of the worst nights a kind of warmth. " Haec olim meminisse juvabit„. Hereafter when I look back on our days and nights together, I shall remember only the warmth and the friendliness of them.

And I shall remember, with the tears very near my eyes, how although I was old enough to be the father of some of you, you made my interests yours, just as I tried to make your interests mine, and indeed made much of me, and always gave me the best of everything.

If there is anything of persuasion in me, as there is surely the will to persuade, then the story of your good humor, your courage and your fineness will lose nothing in my telling of it; and I shall look to hear even generals in command of armies speak with admiration of the men who pick up the wounded under fire.

I pray God that none of you are to be hurt in all this cruel business. I pray Him to bless and keep you all.

A FEW TELEGRAMS

Congratulations on leaving Paris. We miss you on the Grands Boulevards. Don't come back.

General PERSHING.

* *

On the trip down. I lost my voice, my clothes and a thousand francs otherwise. I enjoyed the trip.

G. B. FIFE.

* *

I'm sorry. I didnt see you leave for the front. I must have overslept.

GORDON SARRE.

* *

I declared war on Austria as soon as I heard you had arrived at Milan. Plaese advise me or Colonel House where you expect to go if the army takes over the ambulance service in Italy, so we can arrange for another war declaration.

WOODROW WILSON.

* *

Come and sit at my table the next time you pass through Monte Carlo.

PRINCO OF MONACO.

* *

The following tetegram was received with the name so blurred that the name could not be deciphered. Will the owner please call at the office of the Avanti for the original.

....., Section I, A. R. C. ambulance service

Front page of Section One newspaper *Avanti,* January 1, 1918 (Robert W. Bates Papers).

FIRST AMERICAN PAPER PUBLISHED IN ITALY

COME STÀ

PUBLISHED MONTHLY BY SECTION ONE, AMERICAN RED CROSS.

MARCH 10, 1918

PASSED BY THE ITALIAN MILITARY CENSOR

Chasseurs' Band Serenades
Guests of Section One

Exemplfying the friendship and cordiality of the armies of the nations allied in a common cause, the lawn party and concert held by Section One promises to stand as an important chapter in the Section's annals. It brought together Italian, French and English officers to hear a pleasing concert by the band of a famous Chasseur battalion as the guest of American volunteer ambulance drivers. Distinctions of rank were set aside and differences of language and customs failed to embarrass the gathering as our guests fraternized with one another under the flags of four countries.

As a unique event, the idea of a lawn party on the thirty-first of January may have meant more to the folks at home than to us who are accustomed to balmy days in Northern Italy. But to us, this first real plunge into the inner circles of military society was a satisiying success from the ideal weather to the cordial feeling it engendered.

To Charles Waldispuhl, our always reliable diplomat and envoy extraordinary, is due a large measure of success of the undertaking. It was he who obtained permission for the band to be present and directed the splendid effort of our cuisine. Charles discriminating judgment in the selection of refreshments, food and fluid, met with obvious approval from all.

The following is a copy of the official program :

Concert

execute par la Fanfare du Bataillon de Chasseurs Alpins au camp de la Croix Rouge Amèricaine, 1 e Section le 32 Janvier, 1918, a . . . Italie.

Programme

La St. Cyrienne, marche, clarions	Mougeot
Emblème National Amèricaine	Sousa
Le Flambert, marche	Gourdin
Carmen	Bizet
Louis XIV, marche, clarions	Millet
Stars and Stripes Forever	Souza
Sous la futuaie, polka	Flavel
Quand Madelon	Allier
Tipperary	
Salut a Stenay	Briens
Hymns Nationaux Allies	

THINGS WE WOULD LIKE TO KNOW

What happened to Bob Chambers in Paris
Where Tom Salter got all his luck.
Why Jack Nash doesn't visit us.
Where Charles Waldispuhl got his knowledge of Florence.

Who sends all the packages to Appleyard.
How Lummis spells his name.
When Birmingham is coming.
Why is a three day post.
How Fairbanks would look without a beard.
What happened to packages sent in care of the American Field Service.
Where the new men will sleep when the permissionaires return.
When we're going to find time to get out the next «Come Stà ».
Who wrote those letters.
Who is not going to re-enlist.
When we will hear from Captein Bates next.
When the new cars will arrive.
When the w. w. e.

NOW IT'S COME STA'

We have changed our name.

Following the issue of the opening number of Avanti in January, we anticipated thousands of letters and telegrams of commendation and praise. But they didn't come. The February edition, undoubtedly the cleverest and best paper ever published in English by an American ambulance section in Italy, brought but a scant five hundred letters and telegrams of praise.

An editorial conference followed. The staff was unanimous in the opinion that the papers mailed were failing to reach their destination. How account otherwise for the lack of a veritable storm of public approval ?

Captain Cacciapouti was consulted. He solved the riddle at once.

« Alors ». said he. « Perhaps th Avanti is being confused with a former journal of the Italian socialists, also called the Avanti. It was suppressed at the beginning of the war. Perhaps it would be well to find another name for our paper. N' est-ce pas ? ».

Other Italian mentors and friends of the Section agreed with Captain Cacciapuoti and urged a new name. Personally, we never thought much of the old name anyhow. We considered it too serious for our youthful and frivolous nature and we were always happy when we could blame the christening on Gouverneur Morris and Captain George Utassy.

So from now on it's « Come Stà »

MAYOR OF ROME
Greets Permissionaires

Rome, Feb. 22 : — Convoyed by of the editors of the Come Stà who acted as guide and moral mentor, the first group of permissionaires from Section One arrived here yesterday. In the party were Deacon Volle, Smiley Dickinson, Venti-

---

Front page of Section One newspaper *Come Stà*, March 10, 1918 (Robert W. Bates Papers).

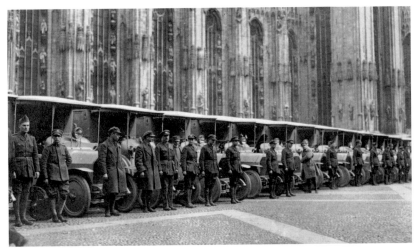

Presentation of Section Four to the Italian government in Milan, April 4, 1918 (Robert W. Bates Papers).

Red Cross parade, New York City, May 18, 1918 (Library of Congress).

Weather report: clear:with bombing moon, possibility of sky becoming overcast before morning with planes,with resulting hail.
N. T. AIRCRAFT

CIAO

MAY 1918

Published by Section IV A. R. C. on the Italian front

ALL THE HYSTERICS

OT SECTION IV

PASSED BY THE

MILITARY CENSOR

And Yet More Driving Power. (cont.)

(Beg pardon, Aesop Ade)

When the Continued-in-our-Next-Number Flashed Across the Screen in this Odessey of the Chosen Band, it Left Our Heroes in the Diminutive Crossroads of Varese. But this Time was not De-Destined to be the Great Tribulation, their Exile was Only a Matter of Hours, and the Same Night the Moon Gazed Silently Down on the Battle of the Galleria with Our Boys Going Over the Top. doubtless we should have Won, had not Sailing Orders been issued the Next Day, Decreeing the Total Disintegration of the section to Far Removed Points on the Fluctuating Battle Line.

Most of us Shook the Milanese Mud Regretfully from Our Heels by Means of the Ten Thirty for Vicenza, which According to the Vogue now Present in Italy did not Cast Off till One. The Boys seemed in Good Form for Propaganding. Sig. S. Schwartz, of Atlantic City Fame, most Altruistically Tried to Lighten the Burden of One Poor Working Man by Temporarily Assuming his Responsibilities. But it was not Written that He should Win the War in ths Manner; the Gentleman in Question was the Baggage-Smasher, and Prospective Customers showed an Obvious Reluctance to Trust their Worldly Goods to Sam.

Other Boys-from-the-Best-Families Equally Distinguished Themselves that Night. Our Hitherto-fore Respected. but Sombulent Confrere Robert Louis Stevenson Rollins Caused even Blasé Milan to Pause and Wonder by Anna Pavloving It. in the Center of the City with a Lady of Questionable Rep. But the Ambulancier's Pet Providence was Working Overtime : the Twentieth Century Drifted Out with All Hands Aboard.

Owing to the Tempory Disentegration of the Restorers-of-the-Trentino as a Unit, many Heroic and Dramatic Events must by Necessity go Unrecorded. No-body got Killed : None of us got Captured : yet in Spite of This, Our Heroes were Fighting True to Form, The Hon. Business Manager of this Publication Relinquished His Ford for Five Minutes in Front of a Hospital and Returned to Watch it Precipitate Itself into the Inevitable Ditch. Another Hero, Noted for his Vivid Imagination saw Some Remarkable Performances in an Avion of Dubious Nationality - not Recorded in the Communiques. The Paen of Joy raised by Section Three on Welcoing Our Delato its Midst Echoed from the Dolomites to the Adriatic.

After we'd Won the War in the Respective Cafes of Rome. Naples and Florence. while on Permission, Again we Presented Ourselves, Ready unto Death. for Ordrs from our Beloved Chef. Every-body Showed Up but Brothers Anthony,

(cont-on-page-two)

Italy and America

To the Italian mind, the words *Amico and Americano* are synonymous. This feeling has a solid historical foundation in such names as Columbus, Verazzano, Vespucci. Rightly every Italian has a sense of proprietorhip in America and all things American.

By reason of internal and external wars in the fifteenth and sixteenth centuries, the small states of Italy vere not in a position to send Columbus to find a new world, and therefore he sailed under the patronage of a neighboring power, Spain. but America will never forget that he was an Italian. For the same reason, Verazzano, a Florintine navigator, sailed on a similar errand under the patronage of France. He skirted the North Atlantic coast, entering various harbors, among them the one that is now called New York, and sighting the river that is now called the Hudson. Thus a Genoese found South America, and a Florentine found North America.

If two Italians found us, a third gave us our name. Amerigo Vespucci a Florentine mathamatician and geographer, was a friend and counsellor of Columbus, and from him the new world received it's name. Notrue son of the West can stand unaffected before the statue of Amerigo Vespucci in Florence, which rerpesents him locking far away toard the declinig sun with an eager, expectant,y earning eye, while at his side is a pillar with the one word, America.

Embarrassing moments of the future:

When we find ourselves sitting on a waterpipe in a street excavation because some unfortunate motorist had a blowout.

When we find ourselves before a policecourt judge because we bellowed Croce Rossa at tre copper who tried to stop us when we were doing sixty.

When we find ourselves lying on our stomach in the gutter because some small boy had an odd sounding whistle.

When we find ourselves in the basement of our girl's home because a mosquito had to hum in the presence of a full moon.

When we find that we have put on our souvenir gasmasks because the family downstairs were preparing cornbeef and cabbage.

Front page of Section Four newspaper, *Ciao*, May 1918 (Robert W. Bates Papers).

Ernest Hemingway (second from left) and other war personnel during a lifeboat drill aboard the *Chicago*, May 1918. (Ernest Hemingway Collection, John F. Kennedy Library).

Palazzo Pigatti in Vicenza, which served as headquarters for Red Cross ambulance and rolling kitchen services on the Italian front (Robert W. Bates Papers).

Italian troops marching past the Red Cross Headquarters at Palazzo Pigatti in Vicenza (Robert W. Bates Papers).

Red Cross ambulance and personnel at a post in the mountain region (Robert W. Bates Papers).

Schio. The American flag indicates Section Four headquarters (Robert W. Bates Papers).

Section Four Chef Charles Griffin and Sous Chef Edward Welch in a staff car (Robert W. Bates Papers).

Section Four lodgings, Schio (Robert W. Bates Papers).

Ernest Hemingway at the wheel of a Section Four ambulance (Ernest Hemingway Collection, John F. Kennedy Library).

Editorial Staff of *Ciao*

Editor — S. G. Fisher,
Bus. Magg. — W. Feder.

Eight men have left section four to enter various branches of the service. They were all bully good fellows, and hawe the best wishes, we know, of the Chef, Sou-chef, and each individual of the Section. We sincerely trust that each shall find his proper niche, and we feel confident that everyone will bring honor to himself in any service to which he shall be at attached. You go on your way with Section Four pulling strong four you.

« Good luck « Dick », Yutch », « Goody », « Woof », « Ship », « Sam », « Stupid », and « Hammie ».

Section Four has been strongly re enforced by the arrival of Twentytwo new menfrm the U-nited States. This Sectioon has always been composed of a fine bunch of men and they have made an enviable reputation on the Italian front. Many of the old men have left for other services. They were good men, veterans of other fronts as well as this one. Their places are being taken by the new men. They have The reputation of the Section to upholdand we feel confident that they will oo so. We are more than glad to welcome the icw en into he Section.

We hope the new men will contribute largely to Ciao. We know that there is talent among them. Ciao is the Section 's paper, and not the sheet of one or a few indivduals. Make a name for Yourself by writing for Ciao.

The six months enlistment for Sectins One; two, and three is already up and we note with regret that so many men have chosen to leave the Service. The time has now come for our own men to make the decision ande we trust that they have chosen wisely. Itt does seem a pity that we should spend the winter, always inactive on any front, in this service, and then when our services are really needed, and could be of some real worth tho say nothing of the attractiveness of the work, that we should pull up stakes. We want to take this opportunyto thank the A. R. C. officials for sending us such a crowd of god fellows, and with our old men as a nucleus, this section 's star of supremacy will be understanding between the men and the officials and we are all pulling together for the good of America and the A. R. C. in Italy.

AL RECEIVES ANOTHER LETTER

Dear Al :

Well Al we are here in this now Italy and now that I am here I am not going to leave it. Not at all if any. And that is not no New Years revolution Al but the truth Well Al I am now and officer and if you would meet me you would have to salute me. What I am is a provisional acting second lieutenant without a commission but the trouble is that all the other fellows are too. There aint no privates in our army Al and the Captain is called a chef. But he dindt look to me as tho he could cook a dam bit. And the next highest officer he is calleda sou chef. And the reason that the call him that is that is chef of the jitneys and has to cook for the 4ds. But he has a soft job Al because there are only three 4ds left.

You see Al they dont like dddds here ond one of the fellows told me that you get promoted if you wreck them. Maybe that is what those ribbons are for that they wear Al. One bar for each Ford wrecked. And every fifth ford they give you a brass rail. One of the fellows had a ribbon with red wgite and green bars on it. Six sets of three colors each and so I guess he must be one of these Ford destroyers that you read about in the newspapers. But you cant believe everything that you read in even the newspapers sometimes. Can you Al?.

It is pretty soft for you back in the states Al because at least you always have plenty to eat and a place to sleep and a wife but this Trench life is hell Al. I would tell you about our hardships Al Al but we mustnt reveal no military secrets even to those that are nerarest and dearest to us. But I can tell you that we have been in two battles Al. The Battle of Milan and the Batile of Paris. That is, a jocke Al and maybe yoou cant understand it but it will show you any way that I am the same old joker Huh Al?

Do you remember that fellow Pease Al that I wrote you about what was our captain? Well he is a p. s. l. A. w. a. c. now just like the rest of us and he speaks to me pretty regular now and yesterd he darn near called me by first name. But what are we fighting for anyway except to make the world safe for the Democrats?

Well Al the dug out that we sleep in they let us sleep unt il 745 that is they did until this guy Moore that is in our bunch began to think that he was Jonahvark or Gerry Baldy Putanm at the battle of Bull run ore some one. He wakes up about six oclock every morning or fivefourty five and says my how fine I slept I never even turned over.

But what he really done is this all nigt long he fights battles and hollers out Load Bayonicks! Fix cartrigdes! Fire faster men! Fire faster Boom Bang. And then he snores over a barrage. That guy sounds like the musical score to the Birt of a Nation Al. And this Jenkins who is a funny guy and looks it he says that this Moores wife must know ahe horros of war all right. But then Al when youx are in the trenches you cant kick.

You know this Dick Hawes Al that won all the money on the boat. Well he lost about 2500 Lire and I'm telling you confidential Al that I am kind of glad he done it because the way he was taking money away from the boys I had begun to think that he was maybe one of these Ardities in disguise. And say speaking of them they are the real rough guys and if you dont let them ridexon your ambulance they stick a knife through you. Loots of the fellows have had that done to them.

And I am going to buy a knife Al becau se that looks like the only way that you can get to ride on one of these ambulnces anyway. Well Al they say I am going to be seventh on cal tomorrow and so I want to get ready because you know me Al always right on the spot all the time so I am not going to take off me clothes tonight Al and any way it isafer because if this moore starts an offensive I can retreat quicker.

So So Long Al

Your Old Pal Steve, now known as the second Gerry Baldy.

Ernest Hemingway's Ring Lardner parody, "Al Receives Another Letter," *Ciao*, June 1918, 2 (Robert W. Bates Papers).

Edward M. McKey (right) next to a rolling kitchen (Library of Congress).

The opening reception at "Gamble's Kitchen," James Gamble's Red Cross canteen post near Monte Grappa (Robert W. Bates Papers).

Italian soldiers at a Red Cross canteen in the mountain region (Robert W. Bates Papers).

Edward McKey's rolling kitchen after it was wrecked by a shell on June 17, 1918, the day after McKey was killed (Robert W. Bates Papers).

Overleaf: Carbon copy of letter from Robert Bates to his family, June 27, 1918. Bates's handwritten annotation states: "Note: This + other such comments in these letters were for the benefit of the Italian Military Censor + did not reflect my true opinion of the fighting qualities of the Italians" (Robert W. Bates Papers).

Vicenza
June 27'18

Dear Family

This is the first chance I have had to sit down and write for some time; will try to tell you about the last few days. When the big offensive started the first word I had of it was a hurry call from the mountains, and I drove out immediately to ------ where the wildest rumors were afloat. One of our cars at the highest poste on the mountains was reported cut off by the enemy and there were other worse rumors yet. I spent the night visiting the postes and the next morning got up over a new and uncompleted road to the top poste; the old road had been cut out. The lost car had in the meantime come down; it had simply been delayed by the explosion of a munitions dump which continued to go off for hours after; excepting for a few dead, and for a lot of pieces of horses, one whole hindquarters hanging from a roof, and a lot of shell holes, there was nothing to see.

The next day I set off for the plains and never dreaming that there was action there too. I took an American girl along with me. She manages the Mary Elizabeth shop in New York, and had come to Vicenza to run our station rest-house and canteen. Imagine my concern, when arrived at the Section, I found a violent attack in progress and more wild rumors afloat. A battery beside the house deafened our ears, and the boys were silent and tired-looking. I was told of the death of one of our lieutenants but could get no definite news as every body had been too busy to look for the body. I determined to ship the girl right back to Vicenza, but she begged so hard to be allowed to stay and work in a soup kitchen serving hot drinks to the wounded which was run by two Scotch girls, that I decided to let her. I put her in charge of the ambulance man directing the loading of the wounded in case of necessity; then I started out to look for McKey. I looked all afternoon, going to places where bodies were collected and looking at faces; at last I found him.

That was a bad night, principally on account of w rumors. We were told that the enemy had broken through and that we had only 15 minutes in which to get out, but fortunately due to the heroic fighting of the Italian soldiers it proved to be untrue. I cannot tell you of our happiness at the magnificent fighting qualities of this great people.

The wounded poured in, walking from the lines in streams and climbing on to the little Ford ambulances until they hung all over the outside, sitting on mudguards and hood; 9, 10, and even 12 wounded came in on a single Ford, and stretchers carried by four men streamed down the roads for lack of machines to carry them. I telegraphed Milan to send out more cars and 6 came; I telegraphed the other two sections until I had every available car mobilized, and every man that could be spared from other Sections. In that one section I had 40 cars and 48 men, and the Section along side of it was working just as hard. Even with those numbers the men were almost dropping with fatigue. Then I got out chocolate and biscuits for the men to eat during the night, and supplies for the English kitchen and surgical dressings for the hospitals. Then I took the car and drove over to

------ and got a man who said he could conduct a burial service.

Morning came and I went up on one of the ambulances to bring in wounded; it was a strange sight to see the equipment that was strewn about the roads, and the dead bodies lying in the ditches, and in farm yards and in the fields. Then I went on a camion to try to bring in the kitchen of the man who had been killed, McKey. It was worth 6000 lire; but a shell had landed on his poste the day before and completely wrecked it, burying his supplies, and upsetting the kitchen which stood outside. We couldn't bring it in. We had also lost 3 ambulances which the Austrians had taken from us.

Then I went on an ambulance and got McKey's body. I had to put it on a stretcher with the help of a soldier; the poor fellow was badly smashed. That afternoon we had the funeral. I had managed to get a coffin made out of some old boards and again I had to help put him in the coffin. It spoiled the whole thing for me, and in spite of the flowers with which we covered him and which hid the rough boards the whole experience was crude and ugly for me. We put him in a little ambulance and four of us walked beside it. About 40 old territorials marched behind as a guard of honor, and two or three of our staff cars brought up the rear. A battery of big guns deafened us during the brief ceremony at the grave. Poor fellow; he was about as good a friend as I have made here and there was nothing of him left. He was always spick and span, fresh gloves in his hand, a little swagger stick, and a smart uniform. I have never before realized that gross clay we are when the spirit of life has left us. I have often thought how unpleasant it would be to have ones friends see one disfigured in death. Now I know that it makes no difference; there was nothing of McKey in that lifeless clod.

That night I drove back to Vicenza to see about more cars; I was tired. The next day I went back and came up the day after; I have forgotten how many days I alternated. The last day I went to the neighboring Section and made the rounds in daylight; the Austrians had been driven back the day before and we went out to the advance post which had been in enemy hands since the beginning of the attack. They were cleaning out dead Austrians from the rooms of our little farm house and sprinkling lime. The Austrians lay by the window, little piles of empty cartridges beside them, and our truck was carrying lime while one of the ambulances collected bodies. It was an ugly sight; many of them had been dead for days. Major Lowell who was with me said that he came very near to being sick; it didn't affect me at all, strange to say. We had a new chauffeur who saw fit to disregard the sentries posted at the bridges and drive across fast. Finally I leaned over and said: "Do you see those little sacks about 3 feet apart? And those wires connecting them? Well the sacks are filled with explosives and the wires are live fuses." He almost stalled the car 3 times going over the next bridge!

I am reaching the end of my page and must quit. Just this minute a man has come in to say that 2 of the section leaders are on the way up here with sure news of more activity, and if its true (the activity I mean) I thank heaven for today's rest; I didn't wake up till 10 A.M.!

Robert Bates (fourth from left) and Captain Felice Cacciapuoti of the Italian army (second from right) along with unidentified soldiers and Red Cross personnel after the recovery of Edward McKey's damaged rolling kitchen (Robert W. Bates Papers).

From left to right: Robert Bates, Felice Cacciapuoti, and an unidentified Red Cross worker at Edward McKey's burial (Library of Congress).

Ernest Hemingway while assigned to the Red Cross emergency *posti di conforto* (canteen posts) near the Piave River (Ernest Hemingway Collection, John F. Kennedy Library).

Italian soldier outside of a Red Cross *posto di conforto,* San Pietro Novello (Library of Congress).

AMERICAN RED CROSS

INTER-OFFICE LETTER

To Mr. E. M. Hemingway   *Date* July 11, 1918

From R. W. Bates

Subject

Dear Hemingway:

I have learned with regret of your accident, and am
very much relieved at the report which Captain Gamble has brought
in. He assures me that your wounds are not serious and that you
will soon recover. I went out to the Piave today with Major
Lowell, and we tried to find the hospital that you were in, but
having no exact information as to just where it was, we were
unable to find it. You will receive good care in Milano, and
I trust that before long you will be back again at the front.

With kind regards and best wishes

R. W. Bates
Captain A.R.C.A.S.

RWB/L

Letter from Robert Bates to Ernest Hemingway, July 11, 1918, three days after
Hemingway was wounded (Ernest Hemingway Collection, John F. Kennedy Library).

Ernest Hemingway seated in a wheelchair in Milan (Ernest Hemingway Collection, John F. Kennedy Library).

6. As previously reported, this service lent 14 men to Consul Carroll at the moment of the offensive in June. The men were used for emergency canteen work, and after the attack were taken over by our Kitchen Service, which continued the more important of the emergency posts. In addition to serving coffee, cigarettes, chocolate, etc. at the points set directly back of the line, the men carried supplies into the front line trenches. During such a trip, E. M. Hemingway of Section 4 was wounded by the explosion of a shell which landed about three feet from him, killing a soldier who stood between him and the point of explosion, and wounding others. Due to the soldier who lost his life and who protected Hemingway somewhat from the explosion, and due also to the fact that the eclats had not yet obtained their full range, Hemingway was only wounded in the legs. He sustained ten fairly serious wounds and two hundred and twenty-seven punctures. He is now in the American Hospital at Milan and has yet to undergo an operation to remove shrapnel from his knee. With him at the hospital are - Coles Seeley, formerly of Section 1, who while attempting to unscrew a shell head was severely wounded in both hands and in his left eye. He is recovering the use of his hands, with the exception of one finger. His eye, however, is still in a precarious condition. - B. F. Rogers of Section 1, who is in a generally run-down condition, and Edward E. Allen, Jr. of Section 3, who is seriously

Earnest Hemmingway – now a well known writer whose stuff I don't care for.

Excerpt from Robert Bates, "Ambulance Report No. 9," July 25, 1918, 2. Bates's handwritten note states "Earnest [sic] Hemingway—Now a well known writer whose stuff I don't care for" (Robert W. Bates Papers).

Robert Bates (front row, far left) with drivers of Section Four in Schio. The photograph was most likely taken after Ernest Hemingway left the unit for service with the *posti di conforto* (Robert W. Bates Papers).

Portrait of Ernest Hemingway in formal attire. In addition to the Sam Brown belt he purchased in Paris, Hemingway is wearing ribbons over his left breast pocket that indicate decorations from the Italian military along with stripes on both sleeves that show his rank of First Lieutenant in the Red Cross, a promotion he received after he was wounded (Ernest Hemingway Collection, John F. Kennedy Library).

of attempts at preventing loss of life by transporting wounded but also the extreme discomfort experienced by those who become accustomed to frequent deaths.

Besides the experiences that influenced depictions in *A Farewell to Arms*, Hemingway's stint as a canteen worker helped him set the scene for "A Way You'll Never Be."[61] When the protagonist travels toward the trenches in the beginning of the story, his route is virtually identical to that which Ernest would have taken from Fornaci through Fossalta di Piave to the frontlines:

> Nick Adams had seen no one since he had left Fornaci, although, riding along the road through the over-foliaged country, he had seen guns hidden under screens of mulberry leaves to the left of the road, noticing them by the heat-waves in the air above the leaves where the sun hit the metal. Now he went on through the town, surprised to find it deserted, and came out on the low road beneath the bank of the river. Leaving the town there was a bare open space where the road slanted down and he could see the placid reach of the river and the low curve of the opposite bank and the whitened, sun-baked mud where the Austrians had dug. It was all very lush and over-green since he had seen it last and becoming historical had made no change in this, the lower river. (307)

Nick's observations on the aftermath of battle parallel what Hemingway could have witnessed along the same journey. He discerns the action of the attack and counteroffensive according to "the position of the dead" which the "weather had swollen" all "alike regardless of nationality," notes "broken" houses and rubble littering the landscape, and describes various material abandoned during the retreat, such as "helmets, rifles, . . . intrenching tools, ammunition boxes," and "star-shell pistols" (306–307). Even the description of the "over-foliaged country" coincides with aspects of the battle zone during June of 1918, as James Edmonds describes in *Military Operations: Italy, 1915–1919:* "The ground west of the Piave was entirely covered with vineyards and cultivation, offering good cover and a ready-made obstacle for the defence, and, being flat, hampered artillery observation."[62] Unlike Ernest, however, Nick is less than eager to experience the war zone again since he is revisiting the front shortly after a traumatic wounding.

Hemingway's depiction of Nick's job duties, which coincide with his work in the canteen unit, helps to illustrate the protagonist's mental instability. Similar to Ernest's assignment with Consul Carroll, Nick's role is designated as "under the American consul" (312). He describes his mission to Captain Paravacini but shows little enthusiasm for his work:

> "I am supposed to move around and let them see the uniform."
> "How odd."
> "If they see one American uniform that is supposed to make them believe others are coming."
> "But how will they know it is an American uniform?"
> "You will tell them."
> "Oh. Yes, I see. I will send a corporal with you to show you about and you will make a tour of the lines."
> "Like a bloody politician," Nick said. (308–309)

Despite his pessimism, Nick still makes an effort to carry out his assignment. When he inadvertently exposes himself to the enemy by walking directly toward the river, however, Paravacini intervenes. The reckless act leads the Italian captain to recognize that Nick is not fit for duty: "I think you should go back," he tells him (313).

Hemingway further emphasizes Nick's mental fatigue through references to the character's lack of adequate provisions. Nick explains that

> I'm supposed to have my pockets full of cigarettes and postal cards and such things. . . . I should have a musette full of chocolate. These I should distribute with a kind word and a pat on the back. But there weren't any cigarettes and postcards and no chocolate. So they said to circulate around anyway. (309)

All things considered, Paravacini tries to convince Nick to leave the front: "I think it would be better if you didn't come up to the line until you had those supplies. There's nothing here for you to do" (313). When Nick talks about going to "San Dona to see the bridge again" instead, the Captain reiterates his suggestion more forcefully: "I won't have you circulating around to no purpose" (313). Paravacini's comment, moreover, calls attention to Nick's erratic behavior as it threatens to unnerve the rest of the men. Nick finally agrees to leave, explaining that "if any supplies have come I'll bring them down tonight. If not, I'll come at night when I have something to bring" (314). Unlike Hemingway's situation, however, Nick's lack of purpose exacerbates his confusion from the psychological effects of his injury as well as the increased anxiety he experiences from witnessing atrocities at the front not long after he has been wounded.

Nick's speech on grasshoppers, moreover, correlates with an unusual article published in the Section One newspaper *Come Stà*. In "Patents Applied For," the editors refer to James Baker's idea for a "grasshopper bomb" devised to

> destroy the wheat crops of Germany and Austria. Mr. Baker's blue prints indicate that an ordinary French Soixante-Quinze shell may be adapted with a few minor changes. A hole is to be drilled behind the fuse cap into which grass hoppers are inserted. Mr. Baker's researches into the life history of the grasshopper lead him to believe that a sufficient number of the long-legged pests would be propagated from the time the shell left the cannon's mouth until it landed on enemy soil to destroy one and three-quarter acres of wheat.[63]

Nick makes reference to the insects as a sort of plague as well, relating them to the promised influx of American combatants: "Soon you will see untold millions wearing this uniform swarming like locusts. The grasshopper, you know, what we call the grasshopper in America, is really a locust" (312). Although Hemingway's fishing experience no doubt offered source material for Nick's oration, Baker's article suggests a parallel for the reference to these insects as a force deployed against the enemy. Whereas the "Patents Applied For" piece serves as a joke, Nick's rambling address leads his listeners to realize that he has become unhinged by the horrors of war.

Hemingway made another reference related to his service in what became one of his most recognized passages from *A Moveable Feast*, as Robert A. Martin has also pointed out.[64] In the chapter titled "Une Génération Perdue," Ernest writes of a conversation with Gertrude Stein about a young mechanic who "had served in the last year of the war."[65] The memory leads him to recall an anecdote that is based on popular attitudes expressed by seasoned drivers who preferred Fiats over Fords:

> I thought about the boy in the garage and if he had ever been hauled in one of those vehicles when they were converted to ambulances. I remembered how they used to burn out their brakes going down the

mountain roads with a full load of wounded and braking in low and finally using the reverse, and how the last ones were driven over the mountainside empty, so they could be replaced by big Fiats with a good H-shift and metal-to-metal brakes. (30)

Hemingway wrote a similar passage in his Ring Lardner parody in June of 1918: "You see Al they dont like dddds [Fords] here and one of the fellows told me that you get promoted if you wreck them."[66] Red Cross reports show careful accounts of the vehicles sent to each section and indicate no descriptions supporting the possibility that men intentionally demolished Ford ambulances by guiding them over cliffs, but the reminiscence makes for a good story nonetheless. Even more, it serves, along with his reference to Ecclesiastes, as the basis for his well-known response to Stein's comment calling him and his contemporaries "a lost generation."[67] Instead, the remembrance leads him to conclude that "all generations were lost by something and always had been and always would be" (30). Although Hemingway avoided explicit reference to the Red Cross, the details of his active duty inform his writing over the course of his entire career.

Even more, his wounding at the Piave and subsequent attitudes toward heroism became defining features of his work. Hemingway began producing fiction related to his trial by fire soon after the incident. One piece written while he was still in Milan tells about Nick Grainger during his convalescence in a Red Cross hospital in Italy.[68] Nick has received a Silver Medal and War Cross, and a crowd outside his window is celebrating the end of the war. His citation explains that he was "wounded twice by the machine guns of the enemy" after which he "continued to advance at the head of his platoon with the greatest coolness and valor until struck in the legs by the shell of a trench mortar." Because he survived his "rendesvous [sic] with Death," however, he felt that "God double crossed" him.[69] Nick hides a bottle of bichloride of mercury in his bedding, and, as Reynolds interprets it, "suicide is preferable to the maimed life he has left to him."[70] Hemingway produced a related piece not long after his homecoming. "The Woppian Way" or "The Passing of Pickles McCarty" tells of "a bum box-fighter" named Nick Neroni who heads off to fight with the Arditi. The narrator, a journalist traveling to the combat zone with Nick, reflects on the exploits of Gabriele d'Annunzio, "the great amourist who had exhausted the love of women and now was wringing the last drops from love of country onto his white hot soul." Looking ahead to the impending battle, the reporter wonders if d'Annunzio will "find the death he was looking for" or "be cheated again."[71] Indeed, Hemingway's early efforts show themes based on romantic notions of heroism and characters who view loss of life as a fitting end to combat.

In 1921, he wrote a poem that dealt with death in more complex terms. Initially, he called the piece "Killed—San Dona di Piave. June 15, 1918," which Reynolds considers as a possible tribute to McKey.[72] The revised title calls to mind Hemingway's wounding instead. Similar to the articles printed about his lectures in Oak Park, "Killed Piave—July 8—1918" alludes to the moments immediately following the explosion:

> Desire and
> All the sweet pulsing aches
> And gentle hurtings
> That were you,
> Are gone into the sullen dark.
> Now in the night you come unsmiling
> To lie with me
> A dull, cold, rigid bayonet
> On my hot-swollen, throbbing soul.[73]

James Mellow suggests that Hemingway is describing "a dead soldier" who is "remembered by his wife and lover."[74] The second person seems rather to indicate that the "you" mentioned in line four, who has "gone into the sullen dark," initially signifies abstractions that represent the injured persona; and the "you" who comes "unsmiling / To lie with me" in lines six and seven refers to the Grim Reaper. Instead of carrying a scythe, death personified wields a rifle blade, which is pressed against the person's soul "in the night." Although the ambiguous point of view is somewhat confusing, the poem significantly prefigures Hemingway's later work associating traumatic injuries with spiritual awareness.

At the same time he composed "Killed Piave," Hemingway worked on brief sketches that dealt with the aftermath for protagonists who returned home. Among the portraits in "Cross Roads," an unfinished collection describing various personalities around Horton Bay, Michigan, where Hemingway spent much of his time in the summer and fall of

1919, "Billy Gilbert" tells about an ex-soldier with wound stripes and ribbons.[75] "Nobody around the Bay" understood what they meant, however, and "all the boys that came back had ribbons on." Even more, anyone "could buy them at the camps where you were discharged" (126). Another piece, "Bob White," portrays a veteran who did not arrive in France until "three days before the armistice."[76] When Bob returns to his hometown, the people are susceptible to believing his war stories despite his lack of experience. Hemingway never completed "Cross Roads," but the "concept of an understated, ironic sketch to reveal attitude, character or situation," as Reynolds has observed, "matured eventually into the brilliant paragraphs" of *in our time*.[77] Moreover, the subject matter focusing on characters who struggle to tell about their war exploits came to occupy a central place in his writing.

Hemingway's journalism in the *Toronto Star* elaborated on these themes from his experiments in fiction. "How to Be Popular in Peace Though a Slacker in War" offered a "few hints" for Canadian men who profited by working in the United States instead of enlisting.[78] In discussing how shirkers can pass for veterans, Hemingway stresses that the "camaraderie of returned men" seemed to be "the main result" of the conflict (10). Explaining how to fit in, he tells them to purchase a "trench coat" and "army issue shoes" and to study a "good history of the war" (10–11). Once "you have firmly established by suggestion your status as an ex-army man and possible hero," he advises, "be modest and unassuming and you will have no trouble." After "you have service at the front, proven patriotism and a commission firmly established," he adds, "take your bankbook out," "read it through," and "remember that that there are fifty-six thousand Canadians dead" (11). An article published the following month provided a similar account of officers who realize that "we didn't get nothing permanent good out of the war except the lieutenant's mustaches."[79] Their stories have become so routine that listeners tend to change the subject whenever the ex-soldiers become "reminiscent" (19). Although these satirical sketches make light of the imitable pose of the veteran, they nonetheless underscore the tragic outcome for those who served.

Hemingway's article about returning to Fossalta deals with similar issues. In "A Veteran Visits Old Front," he does not call attention to the "hero of the Piave" or the "first American wounded in Italy," and the combat injury he describes in second person suggests circumstances shared by many who served in action:[80]

The front is as different from the way it used to be as your highly re-
spectable shin, with a thin, white scar on it now, is from the leg that
you sat and twisted a tourniquet around while the blood soaked your
puttee and trickled into your boot, so that when you got up you limped
with a "squidge" on your way to the dressing station. (176)

Instead of courage under fire, he points out a minor injury that leaves a
barely perceptible blemish. The image effectively underscores that despite the intense battles, reminders of personal sacrifice had already begun to fade from view. Another passage evokes sympathy for countless
numbers of the "poor old boys hoofing it along the side of the road to
ease their bad feet, sweating along under their packs and rifles and the
deadly Italian sun in a long, horrible, never-ending stagger after the battalion" (178). When he tries to appeal to a store clerk by telling her that
he was "here during the war" too, she replies with bitterness to tell him
that "so were many others" (177). Overall, the article avoids talk of hero-
ics and laments the aftermath as a collective tragedy.

Hemingway also elaborated upon war decorations in his journalism.
In April of 1922, he published a brief item after his move to Paris, noting
that "you cannot walk twenty yards on the Grands Boulevards without
seeing the familiar red ribbon of the Legion [of Honor] in someone's
buttonhole."[81] At the end of the following year, he produced a piece on
the trading of medals.[82] After a series of visits to pawn brokers and coin
shops on Adelaide Street in Toronto, he learns that the previously sought-
after awards, which used to be bought and sold on a regular basis, are no
longer popular among shopkeepers trying to turn a profit. Since no one
wishes to purchase them, he concludes that the "market price for valor
remained undetermined" (403). The account ironically suggests that the
courageous acts represented by the decorations hold value, but the em-
blems themselves had become worthless.[83] Taken as a whole, the *Toronto
Star* articles emphasize how recognition for individual acts of heroism
had become outdated. The tone he developed prefigures the way he dealt
with similar themes in subsequent short stories and novels.

Hemingway began publishing fiction dealing with wounded protagonists in *in our time*.[84] Unlike the author's experience, the main character in "chapter 7" of that volume expresses an immediate disavowal of
war upon being injured. After "Nick" has been "hit in the spine," he "sat
against the wall of the church where they had dragged him to be clear

of machine gun fire in the street" (15). As he "looked straight ahead bril-
liantly" and the "sun shone on his face," he sees the Austrian dead and
observes that "things were getting forward in the town. It was going
well" (15). While he waits for stretcher bearers to arrive, Nick "turned
his head carefully and looked down at Rinaldi," who "lay face downward
against the wall" (15). Nick tells him that "you and me we've made a
separate peace," but Rinaldi "lay still in the sun breathing with difficulty"
(15). Nick says "not patriots" and turns his head "carefully away smiling
sweatily" (15). The sketch shows effective use of limited point of view
and clipped dialogue to create, as Kathryn Derounian has observed, "an
exact sequence of events in simple yet forceful language."[85] In contrast
to Hemingway's earlier experiments in fiction, Nick is relieved after his
injury and expresses a wry sense of contentment when he comes to realize that the war is over for him.

Composed the same year *in our time* was published, "Soldier's Home"
shows a veteran struggling with notions of courage in the aftermath.[86]
After serving in the Marines from 1917 until the summer of 1919, Harold
Krebs returns to Oklahoma.[87] By that time, however, "the greeting of
heroes was over," and Krebs has difficulty fitting in with his family and
the community (111). After participating in several major campaigns
in France, at first "he did not want to talk about the war at all." Later,
"he felt the need to talk but no one wanted to hear about it." Indeed,
the people had "heard too many atrocity stories to be thrilled by actu-
alities" (111). Krebs, therefore, tries to appease them by telling lies that
"consisted in attributing to himself things other men had seen, done
or heard of, and stating as facts certain apocryphal incidents familiar
to all soldiers" (111–12). When he meets other veterans, he expresses a
different kind of falsehood: "He fell into the easy pose of the old soldier
among other soldiers: that he had been badly, sickeningly frightened
all the time" (112). Even so, Krebs does not see himself as a coward in
battle. Instead, he took pride in "all of the times that had been able to
make him feel cool and clear inside himself when he thought of them;
the times so long back when he had done the one thing, the only thing
for a man to do, easily and naturally, when he might have done something else" (111). Indeed, "he had been a good soldier," and "that made a
difference" (113). Because he adopts a false persona in order to appease
others, however, Krebs lost "everything" (112). Although he had been
brave on the battlefield, the pressures away from the trenches ultimately

lead him to compromise his values, and he suffers from "nausea" as a result (112).[88] Another limited-point-of-view account, "Soldier's Home" adeptly communicates Krebs's valor without overstating it and epitomizes the struggle of a combatant who has performed well in the war but cannot acclimate once the fighting has ceased.

Hemingway portrayed another veteran as the central figure in *The Sun Also Rises*. Unlike the story of Krebs, however, Jake Barnes's first-person account focuses on his difficulty in achieving a meaningful relationship with the woman he loves. Although Jake says little about his service as an aviator in Italy or the events that led to his embarrassing injury, he alludes to the outcome early in the narrative: "Undressing, I looked at myself in the mirror of the big armoire beside the bed," he relates, "of all the ways to be wounded. I suppose it was funny."[89] Still, the "old grievance" keeps him awake at night as he thinks about his hospitalization and the "liaison colonel" who visited him after hearing about news of the accident: "He made a wonderful speech," Jake explains, "'You, a foreigner . . . have given more than your life.' What a speech! I would like to have it illuminated to hang in the office. He never laughed. He was putting himself in my place, I guess. 'Che mala fortuna! Che mala fortuna!'" (31). Although Jake makes light of the situation by joking about the officer's rhetoric, the true extent of his sacrifice is no laughing matter, especially when he is alone at night. His feelings for Brett Ashley only make things worse: "Probably I never would have had any trouble if I hadn't run into Brett," he supposes (31).

Even so, Jake emphasizes the many ways he tries to move ahead despite his misfortune.[90] He finds a mentor in Count Mippipopolous, who despite being wounded and serving in "seven wars and revolutions" believes that "it is because I have lived very much that now I can enjoy everything so well" (60). Jake also seeks solace in the rituals of Catholicism, devotes much of his time as a bullfight aficionado, and takes pleasure from the pastoral settings he visits while fishing.[91] He reflects on his attempts to find fulfillment in a key passage that underscores the essential theme of the novel: "I did not care what it was all about. All I wanted to know was how to live in it. Maybe if you found out how to live in it you learned from that what it was all about" (148). Overall, Hemingway shows the profound impact of the war on Jake while also demonstrating the protagonist's struggle in the years that follow.[92]

"In Another Country" is another first-person account dealing with a protagonist recovering from a wound.[93] As the narrator relates, "in the fall the war was always there, but we did not go to it any more" (206). Instead, the patients attend regular therapy sessions while recuperating in Milan. Although most of them have earned "the same medals," the narrator does not take his awards very seriously (207). He explains that his citation "really said, with the adjectives removed, that I had been given the medals because I was an American" (208). Rather than a show of valor, he considers that getting injured in battle "was really an accident" (208). After reflecting on the courageous acts that his fellow patients had performed, he admits that "I would never have done such things, and I was very much afraid to die" (208).

An Italian major he meets "did not believe in bravery" either (208). The officer is also skeptical that the machines used for his rehabilitation will actually achieve the desired result. After the major discovers that his wife has died of pneumonia despite waiting to marry until after he was "definitely invalided out of the war," he becomes intent on advising the younger protagonist that "he should not place himself in a position to lose" (209). Similar to *The Sun Also Rises*, "In Another Country" emphasizes that courage "is not measured only on the battlefield," as Arthur Waldhorn puts it, for the protagonist observes how the major must cope with his immense suffering even after he is out of the action.[94] The use of first person, moreover, effectively portrays a younger character as he comes to understand a more profound sense of sacrifice than that referred to in the "beautiful language" of his citation (208).

The protagonist of "Now I Lay Me" is another convalescent who is afraid to die.[95] Nick Adams announces from the outset that his anxiety is based on questions dealing with spirituality. In the opening paragraph, he explains that

I myself did not want to sleep because I had been living for a long time with the knowledge that if I ever shut my eyes in the dark and let myself go, my soul would go out of my body. I had been that way for a long time, ever since I had been blown up at night and felt it go out of me and go off and then come back. I tried never to think about it, but it had started to go since, in the nights, just at the moment of going off to sleep, and I could only stop it by a very great effort. So while now I am fairly sure that it would not really have gone out, yet then, that summer, I was unwilling to make the experiment. (276)

Similar to accounts of Hemingway's lectures in Oak Park and his poem about the Piave, "Now I Lay Me" shows that the protagonist has become aware of his soul after the trauma of his near-death experience. As the title alluding to the popular children's prayer also emphasizes, Nick has become seriously concerned about his safekeeping during the night and is afraid to fall asleep.[96]

Among the ways Nick occupies himself while attempting to stay awake, he recites his prayers "over and over" (277). His difficulty in saying the "Our Father" points to another aspect of the spiritual crisis he undergoes: "I could only get as far as 'On earth as it is in heaven,'" he explains, "and then have to start all over and be absolutely unable to get past that" (278). Nick's inability to complete the prayer suggests that he is held up not by the words that follow, as Flora surmises, but as a result of the implications of what he has already stated: "Thy will be done, on earth as it is in heaven."[97] Considering his proximity to the trenches, Nick's circumstances indicate that he cannot reconcile the living hell of combat with the promise of a peaceful afterlife. As a result, he tries to think about more pleasant things such as girls, trout-fishing, and various people he knows. The eschatological concerns that arise due to his wounding, however, are profoundly troubling.

Hemingway's treatment of themes based on his ordeal by fire culminated in *A Farewell to Arms*. As with depictions of his other protagonists, Frederic Henry's first-person account of the circumstances related to his injuries downplays notions of valor. In the moments immediately following the explosion that incapacitates him, Henry tries to help his fellow driver Passini, but he is unable to do so in time. Once he realizes that the Italian is dead, Frederic discovers that he has also been "hit" and becomes "very afraid" (56). After his cohorts carry him to safety behind the lines, Henry tries to defer medical treatment so that others can receive attention first, but a British officer tells him "don't be a bloody hero" (58). When Rinaldi visits the field hospital, he wants to know if Henry had accomplished "any heroic act," but Frederic explains that "I was blown up while we were eating cheese." Rinaldi insists that Henry must have "carried several people" on his back, but Frederic maintains that "I didn't carry anybody. I couldn't move." Even so, Rinaldi says that "I think we can get you the silver" (63). After Henry recuperates and returns to the front, he explains his dislike for the kind of rhetoric associated with war medals: "abstract words such as glory, honor, courage, or hallow were obscene beside the concrete names of villages, the numbers of roads, the names of rivers, the numbers of regiments and the dates" (185). When he flees the *carabinieri* upon realizing they intend to execute him, he does not think of those actions in grand terms either: "I ducked down, pushed between two men, and ran for the river, my head down. I tripped at the edge and went in with a splash" (225). Afterward, he points out that "it was no point of honor. I was not against them. I was through" (232). Rather than cast himself as a heroic figure, Henry shows how he ultimately chooses to have nothing more to do with the fighting, and he does not look upon his decision as admirable.[98]

Instead of emphasizing exploits in battle, Frederic's narrative focuses on the circumstances that develop for him after he has left the war behind. Similar to Nick in "Now I Lay Me," Frederic's near-death experience also leads to a significant new awareness: "I knew I was dead and that it had all been a mistake to think you just died," he explains, "then I floated, and instead of going on I felt myself slide back. I breathed and I was back" (54). The "most dramatic, the most significant single moment in *A Farewell to Arms*," as Stoneback calls it,[99] Henry's spiritual awakening leads him to commit to his relationship with Catherine: "God knows I had not wanted to fall in love with her," he recalls, "I had not wanted to fall in love with any one. But God knows I had and I lay on the bed in the room of the hospital in Milan and all sorts of things went through my head but I felt wonderful" (93). Indeed, after Count Greffi asks Henry "what do you value most?" Frederic responds by saying "some one I love" (262). "That is a religious feeling," Greffi tells him (263). When Catherine dies, Henry alludes to the emptiness that comes as a result. His final description implies that her spirit has left for good: "It was like saying good-bye to a statue," he explains (332). For Frederic, the aftermath of war is compounded by an emotional loss that is much more difficult to deal with than the pain from physical injuries.

Nick Adams does not pretend to be a hero in "A Way You'll Never Be" either. When Paravacini suggests that Nick is brave, the latter explains that he needs to get drunk to face combat: "I was stinking in every attack," he tells him, and "I'm not ashamed of it" (309). Even more, Nick is trying to deal with nightmares that haunt him after his brush with death. Centering on the image of "a house and a long stable and a canal," his visions lead him to be "more frightened than he had ever been in a bombardment." When Nick returns to the locale where he had been injured, he becomes even more troubled when he realizes that the details of his dreams do not match up with reality: "then where did he go each night and what was the peril, and why would he wake, soaking wet," he wonders (311). As he tries to relax, he imagines the event once again:

> He shut his eyes, and in place of the man with the beard who looked at him over the sights of the rifle, quite calmly before squeezing off, the white flash and clublike impact, on his knees, hot-sweet choking, coughing it onto the rock while they went past him, he saw a long, yellow house with a low stable and the river much wider than it was and stiller. "Christ," he said, "I might as well go." (314)

Similar to the passages in "Now I Lay Me" and *A Farewell to Arms*, "A Way You'll Never Be" implies aspects of an afterlife in the image that appears "in place of the man" who shot him.[100] As in the earlier account of Nick's attempts to stay awake, the prospect is extremely unsettling. In the later story, however, Hemingway added the detail explaining that the "house meant more than anything" and "was what he needed" (310). Although the hallucination is extremely disturbing, the narrator suggests that the protagonist is nonetheless drawn to it.

Almost two decades later, Hemingway's *Across the River and Into the Trees* served as the last word, so to speak, in terms of his fictional treatments inspired by the episode at the Piave. When Colonel Richard Cantwell returns to the site of his injury at Fossalta, he "squatted low, and looking across the river from the bank where you could never show your head in daylight, relieved himself in the exact place where he had determined, by triangulation, that he had been badly wounded thirty years before" (26). There is no mistaking this act for a heroic one either: "'A poor effort,' he said aloud to the river. . . . 'But my own'" (26). Afterward, Cantwell buries a ten thousand lira note and considers it partial payment for "the Medaglia d'Argento al Valore Militare." He calls the end result "a wonderful monument" (27). A little later in the novel, Cantwell suggests, however, that he paid a much higher price when he got "hit properly and for good," reflecting that "the loss of the immortality," after all, is "quite a lot to lose" (39). Indeed, Cantwell clearly articulates the main issue that Hemingway's other protagonists struggle to deal with all along.

Conclusion

Ernest Hemingway's enlistment with the American Red Cross was one of the most formative experiences of his life. In conjunction with existing scholarship, the official reports, letters, and other papers of key figures from that period tell the full story of the ambulance drivers and canteen workers in Italy. Even more, the documents provide specific dates and place names that were previously unclear, resulting in a more accurate chronology of Hemingway's involvement. Altogether, these sources reveal the most complete portrait of the young writer's participation in the Great War.

The opportunity to volunteer came about after a commission was established in response to the devastating aftermath of the Battle of Caporetto. Because leaders of the Allied Cause prioritized troop commitment on the Western front, noncombatants were charged with boosting morale among soldiers fighting in northern Italy. Ambulance drivers and canteen workers were issued U.S. army uniforms, and their leaders emphasized adherence to pseudo-military rules and regulations. Volunteers received honorary status as second lieutenants in the foreign service, and administrators used titles that were typically assigned to officers in armed forces.

While working as a cub reporter at the *Kansas City Star,* Hemingway applied to the Red Cross on February 23, 1918. The positions advertised were filled by other volunteers, and his application was subsequently placed on hold. In the meantime, he served with the Second Regiment of the Missouri Home Guard, which he joined in early November of 1917. On March 25, 1918, he became a member of Company E in the Seventh Regiment of the National Guard, but the unit did not officially receive federal status until May 18. On May 2, he was notified to resume his application to the Red Cross. On May 12, he arrived in New York City where he was issued a uniform and joined other new recruits headed overseas. While quartered at the Hotel Earle in Washington Square, his ten days in Manhattan coincided with publicity underscoring the importance of humanitarian aid to Italy. Before he left, he participated in a parade of seventy-five thousand war workers reviewed by President Woodrow Wilson. Less than a year after graduating from high school, Hemingway began his journey to Europe on May 23 when the *Chicago* set sail for France.

After several days at sea mingling with other personnel amid enthusiasm for the adventure to come, he arrived in Bordeaux on June 3. That night he boarded a train to Paris, where he was lodged at the Hotel Florida, 12 Boulevard Malesherbes. After a few days of sightseeing, during which time he observed the effects of German artillery on the French capital, he embarked for Italy on an overnight train. Upon his arrival in Milan on June 7, he was initiated into the horrors of war when he helped in the aftermath of the Sutter & Thevenot munitions factory explosion in Bollate. The official date for the start of his enlistment was recorded as the same day. Carrying out Robert W. Bates's orders, Meade Detweiler assigned Hemingway to Section Four, attached to the Fifth Army Corps of the First Army. On June 10, Hemingway left for his base at Schio by way of Vicenza headquarters, where he checked in with Captain Bates.

At the time Hemingway joined the ambulance outfit, administrators were eager for new volunteers. As the commanding officer, Bates underscored the importance of Red Cross rules and regulations. He particularly emphasized that the men adhere to stipulations set forth by the military censor. Issues of drunkenness among the drivers had been a cause of concern as well. Major Guy Lowell, who oversaw the operation from Rome, sent dispatches to Bates instructing the men to avoid future embarrassing incidents. A prominent architect, Lowell also spent time obtaining photographs for a book on Italian design over the course of his visits to the sections. Once the intense fighting resumed during the summer months, the overseers counted on the enlistees for providing much needed support to the soldiers.

Most of the experienced drivers from the Western front who stayed on during the summer of 1918 were assigned to Hemingway's unit. Many were well-acquainted with atrocities from the fighting in France and made light of objectives touted by their commanding officers in Italy. Some of them expressed their attitudes in ironic articles they wrote for section newspapers. Hemingway's only publication during the war, "Al Receives Another Letter," appeared in the June edition of *Ciao*, the broadsheet produced at Schio.

Even though Hemingway's ambulance service coincided with the start of the Austrian offensive on June 15, his unit was not close enough to the heavy fighting to engage in serious action. Many of the drivers and vehicles from his base were reassigned to other areas where they could be more useful, but Hemingway initially remained at Schio. Even before the battle had been decided, his colleagues were beginning to receive word about commendations for various acts of bravery performed during combat.

After two weeks with the ambulance corps, Hemingway went to work in the canteen service, the emergency *posti di conforto* organized at the lower Piave. On June 24, after the Austrians had retreated to their former positions on the right bank of the river, he rode with other volunteers in a camion driven by John S. Vanderveer to Mestre. The next day, Hemingway was dropped off at Fornaci, located seven kilometers behind the lines. The workers manning the temporary canteens, which were hastily organized by American Consul B. Harvey Carroll and Venice District Delegate Moses S. Slaughter, were initially unproductive because of a lack of supplies. Once resources began to arrive, Hemingway made regular visits to the trenches beyond Fossalta di Piave, a town which had been previously overrun by the enemy. Lieutenant Edward M. McKey, the first volunteer in the American Red Cross to lose his life in Italy, was highly praised for his sacrifice after he was killed in the same region on June 16. Evidence of carnage from the heavy fighting was widespread. A few days after Hemingway received his assignment, Bates issued a memo cautioning volunteers to avoid risk taking and reminding them that they were prohibited from taking up arms or otherwise becoming involved as combatants.

After six days working amid the soldiers in the trenches, Hemingway was wounded in the frontlines around midnight on July 8, 1918. Bates received word of the incident on July 11 from Captain James Gamble, who oversaw the permanent rolling-kitchen operations. Bates suggested that Hemingway contact home about the incident, and notifications were sent by cable to Ernest's family on July 13.

After several days in a field hospital outside of Treviso, Hemingway had arrived at the American Red Cross Hospital in Milan by July 14. Ted Brumback visited him that day and wrote a letter to Hemingway's father explaining the circumstances. Brumback mentioned in particular that Ernest carried an injured soldier to a first aid dugout. On August

4, Hemingway wrote home to say that he had taken part in a parade in Milan the previous Sunday and was recognized by the Italians as the "American Hero of the Piave." At the same time, he made comments in his letters implying that he took a small part in the action as a combatant. On August 18, he elaborated on his trial by fire in a letter to his family that described another act of bravery in addition to the one mentioned by Brumback. He said that he deferred medical treatment so others could receive aid before him. By the end of August, he was promoted to First Lieutenant in the Red Cross, which also earned him the same honorary status in the Italian army. Guy Lowell commended Hemingway for his actions in a brief item printed on August 5 in the *Red Cross Bulletin*, but administrators did not elaborate upon the circumstances of Hemingway's wounding in their official reports. Even so, the Italian military recognized Ernest for two acts of courage and awarded him the Silver Medal of Military Valor. He also received a War Cross of Merit for his participation in the counteroffensive immediately following the Battle of the Piave.

After his wounding put him out of commission, Hemingway developed a romance with Agnes von Kurowsky and socialized with other volunteers and soldiers. In late September, he took a trip with colleague John Miller to Stresa, situated on Lago Maggiore at the border of Italy and Switzerland. At the start of the Battle of Vittorio Veneto on October 24, 1918, he attempted to rejoin his fellow volunteers at Bassano, but he returned to Milan the following day due to hepatitis. After hostilities ceased, he was released from service on November 16 and considered taking a job in the Red Cross helping with civilian relief during the aftermath. In early December, he observed conditions in the defunct combat zone on a visit to Nervesa. Later that month, he sojourned with Gamble in Taormina, Sicily. On December 31, Robert Perkins signed Hemingway's honorable discharge, and Ernest left for home aboard the *Giuseppe Verdi* on January 4, 1919. Upon his homecoming, reporters printed articles that touted him as a hero and indicated that he served in the Italian army. A few months later, Hemingway wrote to Gamble saying that "all the real heroes are dead."[1]

Hemingway's World War I writing grew directly out of these circumstances, and his Red Cross experience had a profound impact on his work for the rest of his life. Upon his return, he expressed excitement over the prospect of publishing related stories in popular magazines. Living off the income he collected from the insurance policy covering his wounding, "roughly $116 a month," as Michael Reynolds explains, he wrote to friends about his efforts.[2] In a letter to Gamble, he said that "I've written some darn good things . . . and am starting a campaign against your Philadelphia Journal the Sat. Eve Post. I sent them the first story Monday last. . . . Tomorrow another one starts toward them."[3] He planned on sending "so many and such good ones" that "they're going to have to buy them in self defence." Around the same time, he told Bill Horne "I am writing. Honest to God writing." One story "made Brother Jenks [Howell Jenkins] cry, really, and he was cold sober. . . . Really tho I'm writing stuff that I had no idea I could write. I[']m going to land in the post."[4] By the fall of 1919, he had moved to Michigan not far from the family cottage on Walloon Lake to spend the winter writing stories for the slicks.

Despite his efforts, Hemingway's early attempts did not pay off, and he had to find other means to support himself. Although his "Cross Roads" project showed promise, romanticized stories such as "The Woppian Way" were rejected by the magazines.[5] He later recalled that

> I was always known in Petoskey as Ernie Hemingway who wrote for the Saturday Evening Post due to the courtesy of my landlady's son, who described my occupation to the reporter for the Petoskey paper. . . . After Christmas when I was still writing for the Saturday Evening Post and had $20 left of my savings, I was promised a job at the pump factory . . . and was looking forward to laying off writing for the magazines for a time.[6]

When his insurance money ran out, he gave a lecture about his war exploits to the Ladies' Aid Society in Petoskey. Afterward, Harriet Connable offered him "the softest job of his life," as Reynolds explains. She hired Ernest as a "paid companion" to her son Ralph, whose father was the head of the Woolworth stores in Canada.[7] Once he left Michigan to join Ralph at the Connable home, Hemingway gained a position as a reporter for the *Toronto Star*. In the spring of 1920, he published two satires on veterans: "How to Be Popular in Peace Though a Slacker in War" and "Lieutenant's Mustaches the Only Permanent Thing We Got Out of War."[8]

By the end of 1920, Hemingway was living in Chicago and entertaining plans for heading back to Italy. Not long after his homecoming, he wrote to fellow Section Four veteran Lawrence T. Barnett telling him that his family were "wolfing at me to go to college" in Wisconsin, but he wanted to return "to Schio instead."[9] In January of 1921, Gamble offered to cover expenses for five months while Hemingway worked on his writing in Rome. Ernest considered the option, but his courtship of Hadley Richardson took priority.[10] At the end of March, however, Hadley encouraged him to consider the idea once again:

> Think of how in Italy there won't be anything but love and peace to form a background for writing and what with all this seething writhing mass of turbulous creation going on inside of you now and bursting loose now and again in spite of lack of ideal opportunity—why you'll write like a great wonderful sea breeze bringing strong wiffs from all sort of strange interior places you know.[11]

In July, Nick Neroni, a former soldier in the Italian army who was "going back in the fall," offered to help "arrange everything."[12] After Ernest and Hadley were married in September, they were unable to afford the trip at first, but Hadley received an unexpected inheritance when her uncle died and plans were underway once again.

Meanwhile, Hemingway had been relying on specific episodes from his war service as "a source for his fiction."[13] By April of 1921, he had written three chapters of a novel "about a wounded American soldier on the Italian front" that was "closer to his own experience than anything he had yet attempted."[14] He was determined to write accurate dialogue, and Hadley gave him positive feedback: "That's the way for a novel to start," she said, "with real people talking and saying what they really think."[15] In addition to his "Killed Piave" poem, he wrote an ironic lyric about Theodore Roosevelt: "All the legends that he started in his life / Live on and prosper, / Unhampered now by his existence."[16] Another verse, "Mitrailliatrice," compared Hemingway's typewriter to a machine gun.[17] His story about Schio, "The Visiting Team," received commentary from a professional. A friend with experience in the marketplace explained how difficult it was to publish war stories in popular magazines, but he encouraged Ernest nonetheless: "Do as much humor as possible as that sells easiest," he advised.[18] Sherwood Anderson inspired Hemingway to read literary works instead. Later that summer, Ernest wrote to Hadley about recasting his novel as a collection of fragments that would include letters, poems, and sketches. Although Hadley thought the plot was "if anything *too* patchwork," he continued to work at it.[19]

At the end of 1921, Hemingway's plan to go to Italy was significantly altered. When Sherwood Anderson came back from Paris "just in time to change the course of American writing," as Reynolds puts it, he spoke at length about artists such as Gertrude Stein and Ezra Pound who were living on the left bank of the Seine.[20] John Bone of the *Toronto Star* offered Ernest an opportunity to work out of the headquarters in the French capital. At the end of November, the Hemingways made reservations to sail from New York to Le Havre on the *Leopoldina*.[21] Ernest left behind the stories he was unable to publish and took with him the novel he began as well as a few other pieces that were based on events from his days in the Red Cross.[22] At the end of December, he wrote to Sherwood and Tennessee Anderson: "Well here we are," he told them, "and we sit outside the Dome Cafe, oposite the Rotunde." He had Anderson's "letters of introduction" addressed to Stein and Pound and intended to send them out soon "like launching a flock of ships."[23]

Working mostly for the *Toronto Star,* Hemingway's initial publications from Paris were nonfiction. Although Canadian interest in the "old-world tangles" of European politics had become "as dead as a bucket of ashes," he noted in one article, the "people who were in the war are interested in the inside reason for the turn of events that has cost France the sympathy of the world." French leaders spoke of "the next war," he wrote, and "nobody that had anything to do with this war wants to talk about another war."[24] While covering an economic summit in Genoa, he worked at "trying to write an impartially observed account" that was "untinged by propaganda."[25] After his return to the Italian Front with his wife and "Chink" Dorman-Smith in June of 1922, he lamented the spread of Fascism: "The whole business has the quiet and peaceful look of a three-year-old child playing with a live Mills bomb."[26] Another piece, "Did Poincaré Laugh in Verdun Cemetery?" centered on a controversy over whether the French premier showed a lack of respect for battlefield dead.[27] While covering the Greco-Turkish conflict, Hemingway reported on the "silent ghastly procession" of refugees from Eastern Thrace to Macedonia.[28] A related item dealt with the Red Crescent, a group "equivalent to the Red Cross" whose "official reports" on "Greek atrocities" were "used as propaganda."[29] His coverage of the Lausanne peace conference included unflattering portraits of heads of state. He referred to

Benito Mussolini as "Europe's prize bluffer" and Russian diplomat G. V. Chicherin as "the boy who was kept in dresses until he was twelve years old" who "always wanted to be a soldier. And soldiers make empires and empires make wars."[30] Overall, his journalism shows a deepening awareness of politics amid the aftermath.

The histories that Hemingway owned show additional perspectives on the devastating outcome.[31] In *The Story of the American Red Cross in Italy* (1920), Charles Bakewell wrote about the Battle of Caporetto and the factors that inspired "disaffected Italian troops" who were "ready to lay down their arms and walk over to the enemy."[32] Bakewell explained that riots led by "socialists clamoring for peace" in Turin as well as a statement from Pope Benedict XV asking leaders to consider an armistice had contributed to the defeat. When the Central Powers broke through the lines in October, the Second Army fled and "threw away their guns" as they shouted "we are going home. The war is over!" Officers attempted to rally their troops, but "great was the confusion" since "Austrians and Germans disguised in Italian uniforms" had been "giving contrary orders."[33] Panic increased in the ensuing retreat as civilians "rushed to join the moving throng that congested highways." Soldiers who had given up their arms "were caught at the bridge crossings. And more than once, in the early dawn, regiments were drawn up on three sides of a hollow square as these unfortunates were led out before them to face the firing squad."[34] Bakewell summarized the outcome as

> a horrible ending to the sweet dream of peace, which had begun with a song in the distant mountain valleys. In truth, they were neither traitors nor cowards—merely victims of a fair but fatal illusion. Stern measures! But,—*è la guerra*. Stern measures were necessary to bring order out of the chaos of those terrible days.[35]

Although Bakewell's volume is steeped in idealistic rhetoric, his description of Caporetto nonetheless reveals the appalling circumstances that led to the Red Cross presence in Italy.

Hemingway's front received attention as well. Bakewell wrote that the stand against the enemy in November of 1917 was "one of the most glorious pages in Italy's history."[36] In *Our Italian Front* (1920), Warner Allen explained that the subsequent Battle of the Piave, however, devastated the army. Even though they "checked the Austrian advance and eventually drove it back" across the river, "they failed to win the great military success which was almost within their grasp. If they had made one great effort there is little doubt that their losses would have been far lighter than they actually were."[37] As Allen pointed out, the ninety thousand casualties could have been reduced by half if the combatants had been more thoroughly trained.[38] Anticipated reinforcements from the United States never materialized either. Instead, Red Cross workers wearing uniforms resembling military personnel led the Italians to believe that additional armed forces were in their midst. As Bakewell explained, the ambulance drivers who inspired the soldiers to keep fighting were "the visible evidence of the reality of America's war with Austria."[39] Although the Allies were triumphant after the Battle of Vittorio Veneto, countless dead and wounded littered the combat zone as a result of the extended fighting. When negotiations for peace came to a close, Italy's efforts had been spurned and the country was left in ruin.[40]

Hemingway's subsequent fiction reflected the pervading disillusionment. His prose sketches downplayed valor using an ironic point of view and showed the influence of Pound's advice on incorporating imagistic techniques.[41] Among the six pieces Hemingway published in the *Little Review* in the spring of 1923, two were based on stories he had heard from Dorman-Smith about fighting in Mons. The detached narrators talk about soldiers that "we potted" as the enemy troops tried to advance over obstacles. Another tells about drunken men headed off to combat at the Champagne.[42] At the end of the year, *Three Stories & Ten Poems* was issued by Robert McAlmon's Contact Publishing Company. The volume included poems, which Hemingway had placed in *Poetry: A Magazine of Verse* the preceding January, that were likewise related to the theme suggesting "soldiers never do die well."[43]

In 1924, Hemingway published *in our time,* his collection of eighteen vignettes that he had been working on since his arrival in Paris. According to the back cover, the book was the last volume in a series edited by Pound intended as an "inquest into the state of contemporary English prose."[44] In addition to his sketches from the *Little Review*, Hemingway added three new pieces on World War I. The first, "chapter 7," describes Nick's "separate peace."[45] Next in the sequence, "chapter 8" underscores the contrast between a soldier's prayer during a bombardment and his subsequent visit to a brothel. A longer narrative, "chapter 10," provides a third-person account of an unnamed patient convalescing in Milan where he and his girlfriend "wanted to get married" and "make it so they could not lose it" (19). After the armistice, "Ag" writes to say that "theirs had been only a boy and girl affair" (19). Even so, "she hoped he would have a great career, and believed in him absolutely" (19). Subsequently, the protagonist "contracted gonorrhea from a sales girl" while "riding in a taxicab through Lincoln Park" (19). Hemingway told Pound that his plan for the series had been to start "noble" and finish "with the feller who goes home and gets clap."[46] Similar to his earlier vignettes, the sketches he added to *in our time* deal with material related to his personal experience from an ironic point of view.

During the same year *in our time* was published, Hemingway focused on longer works of fiction. Gertrude Stein read the war novel he brought to Paris, but she told him to "begin over again and concentrate."[47] Her advice became even more apt when the manuscript (along with most of the other stories he had written up until then) was stolen after Hadley packed it in a suitcase that she left unattended at the Gare de Lyon in December of 1922. Although Hemingway later admitted in *A Moveable Feast* that "it was probably a good thing that it was lost," starting over was a daunting prospect at the time (76). He still intended to produce a book, he recalled, but "in the meantime" he planned to "write a long story about whatever I knew best." While trying to decide on a subject that he knew about "truly" and cared for "the most," he concluded that "there was no choice at all." At a corner table of the Closerie des Lilas in Montparnasse he began composing a story "about coming back from the war but there was no mention of the war in it" (76). After "Big Two-Hearted River" was finished, it was printed in *This Quarter* in January of 1925.[48] Later that fall, it appeared as the penultimate chapter in *In Our Time.*

His most impressive piece of fiction thus far, "Big Two-Hearted River" serves as an integral component of *In Our Time.*[49] Alluding to a phrase from the Book of Common Prayer, the title of the volume suggests that the sketches and stories each resonate with the statement from which he borrowed: "Give peace in our time, O Lord."[50] The central theme is particularly evident in the development of Nick Adams, who appears first as a boy in "Indian Camp" and later in "Chapter VI," the vignette about the wounding of "Nick" that appeared previously as "chapter 7" in *in our time.* In "Big Two-Hearted River," Nick works at putting the war behind him. Upon his arrival in Seney, Michigan, he observes the effects of a fire that are reminiscent of a battlefield and thinks that "it could not all be burned. He knew that."[51] Nick leaves the charred landscape and hikes through a lush countryside, makes his camp in "the good place," and takes pleasure in cooking a meal (167). In Part Two, he emerges from his tent and spends the day fishing. After losing a trout when his line breaks, Nick feels "a little sick" at first but eventually laughs it off (177). Because he has caught "two big trout," he decides to avoid going into the swamp where "fishing was a tragic adventure" (179, 180). Instead, he heads back "toward the high ground" of his campsite (180). As Hemingway wrote years later in a letter to Charles Poore, the lack of explicit reference to the war in the story "may be one of the things that helps it."[52] Indeed, "Big Two-Hearted River" is one of the best examples of his "theory of omission" put into practice.[53]

Composed the same year that *In Our Time* was published, *The Sun Also Rises* (1926) mentions little about the conflict but likewise deals considerably with the results. Wounded on a "joke front" in Italy, Jake Barnes would rather talk about other subjects:[54] "We would probably have gone on and discussed the war and agreed that it was in reality a calamity for civilization, and perhaps would have been better avoided. I was bored enough" (17). Serving as a "V.A.D." (Voluntary Aid Detachment), Brett Ashley entered an abusive marriage "during the war" after "her own true love had just kicked off with the dysentery" (38, 39). Jake also meets Wilson Harris who explains that "I've not had much fun since the war" (129). Mike Campbell tells stories about his service that "reflect discredit" on him, as in his anecdote about medals he borrowed to wear at a formal dinner because he "never sent in for" his own (135). As it turned out, "no one wore any medals," and afterward he gave them away to girls at a night club (135). Indeed, the epigraphs underscore the theme before the story begins. Hemingway later wrote that he "tried to balance Miss Stein's quotation" stating "you are all a lost generation" with "one from Ecclesiastes" explaining that "one generation passeth away, and another generation cometh; but the earth abideth forever."[55] Likewise, Jake's account speaks to the concerns of many of his contemporaries struggling to find fulfillment in postwar Europe.

The stories in *Men Without Women* (1927) portray wartime episodes as well as the aftermath. An American patient recovering in Milan is vague about his role with the military in "In Another Country," but he clearly shows his fear of combat. The protagonist is also concerned about "how I would be when I went back to the front." Unlike other soldiers who "were like hunting-hawks, . . . I was not a hawk," he adds.[56] "Che Ti Dice La Patria?" is based on a disappointing trip Hemingway took through Mussolini's Italy in 1927. After exiting the inhospitable country and spending the night in the border town of Mentone, the narrator explains that France "seemed very cheerful and clean and sane and lovely" by way of comparison.[57] Set during "late March" when the "snow was higher than the window" of a Major's hut behind the trenches, "A Simple Inquiry" focuses on a nineteen-year-old adjutant named Pinin who refuses a sexual proposition from his commander by telling him that he is in love with "a girl." The officer advises him to "stay on as my servant" anyway. "You've less chance of being killed," he says. In a final twist, the story implies that the younger soldier might not be as naïve as he appears: "The little devil," the major thought, "I wonder if he lied to me."[58] Similar to the concluding story of *In Our Time*, Nick Adams is the subject of "Now I Lay Me," the last piece of the 1927 volume. Nick tries to avoid thoughts of death by fantasizing about a trout stream as he lies awake near the combat zone. He also expresses anxiety over the fate of his comrade prior to the Battle of Vittorio Veneto: "I prayed very often for John in the nights and his class was removed from active service before the October offensive. I was glad he was not there, because he would have been a great worry to me."[59] Reflecting the author's proficiency as a short-story writer, *Men Without Women* explores a variety of themes related to the conflict.

Published two years later, *A Farewell to Arms* shows the culmination of his achievements based on his adventure in Italy. In his 1948 introduction to the novel, Hemingway wrote that "I remember living in the book and making up what happened in it every day. Making the country and the people and the things that happened I was happier than I had ever been."[60] The first five paragraphs crafted in the manner of his vignettes from *in our time* show off some of his finest prose. The retrospective point of view effectively emphasizes the complexity of Frederic Henry's journey. After talking with the priest in one episode, he states that "he had always known what I did not know and what, when I learned it, I was always able to forget. But I did not know that then, although I learned it later."[61] The tragic irony of Henry's failed attempt to achieve a "separate peace" after escaping the chaos following the retreat from Caporetto is underscored when Catherine dies from childbirth (243). Instead of valor in battle, Henry emphasizes the woman he loves as heroic, and he considers death as the ultimate equalizer:

> If people bring so much courage to this world the world has to kill
> them to break them, so of course it kills them. The world breaks every
> one and afterward many are strong at the broken places. But those that
> will not break it kills. It kills the very good and the very gentle and the
> very brave impartially. If you are none of these you can be sure it will
> kill you too but there will be no special hurry. (249)

In the end, his attempt to say good-bye to Catherine "wasn't any good,"
and he walks back to his hotel in the rain (332). The narrative closes in
the spring of 1918, months before the cessation of hostilities. After serving in the Red Cross, reading and writing about the conflict during the
twenties, and developing his literary skills over the course of a decade,
Hemingway produced a tour de force with his second novel.

The critical reception of his work throughout the twenties reflected
his growing reputation. After Hemingway published *Three Stories & Ten
Poems*, Edmund Wilson wrote that the "poems are not particularly important," but the "prose is of the first distinction."[62] Regarding *in our
time*, Wilson thought that the "little book has more artistic dignity than
any other" by "an American about the period of the war."[63] An anonymous reviewer for the *Kansas City Star* said that Hemingway "is recognized, not simply as a journalist, but as one of the most promising young
writers in the English language."[64] After *In Our Time* came out, Ernest
Walsh referred to Hemingway's "growing process" by noting that "he is
of the elect. He belongs."[65] In 1926, Conrad Aiken reviewed *The Sun Also
Rises* declaring that it showed an "extraordinary individuality of style"
and "brilliant" use of dialogue.[66] Allen Tate decided that "the present
novel" supported the "prophecy" that Hemingway "will be the 'big man
in American letters.'"[67] When *Men Without Women* was published, Percy
Hutchinson considered it the achievement of a "master in a new manner
in the short-story form."[68] Dorothy Parker stated that he "is, to me, the
greatest living writer of short stories."[69] The publication of *A Farewell
to Arms* prompted Clifton P. Fadiman to call it Hemingway's "best book
to date," and he thought that the novel should have been awarded the
Pulitzer Prize.[70] Likewise, Malcolm Cowley recognized that Hemingway
"is generally mentioned with the respect that one accords to a legendary
figure."[71] Indeed, by 1930, Hemingway had established himself as an author of significant renown.

Not all of his reviews were positive, however, and *A Farewell to Arms* was even subject to censorship. When the novel was serialized in *Scribner's Magazine*, copies were banned from newsstands in Boston, and a debate ensued over the "moral and aesthetic value" of the work.[72] Owen Wister argued that the book "is full of beauty and variety and nobody in it is garbage."[73] Mary Colum asked "what form of morality is served by bamboozling people as to what goes on at a wartime front?"[74] Robert Herrick, on the other hand, thought that "no great loss to anybody would result if *A Farewell to Arms* had been suppressed."[75] M. K. Hare considered that "possibly this book may not be art, but need it be called 'dirt'?"[76] Robert W. Bates had an opinion on Hemingway's writing as well. The former Red Cross captain noted in his personal papers that Ernest was "now a well-known writer whose stuff I don't care for" and "one of the first to write dirty books."[77] Mussolini was not pleased with the novelist either. According to George Monteiro, the work "was seen as vilifying Italian character and distorting recent Italian history."[78] Indeed, *A Farewell to Arms* did not appear in print in that country until 1945 after the dictator's regime had come to an end.

As Hemingway's fiction became widely read, the author also dealt with issues related to the confluence of his life and art. A review of *Men Without Women* in *Time* magazine noted that "in the War" Hemingway "was severely wounded, serving with the Italian Arditi, of whom he was almost the youngest member."[79] As Kenneth Lynn and Robert Lewis have explained, the dust jackets on Hemingway's books also included blurbs stating that the author was a soldier.[80] In February of 1927, Hemingway wrote to Maxwell Perkins, his editor at Scribners, saying that "I was attached to the Italian infantry for a time as a very minor sort of camp follower." He "was wounded" and had "four Italian decorations" that "were given me not for valorous deeds but simply because I was an American attached to the Italian army." At least one of them "was given me by mistake and the citation mentions an action . . . which I did not participate in." He explained that "for these reasons anyone reading war record or other personal publicity coming from Scribner's and knowing the facts would think I had furnished you with the information and simply regard me as a liar or a fool." He added that "it would be a great favor to me if we could lay off the Biography" as well.[81]

In 1930, Scribners issued a revised edition of *In Our Time* that reflected related concerns. Perkins asked Hemingway to introduce the volume, and "Introduction by the Author," a fictional account inspired by his reporting on the Greco-Turkish war, subsequently appeared as the open-ing piece.[82] Hemingway also took the opportunity to revise "A Very Short Story," which had formerly been designated as "chapter 10" of *in our time*. As it incorporated details from his romance with Agnes von Ku-rowsky, he changed the setting of the hospital from Milan to Padua and substituted the name "Luz" for "Ag." He also added a "legal disclaimer" to the work as a whole:

> In view of a recent tendency to identify characters in fiction with real people, it seems proper to state that there are no real people in this volume: both the characters and their names are fictitious. If the name of any living person has been used, the use was purely accidental.[83]

Although the declaration shows that his success made him a target for charges of libel, it also points to developing trends in critical assessments relying on his work for details about the life of the author.

Two years later, Hemingway tried to clarify his war service again. He wrote to Perkins and asked the editor to "spread this statement around," explaining that

> Mr. Ernest Hemingway has asked his publishers to disclaim the ro-mantic and false military and personal career imputed to him in a re-cent film publicity release. Mr. H., who is a writer of fiction, states that if he was in Italy during a small part of the late war it was only because a man was notoriously less liable to be killed there than in France. He drove, or attempted to drive, an ambulance and engaged in minor camp following activities and was never involved in heroic actions of any sort.[84]

Although Hemingway downplayed his involvement, he did not explain the nature of his service with the Red Cross, and the line between his fic-tion and biography remained unclear. In years to come, critics continued to confuse the circumstances. Robert Penn Warren, Malcolm Cowley, and Philip Young, for example, all referred to the author as an ex-soldier in the Italian army.[85]

In 1933, Hemingway included two well-crafted stories on the war in *Winner Take Nothing*, but reviewers began to grow weary of the subject. "A Way You'll Never Be" is Hemingway's most complex rendering of

Nick Adams's anxiety when he revisits the site of his wounding during battle. "A Natural History of the Dead," previously included at the end of chapter 12 in *Death in the Afternoon* (1932), tells the story of the munitions plant explosion outside of Milan and recounts an episode about a fatally wounded soldier who is placed in a cave among dead combatants. The doctor at a nearby dressing station refuses to permit stretcher bearers to move the man, and a tense dispute ensues. Both works emphasize the psychological effects on characters who witness an overwhelming amount of casualties. At the time, Fadiman claimed that the collection "smells of the early 1920's."[86] T. S. Matthews concurred, noting that "not everything" in the volume "is about the War, but for readers of other generations than Hemingway's the present collection might well have taken the title of one of its stories: 'A Way You'll Never Be.'"[87] Indeed, in the Great Depression, critics were less inclined to appreciate fiction about issues associated with a bygone era.

After World War II began, Hemingway wrote about the current state of affairs from the perspective of the previous conflict. On June 10, 1940, the *New Republic* published an article by Archibald MacLeish criticizing authors who had "educated a generation to believe that all declarations, all beliefs are fraudulent, that all statements of conviction are sales-talk, that nothing men can put into words is worth fighting for."[88] MacLeish claimed that writers such as Hemingway "must face the fact that the books they wrote in the years after the war have done more to disarm democracy in the face of fascism than any other single influence."[89] The article points to Frederic Henry's comment about his embarrassment over words such as "sacred, glorious, and sacrifice" as a statement that had "borne bitter and dangerous fruit" in the years that followed.[90] Two weeks later *Life* magazine printed Hemingway's response. Claiming to have "fought fascism in every way that I know how" he pointed out that

> young men wrote of the first war to show truly the idiocies and murderous stupidity of the way it was conducted by the Allies and Italy. Other young men wrote books that showed the same thing about the German conduct of the war. All agreed on war's vileness and undesirability.[91]

In 1942, he commented further in his introduction to *Men at War:* "The last war, during the years 1915, 1916, 1917, was the most colossal, murderous, mismanaged butchery that has ever taken place on earth. Any writer who said otherwise lied."[92] There are "worse things than war," he added, "and all of them come with defeat. . . . We who took part in the last war to end wars are not going to be fooled again."[93] Eight years later, he published *Across the River and Into the Trees*. Cowley thought the work "below the level" of Hemingway's previous novels but considered the protagonist "in some ways the most fully realized of Hemingway's heroes."[94] After visiting the Piave where he was wounded in 1918, Cantwell thinks that "this country meant very much to him, more than he could, or would ever tell anyone."[95] A few days later, he quotes the dying words of Stonewall Jackson and succumbs to a fatal heart attack while being chauffeured on a road between Venice and Trieste.

The Red Cross mission that Hemingway embarked upon as an eighteen-year-old inspired to seek adventure amid the battlefields of Europe influenced his entire career. The ironic tone of his work reflects attitudes expressed by the men in the section newspapers. His characterization of Frederic Henry suggests that several of the volunteers in the corps served as sources. Many of his settings incorporate details from his time spent at various locales near the front. The propaganda mission he took part in paved the way for his writing that later criticized the use of misleading publicity for enlisting support in a cause. His ideas were significantly impacted when the rhetoric of the war to end all wars failed to achieve a lasting peace. Although Hemingway did not become "reformed out of the war" immediately after his wounding, the concept of the "separate peace" nonetheless stems from the author's involvement in the Red Cross.[96] The downplayed notions of valor in his fiction were influenced by his incident at the Piave and his subsequent convalescence. As a result, his protagonists are tested not on the battlefield but in the aftermath. Their most significant struggle comes with surviving a near-fatal wounding that leads to a profound awareness of the inevitability of death.

Hemingway's work is significantly informed by personal experience and historical research, both of which he transformed into fiction according to a highly crafted literary technique. His narrative method, understated prose, and precise use of language all underscore the complexity of his themes. His short stories and novels are supreme works of art that resulted in a well-earned place of prominence in American letters.

Notes

Introduction

1. Ernest Hemingway, *Green Hills of Africa* (New York: Touchstone, 1996), 70.

2. *Green Hills of Africa* initially appeared in serial form in *Scribner's Magazine* from May to November of 1935. See Audre Hanneman, *Ernest Hemingway: A Comprehensive Bibliography* (Princeton, NJ: Princeton UP, 1967), 151.

3. Malcolm Cowley, "Not Yet Demobilized," in *Ernest Hemingway: The Critical Reception*, ed. Robert O. Stephens (New York: Burt Franklin & Co., 1977), 74. Reprinted from *New York Herald Tribune Books*, October 6, 1929, 1, 6.

4. T. S. Matthews, "Nothing Ever Happens to the Brave," in Stephens, *Ernest Hemingway: Critical Reception*, 77. Reprinted from *New Republic*, October 9, 1929, 208–10.

5. John Dos Passos, "Books," in Stephens, *Ernest Hemingway*, 95. Reprinted from *New Masses*, December 1, 1929, 16.

6. Ernest Hemingway, "How to Be Popular in Peace Though a Slacker in War," *Toronto Star Weekly*, March 13, 1920, 11. Reprinted in *Dateline: Toronto, the Complete "Toronto Star" Dispatches, 1920–1924*, ed. William White (New York: Scribners, 1985), 10–11; Ernest Hemingway, "A Veteran Visits Old Front, Wishes He Had Stayed Away," *Toronto Daily Star*, July 22, 1922, 7. Reprinted in *Dateline: Toronto*, 176–80.

7. Ernest Hemingway, *Death in the Afternoon* (New York: Scribners, 1960), 2.

8. Charles A. Fenton, *The Apprenticeship of Ernest Hemingway: The Early Years* (New York: Viking Press, 1954), 50–73.

9. Carlos Baker, *Ernest Hemingway: A Life Story* (New York, Scribners, 1969), 36–56.

10. See Scott Donaldson, *By Force of Will: The Life and Art of Ernest Hemingway* (New York: Viking, 1977), 125–43; Jeffrey Meyers, *Hemingway: A Biography* (New York: Harper & Row, 1985), 22–44; Peter Griffin, *Along with Youth: Hemingway, the Early Years* (New York: Oxford, 1985), 62–120; Kenneth S. Lynn, *Hemingway* (New York: Simon and Schuster, 1987), 66–100; and James Mellow, *Hemingway: A Life without Consequences* (New York: Houghton Mifflin, 1992), 47–100.

11. Michael Reynolds, *Hemingway's First War: The Making of "A Farewell to Arms"* (New York: Basil Blackwell, 1987), 160–80.

12. Bernard Oldsey, *Hemingway's Hidden Craft: The Writing of "A Farewell to Arms"* (University Park, PA: Pennsylvania State UP, 1979), 54.

13. Robert W. Lewis, "Hemingway in Italy: Making it Up," *Journal of Modern Literature* 9, no. 2 (1982): 209–36.

14. Charles M. Oliver, "History and Imagined History," in *Teaching Hemingway's "A Farewell to Arms*," ed. Lisa Tyler (Kent, OH: Kent State UP, 2008), 3.

15. Ibid.

16. Frederic J. Svoboda, "On Teaching Hemingway's *A Farewell to Arms* in Contexts," in Tyler, *Teaching Hemingway's "A Farewell to Arms*,"19.

17. Ernest Hemingway, "Introduction," in *Men at War: The Best War Stories of All Time*, ed. Ernest Hemingway (New York: Bramhall House, 1979), xiv.

1. Esprit de Corps

1. Arlen J. Hansen, *Gentlemen Volunteers: The Story of the American Ambulance Drivers in the Great War, August 1914–September 1918* (New York: Arcade Publishing, 1996), 3.

2. See ibid., 3–55.

3. James Nagel, "Hemingway and the Italian Legacy," in *Hemingway in Love and War: The Lost Diary of Agnes von Kurowsky, Her Letters, and Correspondence of Ernest Hemingway*, ed. Henry S. Villard and James Nagel (Boston: Northeastern UP, 1989), 206.

4. Hansen, *Gentlemen Volunteers*, 28; see also Henry James, *The American Volunteer Motor-Ambulance Corps in France: A Letter to the Editor of an American Journal* (London: Macmillan, 1914) and Nagel, "Hemingway and the Italian Legacy," 206.

5. Janet Hobhouse, *Everybody Who Was Anybody: A Biography of Gertrude Stein* (New York: G. P. Putnam's Sons, 1975), 108.

6. Nagel, "Hemingway and the Italian Legacy," 208.

7. Quoted in Robert W. Bates, letter to "Dear Family," July 8, 1918, Robert W. Bates Papers, private collection.

8. Charles A. Fenton, "Ambulance Drivers in France and Italy: 1914–1918," *American Quarterly* 3, no. 4 (1951): 327.

9. Robert W. Bates, letter to "Dear Mama," April 19, 1916, Robert W. Bates Papers, private collection.

10. Hansen, *Gentlemen Volunteers*, 53.

11. Fenton, "Ambulance Drivers in France and Italy," 335.

12. Quoted in Hansen, *Gentlemen Volunteers*, 39–40.

13. Malcolm Cowley, *Exiles Return: A Literary Odyssey of the 1920s* (New York: The Viking Press, 1951), 38.

14. Ibid., 37.

15. See M. A. DeWolfe Howe, ed., *The Harvard Volunteers in Europe: Personal Records of Experience in Military, Ambulance, and Hospital Service* (Cambridge, MA: Harvard UP, 1916).

16. Hansen, *Gentlemen Volunteers*, 161–81.

17. Michael Reynolds, *The Young Hemingway* (New York: Norton, 1998), 14–15; Steve Paul, "'Drive,' He Said: How Ted Brumback Helped Steer Ernest Hemingway into War and Writing," *Hemingway Review* 27, no. 1 (2007): 31.

18. See Steve Paul, "Preparing for War and Writing: What the Young Hemingway Read in the *Kansas City Star*, 1917–1918," *Hemingway Review* 23, no. 2 (2004): 5–20.

19. "Deeper into Italy," *Kansas City Star*, October 28, 1917, 1.

20. "The Cavalry Saved Italy," *Kansas City Star*, November 4, 1917, A8.

21. "Italy on Its New Line," *Kansas City Star*, November 19, 1917, 1.

22. "Italian Line Is Holding," *Kansas City Star*, November 15, 1917, 8; "British Now in Italy," *Kansas City Star*, November 17, 1917, 1.

23. "Italy Calls on America," *Kansas City Star*, November 4, 1917, 1.

24. "Blames Italian Leaders," *Kansas City Star*, November 30, 1917, A15; "No Delay on Austria," *Kansas City Star*, December 5, 1917, 1.

25. See "Belgium Scorned Peace," *Kansas City Star*, October 29, 1917, 1; "Slavs Still in War," *Kansas City Star*, November 2, 1917, 1; and Frank H. Simonds, "It's Win or Lose for Italy," *Kansas City Star*, November 18, 1917, C14.

26. "To Send Troops to Italy," *Kansas City Star*, December 6, 1917, 1.

27. "To Aid Till Italy Wins," *New York Times*, December 13, 1917, 4.

28. Burris Jenkins, "Italy, a Country of Song," *Kansas City Star*, October 25, 1917, 8. See also Paul, "Preparing for War and Writing," 8–13.

29. Burris Jenkins, "Italian Front a Keystone," *Kansas City Star*, October 24, 1917, 6. See also Paul, "Preparing for War and Writing," 9.

30. Jenkins, "Italian Front a Keystone," 6.

31. Burris Jenkins, "Trieste Is Key to Victory," *Kansas City Star*, October 26, 1917, A8.

32. Jenkins, "Italian Front a Keystone," 6.

33. Jenkins, "Italy, a Country of Song," 8.

34. See Paul, "Preparing for War and Writing," 8–13.

35. "Red Cross Commission to Italy," *Red Cross Bulletin*, August 4, 1917, 1.

36. Ibid.

37. Charles M. Bakewell, *The Story of the American Red Cross in Italy* (New York: MacMillan, 1920), 17.

38. "Aid for Italy Is Hastened by American Red Cross," *Red Cross Bulletin*, November 13, 1918, 2. See also Henry P. Davison, *The American Red Cross in the Great War* (New York: The Macmillan Company, 1920), 205–19.

39. Michael Reynolds, *Hemingway's First War: The Making of "A Farewell to Arms"* (New York: Basil Blackwell, 1987), 164.

40. Ibid., 161.

41. Hansen, *Gentlemen Volunteers*, 161–81.

42. Jack Nash, "From Paris to the Italian Front," *Avanti*, January 1, 1918, 4.

43. George Buchanon Fife, "Section One, Italy: The Chronicle of an Eventful Run Through France," 1, box 881, folder 954.11/08, Records of the American National Red Cross, National Archives, College Park, MD. For a description of Fife's career and involvement in the war, see "George Fife Dies; Newspaper Man," *New York Times*, March 13, 1939, 21.

44. Nagel, "Hemingway and the Italian Legacy," 209; Beverly R. Myles, "The American Red Cross Ambulance Services in Italy: Report to Major Prentice on Work Accomplished and Recommendations for the Permanent Organization of the Service," 27, box 881, folder 954.11/08, Records of the American National Red Cross, National Archives, College Park, MD.

45. Fife, "Section One, Italy," 1.

46. Myles, "The American Red Cross Ambulance Services in Italy," 28.

47. Fife, "Section One, Italy," 2.

48. Reynolds, *Hemingway's First War*, 165, 163.

49. Fife, "Section One, Italy," 3–8.

50. Nash, 4; George Buchanon Fife, "Answering Italy's Cry for Help: With the Red Cross Ambulance on their Dash from Paris to Milan," *Red Cross Magazine*, 13, no. 5 (May 1918): 37.

51. "Official Communiqué," *Avanti*, January 1, 1918, 2.

52. Fife, "Answering Italy's Cry for Help," 37–41.

53. Bakewell, *The Story of the American Red Cross in Italy*, 29.

54. "Italy Gets Sixty Ambulances," *New York Times*, December 17, 1917, 2.

55. Guy Lowell, "Report of the Department of Military Affairs for the Month of January, 1918," 6, box 881, folder 954.11/08, Records of the American National Red Cross, National Archives, College Park, MD.

56. Carlos Baker, *Ernest Hemingway: A Life Story* (New York, Scribners, 1969), 41.

57. Henry Serrano Villard, "Red Cross Driver in Italy," in Villard and Nagel, *Hemingway in Love and War*, 13–14.

58. Bakewell, *The Story of the American Red Cross in Italy*, 221, 223–24.

59. John Dos Passos, *The Fourteenth Chronicle: Letters and Diaries of John Dos Passos*, ed. Townsend Ludington (Boston: Gambit Incorporated, 1973), 81; John Dos Passos, *The Best Times* (New York: The New American Library, 1966), 41–78.

60. Myles, "The American Red Cross Ambulance Services in Italy," 5, 7, 9, 30.

61. Robert W. Bates, diary entry, January 25, 1918, Robert W. Bates Papers, private collection.

62. Baker, *A Life Story*, 48; two articles deal with Bates more substantially. See Steven Florczyk, "A Captain in Hemingway's Court? The Story of Ernest Hemingway, *A Farewell to Arms*, and the Unpublished Papers of Robert W. Bates," in *Hemingway's Italy: New Perspectives*, ed. Rena Sanderson (Baton Rouge, LA: Louisiana State UP, 2006), 62–72; and Stephen Bates, "'Unpopularity Is the Least of My Worries': Captain R. W. Bates and Lieutenant E. M. Hemingway," *Hemingway Review* 29, no. 1 (2009): 47–60.

63. Robert W. Bates, letter to "Dear Edward," April 28, 1918, Robert W. Bates Papers, private collection.

64. Robert W. Bates, letter to "H. Walton Gay" [H. Nelson Gay], February 13, 1918, Robert W. Bates Papers, private collection.

65. Dos Passos, *The Best Times*, 62–63.

66. Robert W. Bates, letter to "Dear Harry," February 28, 1918, Robert W. Bates Papers, private collection.

67. Quoted in Nagel, "Hemingway and the Italian Legacy," 252.

68. Bates, letter to "Dear Harry," February 28, 1918, Robert W. Bates Papers, private collection.

69. Bates, letter to "Dear Harry," February 28, 1918, Robert W. Bates Papers, private collection.

70. Robert W. Bates, letter "Bates to Lowell," c. May 1918, in *The Fourteenth Chronicle: Letters and Diaries of John Dos Passos*, ed. Townsend Ludington (Boston: Gambit Incorporated, 1973), 149–50.

71. Bates kept a copy of the letter, which he labeled "Dos Passos letter which sent him back to U.S.!" Robert W. Bates, addendum to John Dos Passos, letter to José Giner Pantoja, "February 24th, 25, or is it 26th?" [1918], Robert W. Bates Papers, private collection.

72. Bates, letter to "Dear Harry," February 28, 1918, Robert W. Bates Papers, private collection.

73. Robert W. Bates, diary entry, August 22, 1918, Robert W. Bates Papers, private collection.

74. Robert W. Bates, "Ambulance Report No. 7: May 1–31," June 6, 1918, Robert W. Bates Papers, private collection.

75. Guy Lowell, "Report of the Department of Military Affairs for the Month of May, 1918," 4, box 881, folder 954.04, Records of the American National Red Cross, National Archives, College Park, MD.

76. Bates, "Ambulance Report No. 7: May 1–31," June 6, 1918, 1, Robert W. Bates Papers, private collection.

77. Ernest Hemingway, *A Farewell to Arms* (New York: Scribners, 1995), 184.

78. Gwendolyn C. Shealy, *A Critical History of the American Red Cross, 1882–1945: The End of Noble Humanitarianism* (Lewiston, NY: Edwin Mellen Press, 2003), 78.

79. Paul Fussell, *The Great War and Modern Memory* (London: Oxford UP, 1975), 21.

80. George Monteiro, "Introduction," *Critical Essays on Ernest Hemingway's "A Farewell to Arms,"* ed. George Monteiro (New York: G. K. Hall & Co., 1994), 13.

2. Journey to War

1. Ernest Hemingway, "Introduction" in *Men at War*, ed. by Ernest Hemingway (New York: Bramhall House, 1979), xii.

2. Steve Paul, "Preparing for War and Writing: What the Young Hemingway Read in the *Kansas City Star*, 1917–1918," *Hemingway Review* 23, no. 2 (2004): 7.

3. Ernest Hemingway, letter to Marcelline Hemingway, postmarked November 6, 1917, written "1 Week Be Fore Being Mailed," with a postscript added "a week later," in *The Letters of Ernest Hemingway, 1907–1922*, ed. Sandra Spanier and Robert W. Trogdon (Cambridge: Cambridge UP, 2011), 59. Quotations from Hemingway's letters retain misspellings and grammar errors denoting his use of colloquialisms.

4. H. E. Poor, "The Seventh Missouri Infantry," *History of the Missouri National Guard*, ed. Missouri National Guard (Jefferson City, MO: Military Council, Missouri National Guard, 1934), 147; See also James Nagel, "The Hemingways and Oak Park, Illinois: Background and Legacy," *Ernest Hemingway and the Oak Park Legacy*, ed. James Nagel (Tuscaloosa, AL: The U of Alabama P, 1996), 8–9 and Michael Culver, "The 'Short-Stop Run': Hemingway in Kansas City," *Hemingway Review* 2, no. 1 (1982): 79.

5. Harvey C. Clark, *Report of the Adjutant General of Missouri, January 1, 1917–December 31, 1920* (Jefferson City, MO: Office of the Adjutant General, 1921), 27, 37.

6. James Nagel, "Hemingway and the Italian Legacy," *Hemingway in Love and War: The Lost Diary of Agnes von Kurowsky, Her Letters, and Correspondence of Ernest Hemingway*, ed. Henry S. Villard and James Nagel (Boston: Northeastern UP, 1989), 202.

7. Michael Reynolds, *The Young Hemingway* (New York: Norton, 1998), 45.

8. Ibid., 45; Nagel, "Hemingway and the Italian Legacy," 283n11.

9. Hemingway, letter to Marcelline Hemingway, postmarked November 6, 1917, in *The Letters of Ernest Hemingway, 1907–1922*, 59; Peter Griffin, *Along with Youth: Hemingway, the Early Years* (New York: Oxford UP, 1985), 51.

10. Culver, "The 'Short-Stop Run,'" 79.

11. See Poor, "The Seventh Missouri Infantry," 147; See also Clark, *Report of the Adjutant General of Missouri, January 1, 1917–December 31, 1920*, 27; "Test for Home Guard," *Kansas City Star*, March 24, 1918, 4; and "Need 74 Men for the 7th," *Kansas City Star*, March 26, 1917, 1. Hemingway refers to his membership in the Second in a letter home as well: "Today The 2nd Mo. were reviewed by GoV. Gardner and we had a big review and parade and so I did not work in the A.M." See Ernest Hemingway, letter to "Dear Mother," February 23, 1918, in *The Letters of Ernest Hemingway, 1907–1922*, 84.

12. See Hemingway's enlistment record in the Missouri State Archives, Jefferson City, MO.

13. Clark, *Report of the Adjutant General of Missouri, January 1, 1917–December 31, 1920*, 37–38.

14. See "Will Review the Guard," *Kansas City Star*, February 18, 1918, 3; See also, Hemingway, letter to "Dear Mother," February 23, 1918, in *The Letters of Ernest Hemingway, 1907–1922*, 84.

15. Ernest Hemingway, letter to "Dear Kids," November 5, 1917, in *The Letters of Ernest Hemingway, 1907–1922*, 57.

16. Hemingway, letter to Marcelline, postmarked November 6, 1917, in *The Letters of Ernest Hemingway, 1907–1922*, 59.

17. Ernest Hemingway, letter to "Dear Dad and Mother," November 15, 1917, in *The Letters of Ernest Hemingway, 1907–1922*, 60–61.

18. Ernest Hemingway, letter to "Dear Folks," c. November 28, 1917, in *The Letters of Ernest Hemingway, 1907–1922*, 66.

19. Ernest Hemingway, letter to "Dear Dad," November 30, 1917, in *The Letters of Ernest Hemingway, 1907–1922*, 67–68.

20. See Kenneth S. Lynn, *Hemingway* (New York: Simon and Schuster, 1987), 72. See also Hemingway, letter to "Dear Dad and Mother," November 15, 1918, in *The Letters of Ernest Hemingway, 1907–1922*, 61.

21. Steve Paul, "'Drive,' He Said: How Ted Brumback Helped Steer Ernest Hemingway into War and Writing," *Hemingway Review* 27, no. 1 (2007): 31; Ernest Hemingway, letter to "Dear Folks," January 2, 1918, in *The Letters of Ernest Hemingway, 1907–1922*, 71.

22. Paul, "'Drive,' He Said," 32.

23. "Red Cross Calls Men," *Kansas City Star*, February 22, 1918, 3.

24. Ibid.

25. Ibid.

26. Charles Pettus, letter to Ernest Hemingway, February 26, 1918, Ernest Hemingway Collection, John F. Kennedy Library, Boston. The timeline of Hemingway's initial involvement with the Red Cross has been a point of confusion. Carlos Baker has reported that "by Christmas, Ted and Ernest had made a pact with Wilson Hicks: as soon as possible after New Year's, they would apply to the Red Cross as ambulance drivers." Jeffrey Meyers states that Hemingway had offered his services prior to January 1: "Following Brumback's example, he volunteered as a Red Cross ambulance driver in December 1917, was accepted for service and left the *Star* after seven months, on April 30." Lynn suggests a date similar to Baker's, noting that "early in January, both boys volunteered for overseas duty with the American Red Cross. . . . Four months later, they received notice that they would be assigned as second lieutenants in an ambulance unit in Italy if they could pass a physical exam at Red Cross headquarters in New York." Charles Fenton places the enrollment well after the dates provided in other sources:

In April the opportunity finally presented itself. Hemingway and Brumback were able to capitalize on it, appropriately, because of their connection with the *Star*. The legend was that when one day a wire service story came to the telegraph desk, dealing with the Red Cross's need for volunteers with the Italian Army, the two young men cabled applications before the paper used the item.

James Mellow's account is vague about the exact timing of enlistment, noting that "early in 1918" Hemingway and Brumback "were ready to sign up"; after "having been accepted," the two "planned to quit at the end of April," but "there was no telling exactly when he would be called up." Paul clearly shows that the Red Cross announcement capturing Ernest's attention via the *Kansas City Star* was printed on February 22, but his essay lacks information on the circumstances that occurred between February 23, when Ernest first submitted his request for service, and May 2, the day that he was finally notified regarding the reinstatement of his application. See Carlos Baker, *Ernest Hemingway: A Life Story* (New York: Scribners, 1969), 36; Jeffrey Meyers, *Hemingway: A Biography* (New York: Harper & Row, 1985), 26; Lynn, *Hemingway*, 73; Charles A. Fenton, *The Apprenticeship of Ernest Hemingway: The Early Years* (New York: The Viking Press, 1954), 48; James Mellow, *Hemingway: A Life Without Consequences* (Boston: Houghton Mifflin, 1992), 48; and Paul, "'Drive,' He Said," 32.

27. Pettus, letter to Ernest Hemingway, February 26, 1918, JFK Library. Pettus wrote to Hemingway's father toward the end of May with similar information: "Before any applications from this section of the country could reach Washington, the call for Italian ambulance drivers was withdrawn." See Charles Pettus, letter to Dr. Clarence E. Hemingway, May 20, 1918, Ernest Hemingway Collection, John F. Kennedy Library, Boston.

28. Ernest Hemingway, letter to "D[ea]r Kid Swester," March 2, 1918, in *The Letters of Ernest Hemingway, 1907–1922*, 86–87.

29. See American Red Cross, List of Personnel, Robert W. Bates Papers, private collection.

30. Robert W. Bates, "Ambulance Report No. 6: April 12–May 1," c. May, 1918, 3, Robert W. Bates Papers, private collection.

31. Thomas Nelson Page, *Italy and the World War* (New York: Charles Scribner's Sons, 1920), 357.

32. Bates, "Ambulance Report No. 6," 3, Robert W. Bates Papers, private collection.

33. Pettus, letter to Ernest Hemingway, February 26, 1918, JFK Library.

34. "Red Cross in Italy," *New York Times*, April 14, 1918, E3.

35. Pettus, letter to Dr. Clarence E. Hemingway, May 20, 1918, JFK Library.

36. Robert W. Bates, diary entry, August 22, 1918, Robert W. Bates Papers, private collection.

37. "Red Cross Draws Many," *Kansas City Times*, April 23, 1918, 5; "Recruit for Red Cross," *Kansas City Star*, April 21, 1918, A3.

38. Charles Pettus, telegram to Ernest Hemingway, May 2, 1918. Ernest Hemingway Collection, John F. Kennedy Library, Boston.

39. Nagel, "Hemingway and the Italian Legacy," 226.

40. Henry S. Villard, letter to his parents, April 30, 1918, quoted in Nagel, "Hemingway and the Italian Legacy," 227.

41. Robert W. Bates, "Ambulance Report No. 7: May 1–31," June 6, 1918, 1, Robert W. Bates Papers, private collection.

42. Ernest Hemingway, letter to "Dear Folks," March 23, 1918, in *The Letters of Ernest Hemingway, 1907–1922*, 91.

43. Clark, *Report of the Adjutant General of Missouri, January 1, 1917–December 31, 1920*, 27–28.

44. Poor, "The Seventh Missouri Infantry," 147.

45. See Hemingway's enlistment record in the Missouri State Archives, Jefferson City, MO.

46. Reynolds, *The Young Hemingway*, 45.

47. Lynn, *Hemingway*, 73.

48. "Need 74 Men for the 7th," 1.

49. Clark, *Report of the Adjutant General of Missouri, January 1, 1917–December 31, 1920*, 27.

50. Quoted in Scott Donaldson, *By Force of Will: The Life and Art of Ernest Hemingway* (New York: The Viking Press), 125.

51. Robert W. Bates, diary entry, May 18, 1916, Robert W. Bates Papers, private collection.

52. Arlen J. Hansen, *Gentlemen Volunteers: The Story of the American Ambulance Drivers in the Great War, August 1914–September 1918* (New York: Arcade Publishing, 1996), 93.

53. Nagel, "The Hemingways and Oak Park," 9–10.

54. Morris Buske, "What if Ernest Had Been Born on the Other Side of the Street?" in *Ernest Hemingway: The Oak Park Legacy*, ed. James Nagel, 213.

55. Ernest Hemingway, letter to "Dearest Grandmother," February 12, 1918, in *The Letters of Ernest Hemingway, 1907–1922*, 82.

56. Marcelline Sanford, *At the Hemingways: With Fifty Years of Correspondence Between Ernest and Marcelline Hemingway* (Moscow, ID: U of Idaho P, 1999), 170.

57. Nagel, "The Hemingways and Oak Park," 10.

58. Buske, "What if Ernest Had Been Born on the Other Side of the Street?" 214–15.

59. Quoted in Jean Guarino, *Yesterday: A Historical View of Oak Park, Illinois* (Oak Park, IL: Oak Ridge Press, 2000), 88.

60. Larry E. Grimes, "Hemingway's Religious Odyssey: The Oak Park Years," in *Ernest Hemingway: The Oak Park Legacy,* 54; see also Reynolds, *The Young Hemingway,* 10–12.

61. Reynolds, *The Young Hemingway,* 11.

62. William E. Barton, *The Praise of the Wrath of Man and The Rebuilding of the World, Two Sermons* (Oak Park, IL: First Congregational Church, 1918), 14.

63. William E. Barton, *Our Fight for the Heritage of Humanity* (Oak Park, IL: First Congregational Church, 1917), 6.

64. Quoted in Reynolds, *The Young Hemingway,* 29.

65. Nagel, "The Hemingways and Oak Park," 12–14.

66. See Paul, "'Drive,' He Said," 21–38.

67. "Oak Park in the War," *Oak Leaves,* April 14, 1917, 6.

68. "We're Doing Our Bit," *Oak Leaves,* May 5, 1917, 18.

69. "War Time Days," *Oak Leaves,* June 23, 1917, 18.

70. "Go Together From the *Star* to the Italian Front," *Kansas City Star,* May 13, 1918, 4. See also Paul, "'Drive,' He Said," 33.

71. Quoted in Theodore Brumback, "With Hemingway Before *A Farewell to Arms,*" *Kansas City Star,* December 6, 1936, C1.

72. Quoted in Reynolds, *The Young Hemingway,* 23. See also Nagel, "Hemingway and the Italian Legacy," 199–200.

73. Ernest Hemingway, "Class Prophecy," *Hemingway at Oak Park High: The High School Writings of Ernest Hemingway, 1916–1917,* ed. Cynthia Maziarka and Donald Vogel Jr. (Oak Park, IL: Oak Park and River Forest High School, 1993), 57–62. Reprinted from Ernest Hemingway, "Class Prophecy," *Senior Tabula* (1917): 57–62.

74. E. E. Persons, "The Ambulance Service," *New York Times,* July 10, 1917, 11.

75. Theodore Roosevelt, introduction to "With the American Ambulance in France" by J. R. McConnell, *Outlook,* September 15, 1915, 125.

76. Quoted in "Roosevelt Speeds California Men," *New York Times,* May 12, 1917, 11.

77. Ernest Hemingway, letter to "Dear Folks," April 19, 1918, in *The Letters of Ernest Hemingway, 1907–1922,* 95.

78. Pettus, telegram to Ernest Hemingway, May 2, 1918. JFK Library.

79. See Ted Brumback, letter to Ernest Hemingway, May 4, 1918, Ernest Hemingway Collection, John F. Kennedy Library, Boston.

80. Ernest Hemingway, postcard to "Dear Grandfather and Grandmother" [Hemingway], May 12, 1918, in *The Letters of Ernest Hemingway, 1907–1922,* 95.

81. See Grace Hemingway, letter to Ernest Hemingway, April 17, 1918, quoted in Griffin, *Along with Youth,* 52.

82. Brumback, letter to Ernest Hemingway, May 4, 1918, JFK Library.

83. Mellow, *Hemingway,* 49.

84. Sanford, *At the Hemingways*, 159.

85. Mellow, *Hemingway*, 49.

86. "Wilson to Be Patron: President Indorses Plan to Celebrate Italy-America Day," *New York Times*, May 13, 1918, 12.

87. "Plan for Italy Day," *New York Times*, May 15, 1918, 12.

88. Ernest Hemingway, *A Farewell to Arms* (New York: Scribners, 1995), 9.

89. "Baker Will Be Orator on Italy-America Day," *New York Times*, May 19, 1918, 5.

90. "First $100,000 Gift in Red Cross Drive" *New York Times*, May 14, 1918, 13.

91. "Red Cross Benefits," *New York Times*, May 19, 1918, 56.

92. Ernest Hemingway, letter to "Dear Folks," May 17–18, 1918, in *The Letters of Ernest Hemingway, 1907–1922*, 101.

93. "Red Cross to March by President Today," *New York Times*, May 18, 1918, 11.

94. "5,000,000 in Day's Parade," *New York Times*, May 19, 1918, 9.

95. "Red Cross Aid to Italy," *New York Times*, May 21, 1918, 24.

96. Hemingway, letter to "Dear Folks," May 17–18, 1918, in *The Letters of Ernest Hemingway, 1907–1922*, 100.

97. Ibid.

98. Ibid., 101.

99. Ibid., 100.

100. Ernest Hemingway, letter to "Dear Folks," May 20, 1918, in *The Letters of Ernest Hemingway, 1907–1922*, 106.

101. Ernest Hemingway, letter to "Dear Wilse," May 19, 1918, in *The Letters of Ernest Hemingway, 1907–1922*, 104.

102. See American Red Cross, "Outfit for Men," the Ernest Hemingway Collection, John F. Kennedy Library, Boston. See also J. Leo Skelley, letter to "Whom It May Concern," May 16, 1918, Ernest Hemingway Collection, John F. Kennedy Library, Boston.

103. Hemingway, letter to "Dear Folks," May 17–18, 1918, in *The Letters of Ernest Hemingway, 1907–1922*, 100.

104. See "President Leads Red Cross Parade," *New York Times*, May 19, 1918, 8.

105. "Red Cross to March by President Today," *New York Times*, May 18, 1918, 11.

106. Quoted in Lynn, *Hemingway*, 75.

107. Ernest Hemingway, letter to "Dear Folks," May 14, 1918, in *The Letters of Ernest Hemingway, 1907–1922*, 98.

108. Nagel, "Hemingway and the Italian Legacy," 202–4.

109. Ernest Hemingway, letter to "D[ea]r Kid Swester," March 2, 1918, in *The Letters of Ernest Hemingway, 1907–1922*, 86.

110. Nagel, "Hemingway and the Italian Legacy," 204.

111. Grace Hemingway, letter to Ernest Hemingway, May 16, 1918, quoted in Griffin, *Along with Youth*, 58.

112. Lynn, *Hemingway*, 75.

113. As Nagel notes, biographies are inconsistent on the day of departure and suggest a range of dates from May 21 to May 28, 1918. Hemingway's letters help clarify

the issue. His missive to Clarence on May 19, 1918, states that "we sail Wednesday," May 22. On the next day, Ernest wrote his parents again to tell them "our sailing has been delayed by one day," indicating that the departure occurred on May 23. See Nagel, "Hemingway and the Italian Legacy," 284n21; Ernest Hemingway, letter to "Dear Dad," May 19, 1918, in *The Letters of Ernest Hemingway, 1907–1922*, 102; Hemingway, letter to "Dear Folks," May 20, 1918, in *The Letters of Ernest Hemingway, 1907–1922*, 106.

114. Col. C. E. Frazer Clark, "This Is the Way it Was on the *Chicago* and At the Front: 1917 War Letters," *Fitzgerald/Hemingway Annual* (1970), 153; Nagel, "Hemingway and the Italian Legacy," 204.

115. Ernest Hemingway, letter to "Dear Folks," c. May 30, 1918, in *The Letters of Ernest Hemingway, 1907–1922*, 107. Spanier and Trogdon suggest that the main text of this letter was composed "c. 31 May" of 1918. In *Ernest Hemingway: Selected Letters, 1917–1961*, Carlos Baker estimates May 27. Hemingway wrote that "we are expected to land over seas about four days from now." On June 2, he added a postscript stating "we are getting into Port tomorrow." All things considered, it is more likely that Hemingway wrote the statement in the body of the letter on May 30. See *The Letters of Ernest Hemingway, 1907–1922*, 107–9; and *Ernest Hemingway: Selected Letters, 1917–1961*, ed. Carlos Baker (New York: Charles Scribner's Sons, 1981), 9.

116. "German Sea Raider Chased the *Chicago*," *New York Times*, February 23, 1916, 3; "Liner *Chicago* Afire, Reaches the Azores," *New York Times*, October 28, 1916, 1; "Three More Elude U-Boats," *New York Times*, March 5, 1917, 2.

117. "Loss of U-Boats Exceeds Output," *New York Times*, May 14, 1918, 3; "Five U-Boats Sunk in a Single Week," *New York Times*, May 16, 1918, 5; "A Poor Month for the U-Boats," *New York Times*, May 23, 1918, 12.

118. Brumback, "With Hemingway," C1.

119. Richard Harding Davis, "Lifeboat Drills on Ships in the War Zone," *New York Times*, November 21, 1915, SM15.

120. Robert W. Bates, diary entry, April 26, 1918, Robert W. Bates Papers, private collection.

121. Col. C. E. Frazer Clark, "This Is the Way it Was on the *Chicago* and At the Front," 157.

122. Hemingway, letter to "Dear Folks," May 20, 1918, in *The Letters of Ernest Hemingway, 1907–1922*, 106–7.

123. Hemingway, letter to "Dear Folks," c. May 30, 1918, in *The Letters of Ernest Hemingway, 1907–1922*, 107.

124. Brumback, "With Hemingway," C1.

125. Fenton, *The Apprenticeship*, 56.

126. Robert W. Bates, letter to "Dear Mama, Dorothea, and Edward," April 29, 1916, Robert W. Bates Papers, private collection.

127. Baker, *A Life Story*, 40; Hemingway, letter to "Dear Folks," c. May 30, 1918, in *The Letters of Ernest Hemingway, 1907–1922*, 108.

128. See Nagel, "Hemingway and the Italian Legacy," 204; See also Hemingway, letter to "Dear Folks," c. May 30, 1918, in *The Letters of Ernest Hemingway, 1907–1922*, 108.

129. Brumback, "With Hemingway," C1.

130. Griffin has reported that the *Chicago* arrived at Bordeaux on June 1, 1918, but Hemingway's letters indicate that he landed on June 3. A postscript Ernest wrote while still at sea, and dated "June 2," notes that "we are getting into port tomorrow." See Griffin, *Along with Youth,* 63; and Hemingway, letter to "Dear Folks," c. May 30, 1918, with a postscript added June 2, 1918, in *The Letters of Ernest Hemingway, 1907–1922,* 109.

131. Baker, *A Life Story,* 40.

132. Robert W. Bates, diary entry, May 6, 1916, Robert W. Bates Papers, private collection.

133. John Bauby, letter to Warren Roberts, April 18, 1963, box 3, folder 11, Ernest Hemingway Collection, Harry Ransom Humanities Research Center, Austin, TX.

134. Ernest Hemingway, letter to his parents, c. June 5, 1918, in *The Letters of Ernest Hemingway, 1907–1922,* 110. Spanier and Trogdon approximate the date of this letter, which Hemingway wrote while in Paris, as "c. 3 June 1918." Evidence suggests that it was likely composed on June 5, 1918. In the June 2 postscript to his letter written while at sea, Hemingway states that "we are getting into Port tomorrow," indicating that he was scheduled to disembark the *Chicago* at Bordeaux on Monday, June 3, before traveling by train to Paris later that night. In his letter from the French capital, Hemingway describes activities that occurred after spending at least one full day in the city. He writes about hearing "our first shell arrive soon after Breakfast," an afternoon of sightseeing, some shopping, and a nighttime visit to the Folies Bergère, all of which must have occurred on Tuesday, June 4, at the earliest. Additionally, he explains that "we leave for Milan tomorrow" night; his handwriting specifying the exact weekday of departure, however, is difficult to decipher. Spanier and Trogdon transcribe the word as "Tuesday" night, but the comment Hemingway made anticipating his landing in Bordeaux on Monday and his description of activities after his first entire day in Paris suggest that he wrote "Thursday" night instead. Subsequent events indicate likewise. A few days later, Hemingway commented in a postcard sent from Milan that he had his "baptism of fire my first day here," referring to his assistance in the aftermath of an explosion at a munitions factory, which occurred on Friday, June 7. Therefore, Hemingway would most likely have composed the letter from Paris on Wednesday, June 5, before departing for Milan on Thursday, June 6, and assisting in the aftermath of the explosion not long after his arrival on Friday, June 7. See Hemingway, letter to "Dear Folks," c. May 30, 1918, with a postscript added June 2, 1918, in *The Letters of Ernest Hemingway, 1907–1922,* 109; see also the copy of Hemingway's handwritten letter to his parents, c. June 5, 1918, Hemingway Mss. III, The Lilly Library, Bloomington, IN; and Hemingway's postcard to friends at the *Kansas City Star,* June 9, 1918—quoted in "Wounded on Italy Front," *Kansas City Star,* July 14, 1918, A5, and reprinted in *The Letters of Ernest Hemingway, 1907–1922,* 112.

135. Baker, *A Life Story,* 40.

136. Ernest Hemingway, postcard to "Dear Dad," postmarked June 9, 1918, in *The Letters of Ernest Hemingway, 1907–1922,* 111.

137. Eric Hungerford, *With the Doughboy in France* (New York: the Macmillan Company, 1920), 17.

138. See ibid. See also H. R. Stoneback, *Reading Hemingway's "The Sun Also Rises": Glossary and Commentary* (Kent, OH: The Kent State UP, 2007), 61.

139. Hemingway, letter to his parents, c. June 5, 1918, in *The Letters of Ernest Hemingway, 1907–1922*, 110.

140. Nagel states that Hemingway "stayed at the hotel designated for arriving Red Cross drivers, the Hôtel Alexandria, 29, Boulevard Bourdon." Lynn indicates the Hotel Florida at 12 Boulevard Malesherbes. See Nagel, "Hemingway and the Italian Legacy," 204–5; Lynn, *Hemingway*, 76; and Hemingway, letter to his parents, c. June 5, 1918, in *The Letters of Ernest Hemingway, 1907–1922*, 110.

141. Hemingway, letter to his parents, c. June 5, 1918, in *The Letters of Ernest Hemingway, 1907–1922*, 110.

142. Baker, *A Life Story*, 40.

143. Brumback, "With Hemingway," C2.

144. Hemingway, letter to his parents, c. June 5, 1918, in *The Letters of Ernest Hemingway, 1907–1922*, 110.

145. Hemingway, letter to his parents, c. June 5, 1918, in *The Letters of Ernest Hemingway, 1907–1922*, 110.

146. Jennifer D. Keene, *Doughboys, the Great War, and the Remaking of America* (Baltimore, MD: John Hopkins UP, 2001), 137.

147. "'Sam Browne' Belts Are Barred Here," *New York Times*, October 18, 1917, 18.

148. "We Saw it Ourselves," *Come Stà*, March 10, 1918, 3.

149. See Hemingway's postcard, June 9, 1918, quoted in "Wounded on Italy Front," *Kansas City Star*, July 14, 1918, A5, reprinted in *The Letters of Ernest Hemingway, 1907–1922*, 112; and Luca Gandolfi, "The Outskirts of Literature: Uncovering the Munitions Factory in 'A Natural History of the Dead,'" *Hemingway Review* 19, no. 2 (2000): 105–7.

150. Gandolfi, "The Outskirts of Literature," 106.

151. See also Nagel, "Hemingway and the Italian Legacy," 205.

152. Ernest Hemingway, "A Natural History of the Dead," in *Death in the Afternoon* (New York: Scribners, 1960), 135–36.

153. Quoted in "Wounded on Italy Front," *Kansas City Star*, July 14, 1918, A5, reprinted in *The Letters of Ernest Hemingway, 1907–1922*, 112.

154. Bates, "Ambulance Report No. 7," Robert W. Bates Papers, private collection.

155. Hemingway, postcard to "Dear Dad," June 9, 1918, in *The Letters of Ernest Hemingway, 1907–1922*, 111.

3. Active Duty

1. Ernest Hemingway, letter to "Dear Folks," c. May 30, 1918, *The Letters of Ernest Hemingway, 1907–1922*, ed. Sandra Spanier and Robert W. Trogdon (Cambridge: Cambridge UP, 2011), 109.

2. Alternatively, Carlos Baker and Michael Reynolds have stated that Hemingway

served for "three weeks" as an ambulance driver, and Peter Griffin implies that Ernest spent seven days as a canteen worker. See Carlos Baker, *Ernest Hemingway: A Life Story* (New York, Scribners, 1969), 42; Michael Reynolds, *Hemingway's First War: The Making of "A Farewell to Arms"* (New York: Basil Blackwell, 1987), 4; and Peter Griffin, *Along with Youth: Hemingway, the Early Years* (New York: Oxford, 1985), 72.

3. Reynolds acknowledges the firsthand experience as "the most obvious source" for the fiction, but the main focus of his study is the situation on the Italian front that preceded Hemingway's involvement. See Reynolds, *Hemingway's First War*, 3, 138. James Nagel explains that "the Italian Journey would eventually provide the background for ten of [Hemingway's] early short stories and one of the great novels in English, *A Farewell to Arms*." See James Nagel, "Hemingway and the Italian Legacy," in *Hemingway in Love and War: The Lost Diary of Agnes von Kurowsky, Her Letters, and Correspondence of Ernest Hemingway*, ed. Henry S. Villard and James Nagel (Boston: Northeastern UP, 1989), 198.

4. Nagel, "Hemingway and the Italian Legacy," 207.

5. Robert W. Bates, "Ambulance Report No. 8: June 1–30" July 8, 1918, 3, Robert W. Bates Papers, private collection.

6. Robert W. Bates, diary entry, August 22, 1918, Robert W. Bates Papers, private collection.

7. James Mellow, *Hemingway: A Life Without Consequences* (Boston: Houghton Mifflin, 1992), 58.

8. Bates, "Ambulance Report No. 8," 3, Robert W. Bates Papers, private collection.

9. Robert W. Bates, "Ambulance Report No. 3: March 10–16," c. March 1918, 1, Robert W. Bates Papers, private collection.

10. See Robert W. Bates, "Ambulance Report No. 5: March 28–April 12," c. April, 1918, 2–3, Robert W. Bates Papers, private collection. See also Guy Lowell, "Report of the Department of Military Affairs for the Month of April, 1918," 3, box 881, folder 954.11/08, Records of the American National Red Cross, National Archives, College Park, MD. Carlos Baker discusses the accommodations in *A Life Story*, 41, and Nagel mentions the vehicles in "Hemingway and the Italian Legacy," 208.

11. Guy Lowell, "Report of the Department of Military Affairs for the Month of February, 1918," 3, box 881, folder 954.11/08, Records of the American National Red Cross, National Archives, College Park, MD.

12. Robert W. Bates, "Ambulance Report No. 9," July 25, 1918, 2, Robert W. Bates Papers, private collection.

13. Robert W. Bates, memorandum to "Section Leaders," June 7, 1918, Robert W. Bates Papers, private collection.

14. Carlos Baker mentions Dos Passos's claim about meeting Hemingway in *A Life Story*, 42.

15. Hemingway, letter to "Dear Folks," c. May 30, 1918, in *The Letters of Ernest Hemingway, 1907–1922*, 109.

16. John Dos Passos, diary entry, June 1, [1918], quoted in *The Fourteenth Chronicle: Letters and Diaries of John Dos Passos*, ed. Townsend Ludington (Boston: Gambit Incorporated, 1973), 186.

17. John Dos Passos, letter to Arthur McComb, c. June 6, 1918, quoted in John Dos Passos, *The Best Times: An Informal Memoir* (New York: The New American Library, 1966), 68.

18. Robert W. Bates, letter to "[Guy] Lowell," c. March 1918, in Ludington, *The Fourteenth Chronicle*, 151–52. See also Stephen Bates, "'Unpopularity Is the Least of My Worries': Captain R. W. Bates and Lieutenant E. M. Hemingway," *Hemingway Review* 29, no. 1 (2009): 56.

19. John Dos Passos, letter to [Rumsey Marvin], c. June, 1918, in *The Fourteenth Chronicle*, 188.

20. John Dos Passos, letter to [Rumsey Marvin], July 17, [1918], in *The Fourteenth Chronicle*, 192.

21. See Robert W. Bates, "Ambulance Report No. 7: May 1–May 31," June 6, 1918, 1, Robert W. Bates Papers, private collection. Mellow writes that "later in life, Hemingway and Dos Passos would convince themselves that they had met each other" in 1918, despite the fact that Dos Passos "left the Bassano region . . . more than a week before Hemingway had even arrived in Italy." See Mellow, *Hemingway* 58–59.

22. Ernest Hemingway, postcard to "Dear Dad," postmarked June 9, 1918, in *The Letters of Ernest Hemingway, 1907–1922*, 111. Biographies vary in recording the date Hemingway and his colleagues left Milan for Schio via Vicenza. Carlos Baker has written that "two days after the munitions explosion, they got aboard the train for Vicenza," implying they arrived in Schio on June 9. Kenneth Lynn states that "on or about June 6, Ernest joined his ambulance unit." See Carlos Baker, *A Life Story*, 41. See also Kenneth Lynn, *Hemingway* (New York: Simon and Schuster, 1987), 77.

23. Red Cross headquarters for ambulance and canteen services were located at Palazzo Pigatti when Hemingway first arrived in Vicenza. The center of operations was subsequently transferred to Palazzo Folco in a move that began June 15 but was not completed until the end of July. See Bates, "Ambulance Report No. 8: June 1–30," 3, Robert W. Bates Papers, private collection.

24. American Red Cross, List of Personnel, 7, Robert W. Bates Papers, private collection.

25. Ernest Hemingway, letter to "Dear Old Bill," July 17–18, 1923, in *Ernest Hemingway: Selected Letters, 1917–1961*, ed. Carlos Baker (New York: Charles Scribner's Sons, 1981), 85.

26. Bates, "Ambulance Report No. 8," 1, Robert W. Bates Papers, private collection.

27. Robert W. Bates, letter to "Dear Family," June 2, 1918, Robert W. Bates Papers, private collection.

28. For another account of Robert W. Bates, see Stephen Bates's portrait of his grandfather in "'Unpopularity Is the Least of My Worries,'" 47–60. See also Steven Florczyk, "A Captain in Hemingway's Court? The Story of Ernest Hemingway, *A Farewell to Arms*, and the Unpublished Papers of Robert W. Bates," *Hemingway's Italy: New Perspectives*, ed. Rena Sanderson (Baton Rouge, LA: Louisiana State UP, 2006), 62–72.

29. Robert W. Bates, diary entry, August 7, 1914, Robert W. Bates Papers, private collection.

30. Robert W. Bates, diary entry, May 8, 1915, Robert W. Bates Papers, private collection.

31. Robert W. Bates, diary entry, February 28, 1916, Robert W. Bates Papers, private collection.

32. Robert W. Bates, diary entry, May 8, 1916, Robert W. Bates Papers, private collection.

33. Robert W. Bates, diary entry, June 14, 1916, Robert W. Bates Papers, private collection.

34. Ibid.

35. Robert W. Bates, letter to "Dear Harry and Oliver," June 25, 1916, Robert W, Bates Papers, private collection.

36. Robert W. Bates, diary entry, June 19, 1916, Robert W. Bates Papers, private collection.

37. Bates, letter to "Dear Harry and Oliver," June 25, 1916, Robert W. Bates Papers, private collection.

38. Ibid.

39. Robert W. Bates, diary entry, January 14, 1918, Robert W. Bates Papers, private collection. Stephen Bates adds another detail about an "aide" who "collared [Robert] Bates and told him he was 'a damned efficient man and a live wire and just the fellow they needed.'" See Stephen Bates, "'Unpopularity Is the Least of My Worries,'" 51.

40. Robert W. Bates, diary entry, January 30, 1918, Robert W. Bates Papers, private collection.

41. Bates, diary entry, August 22, 1918, Robert W. Bates Papers, private collection.

42. See also Stephen Bates, "'Unpopularity Is the Least of My Worries,'" 57.

43. Robert W. Bates, "American Red Cross Ambulance Service General Notice Number 10," February 7, 1918, Robert W. Bates Papers, private collection.

44. Robert W. Bates, "American Red Cross Ambulance Service General Order Number 11," February 7, 1918, Robert W. Bates Papers, private collection.

45. Bates, letter to "Dear Family," June 2, 1918, Robert W. Bates Papers, private collection.

46. See also Nagel, "Hemingway and the Italian Legacy," 207.

47. Stephen Bates also notes that Lowell was a "renowned architect." Stephen Bates, "'Unpopularity Is the Least of My Worries,'" 51.

48. Guy Lowell, *More Small Italian Villas and Farmhouses* (New York: Architectural Book Publishing Company, 1920), ii.

49. Stephen Bates refers to Lowell's earlier volume published in 1916, *Smaller Italian Villas and Farmhouses*. See Stephen Bates, "'Unpopularity Is the Least of My Worries,'" 51–52.

50. Lowell, *More Small Italian Villas and Farmhouses*, 39.

51. Ernest Hemingway, letter to "Dear Folks and Ivory," August 7, 1918, in *The Letters of Ernest Hemingway, 1907–1922*, 126.

52. Robert W. Bates, letter to "H. Walton Gay" [H. Nelson Gay], February 13, 1918, Robert W. Bates Papers, private collection.

53. Robert W. Bates, "Ambulance Report No. 1: Feb. 19–26," c. February 1918, 1, Robert W. Bates Papers, private collection.

54. "Now It's Come Stà," *Come Stà*, March 10, 1918, 1.

55. Bates, "Ambulance Report No. 3," Robert W. Bates Papers, private collection.

56. Bates, diary entry, August 22, 1918, Robert W. Bates Papers, private collection.

57. Angelo L. Pirocchi, *Italian Arditi Elite Assault Troops 1917–20* (Oxford: Osprey Publishing, 2004), 19.

58. Ernest Hemingway, "Al Receives Another Letter," *Ciao*, June 1918, 2. Quotations from the section newspapers retain misspellings and other errors, many of which were intended to be humorous.

59. Alternatively, biographies indicate that Hemingway's fascination with the Arditi did not take effect until October of 1918. See Carlos Baker, *A Life Story*, 53; Mellow, *Hemingway*, 78; and Lynn, *Hemingway*, 89.

60. Gale Hunter, "Weekly Report: April 1–7, Section 1," Robert W. Bates Papers, private collection.

61. Guy Lowell, "Report of the Department of Military Affairs for the Month of June, 1918," 2, box 881, folder 954.11/08, Records of the American National Red Cross, National Archives, College Park, MD. Nagel refers to the "three kinds of services" in "Hemingway and the Italian Legacy," 209.

62. Hemingway, "Al Receives Another Letter," 2.

63. Bates, letter to "H. Walton Gay" [H. Nelson Gay], February 13, 1918, Robert W. Bates Papers, private collection.

64. See Robert W. Bates, letter to "Dear Harry," February 28, 1918, Robert W. Bates Papers, private collection.

65. See "Editorial Staff," *Ciao*, June 1918, 2.

66. Quoted in Griffin, *Along with Youth*, 70.

67. See Theodore Brumback, "With Hemingway Before *A Farewell to Arms*," *Kansas City Star*, December 6, 1936, C1–C3.

68. Lynn, *Hemingway*, 77.

69. Quoted in Griffin, *Along with Youth*, 70.

70. "Our Day," *Ciao*, June 1918, 3; see also Carlos Baker, *A Life Story*, 41–42.

71. Robert W. Bates, "Ambulance Report No. 4: March 17–27," 1, Robert W. Bates Papers, private collection.

72. Quoted in Robert W. Bates, "Memorandum to Section Leaders," April 30, 1918, Robert W. Bates Papers, private collection.

73. Robert W. Bates, "Memorandum to Section Leaders," May 7, 1918, Robert W. Bates Papers, private collection.

74. Robert W. Bates, "General Notice No. 28 to Sections: Regulations for Trips to Milan," April 27, 1918, Robert W. Bates Papers, private collection.

75. Bates, "Ambulance Report No. 8," 2, Robert W. Bates Papers, private collection.

76. See, for example, "Our Day," *Ciao*, June 1918, 3.

77. Ernest Hemingway, letter to "Dear Old Chieftain," March 3, 1919, in *The Letters of Ernest Hemingway, 1907–1922*, 170.

78. Quoted in Bates, "Memorandum to Section Leaders," April 30, 1918, Robert W. Bates Papers, private collection.

79. Bates, "Ambulance Report No. 5," 3, Robert W. Bates Papers, private collection.

80. "My Elegy (Grey's Apologies to Me)," *Ciao*, May 1918, 3.

81. "Rollins Mixture," *Ciao*, May 1918, 3.

82. Charles Fenton, Carlos Baker, and Michael Reynolds have discussed *Ciao* and its significance as the periodical containing Hemingway's only publication during the war. See Charles A. Fenton, *The Apprenticeship of Ernest Hemingway: The Early Years* (New York: Viking Press, 1954), 58–60; Carlos Baker, *A Life Story*, 42; and Reynolds, *Hemingway's First War*, 165.

83. Laurence Fisher, "Editorial Staff," *Ciao*, May 1918, 2.

84. "Italy and America," *Ciao*, May 1918, 1.

85. "And Yet More Driving Power," *Ciao*, April 1918, 1. Reynolds also refers to the "war weariness" evident in this article. Reynolds, *Hemingway's First War*, 165.

86. Alternatively, Henry Villard has suggested that *"Ciao's* inspiration may have been a British Expeditionary Force sheet that began to circulate in France" called the *"B.E.F. Times."* See Henry Serrano Villard, "Red Cross Driver in Italy," Villard and Nagel, *Hemingway in Love and War*, 18.

87. "Official Communiqué," *Avanti*, January 1, 1918, 3.

88. See the masthead of *Soixante Trois*, August 26, 1917, 1.

89. "Official Communiqué," *Avanti*, January 1, 1918, 3.

90. "Editorial Staff," *Ciao*, June 1918, 2.

91. Carlos Baker and Charles Fenton note that the article also grew out of Ernest's experience writing similar pieces for his high school newspaper. See Carlos Baker, *A Life Story*, 42; and Fenton, *The Apprenticeship*, 59–60.

92. Fenton, *The Apprenticeship*, 59.

93. "Beg Pardon, Ring!" *Avanti*, February 1, 1918, 4.

94. "Al on Permission," *Come Stà*, April 10, 1918, 3.

95. Charles Fenton, "Ambulance Drivers in France and Italy: 1914–1918," *American Quarterly* 3, no. 4 (1951): 336.

96. "Who's Who in Section One," *Come Stà*, April 10, 1918, 2.

97. "Humor," *Soixante Trois*, August 5, 1917, 2.

98. Morris never wrote about Section One per se, but some of his work dealt with the war. *His Daughter*, for example, tells about Frederick Dayton, an ambulance driver and aviator in France. An anonymous reviewer for the *New York Times* said that the novel had "touches that reflect life and human nature truly" even though it was mostly full of "shallowness, artificiality, and distorted pictures of life." The theme stressing "the refining and ennobling effect of participation in the great war" might have been more compelling if Morris "did not ride it quite so hard." See Gouverneur Morris, "To the First Section," *Avanti*, January 1, 1918, 1; Gouverneur Morris, *His Daughter* (New York: Scribners, 1918); and "From New Jersey Artists to War: A Wide Range of Interest in Some of the Latest Fiction by William McFee, Gouverneur Morris, J. O. Curwood, and Others," *New York Times*, February 24, 1918, 59.

99. See also Arlen J. Hansen, *Gentlemen Volunteers: The Story of the American Ambulance Drivers in the Great War, August 1914–September 1918* (New York: Arcade Publishing, 1996), 159–60.

100. Bates, "Ambulance Report No. 8," 1, Robert W. Bates Papers, private collection.

101. Robert W. Bates, "Supplementary to Ambulance Report No. 9," July 25, 1918, Robert W. Bates Papers, private collection.

102. See, for example, in this volume the photograph, "Ernest Hemingway at the wheel of a Section Four ambulance." Hansen reaches a similar conclusion calculating that Hemingway "drove an ambulance either one or, at most, two days," but his speculation is based on inaccurate dates for Hemingway's service and relies on a vague passage in *A Moveable Feast* as evidence that Hemingway must have driven only a Fiat. See Hansen, *Gentlemen Volunteers*, 159–60, 225n9.

103. The Supreme Command of the Royal Italian Army, *The Battle of the Piave: (June 15–23, 1918)*, trans. Mary Prichard Agnetti (London: Hodder and Stoughton, Ltd., 1919), 45–48.

104. Bates, "Ambulance Report No. 8," 2, Robert W. Bates Papers, private collection.

105. Ibid.

106. Bates, diary entry, August 22, 1918, Robert W. Bates Papers, private collection.

107. Bates, "Ambulance Report No. 8," 2, Robert W. Bates Papers, private collection.

108. Ibid.

109. "Our Part in the Big Drive," *Ciao*, June 1918, 4.

110. Brumback, "With Hemingway," C2; See also Carlos Baker, *A Life Story*, 42.

111. Brumback, "With Hemingway," C2.

112. Hemingway, "Al Receives Another Letter," 2.

113. Ibid.

114. Scholars have reported various dates for the start of Hemingway's work with the canteens. Reynolds notes that "in July he asked to be transferred to the canteen operation along the more active Piave River front." Griffin mentions "July 1, 1918" as the day that Ernest "left Schio." According to Lynn, Hemingway volunteered "by the fourth week in June." See Reynolds, *Hemingway's First War*, 5; Griffin, *Along with Youth*, 72; and Lynn, *Hemingway*, 78.

115. Scholars have indicated the nearby town of Fossalta di Piave as the site of Hemingway's post. While Ernest frequented Fossalta, Red Cross records indicate that he was based at Fornaci. See Carlos Baker, *A Life Story*, 43; Griffin, *Along with Youth*, 73; Lynn, *Hemingway*, 78; and Mellow, *Hemingway*, 59; See also Bates, "Ambulance Report No. 8," 3; and Moses S. Slaughter, "Report on emergency posti di conforto," July 26, 1918, 1–3, Robert W. Bates Papers, private collection.

116. Much of the background information on the canteens is drawn from reports by Robert W. Bates from February to June of 1918, located in the Robert W. Bates Papers, private collection. For other accounts of the service, see Nagel, "Hemingway and the Italian Legacy," 209–12; Charles M. Bakewell, *The Story of the American Red Cross in Italy* (New York: The Macmillan Company, 1920): 72–85; and Stephen Bates, "'An Apostle for His Work': The Death of Lieutenant Edward Michael McKey," *Hemingway Review* 29, no. 2 (2010): 61–73.

117. On June 2, 1918, Bates wrote that "Rome has at last listened to me and has appointed a man on my recommendation as Captain of the Cucina Service. He has just this minute come in from the mountains and it was such a pleasure to see his

delight when I told him." Bates's final kitchen report concluded by indicating that "the Service is fortunate in having such a man as Mr. Gamble to lead it." See Bates, letter to "Dear Family," June 2, 1918, Robert W. Bates Papers, private collection; see also Robert W. Bates, "Kitchen Report No. 6: May 1–31," June 4, 1918, 3, Robert W. Bates Papers, private collection.

118. Bates, letter to "Dear Family," June 2, 1918, Robert W. Bates Papers, private collection.

119. Robert W. Bates, "Cucine Report No. 5: April 12–May 1," May 2, 1918, 1, Robert W. Bates Papers, private collection.

120. Edward M. McKey, "Weekly Report on Cucina No. 1," March 9, 1918, 1, Robert W. Bates Papers, private collection.

121. McKey, "Weekly Report on Cucina No. 1," 1, Robert W. Bates Papers, private collection.

122. Robert W. Bates, "Cucine Report Number 4: March 26–April 12," 1, Robert W. Bates Papers, private collection.

123. McKey, "Weekly Report on Cucina No. 1," 1, Robert W. Bates Papers, private collection.

124. Bates, "Cucine Report No. 5," 2, Robert W. Bates Papers, private collection.

125. Bates, "Ambulance Report No. 9," Robert W. Bates Papers, private collection. Villard mentions Seeley's injury as well in "Red Cross Driver in Italy," 13. Hemingway alludes to the incident in *A Farewell to Arms*. See Ernest Hemingway, *A Farewell to Arms* (New York: Scribners, 1995), 108.

126. Bates, "Kitchen Report No. 6," 2, Robert W. Bates Papers, private collection.

127. Bates, "Cucine Report No. 5," 3, Robert W. Bates Papers, private collection.

128. Ibid.

129. Guy Lowell, "Report of the Department of Military Affairs, January, 1918, to February, 1919," 23–24, Robert W. Bates Papers, private collection.

130. Guy Lowell, "Report of the Department of Military Affairs for the Month of July, 1918," 8, box 881, folder 954.11/08, Records of the American National Red Cross, National Archives, College Park, MD.

131. Bates, "Kitchen Report No. 6," 3, Robert W. Bates Papers, private collection.

132. James Gamble, "Cucina Report No. 6: June," July 30, 1918, 2, Robert W. Bates Papers, private collection. Incorrectly titled, Gamble's report follows "Kitchen Report No. 6" and is actually seventh in the sequence established by Bates.

133. See, for example, Carlos Baker, *A Life Story*, 43; Lynn, *Hemingway*, 78; Nagel, "Hemingway and the Italian Legacy," 210; and Mellow, *Hemingway*, 59.

134. See Slaughter, "Report on emergency posti di conforto," 1, Robert W. Bates Papers, private collection; See also Gamble, "Cucina Report No. 6," 2, Robert W. Bates Papers, private collection.

135. Reynolds notes that Hemingway "was assigned to the same area that McKey had been in charge of when he was killed." See Reynolds, *Hemingway's First War*, 148; Nagel explains likewise in "Hemingway and the Italian Legacy," 216.

136. Gamble, "Cucina Report No. 6," 1, Robert W. Bates Papers, private collection.

137. Ibid., 2.

138. Ibid., 1.

139. Robert W. Bates, letter to "Dear Family," June 27, 1918, Robert W. Bates Papers, private collection.

140. Fenton, however, has suggested that Hemingway "took charge" of "a canteen" that included a "small hut" containing the volunteer's quarters along with "a kitchen and large rest room for the Italian soldiers." Fenton, *The Apprenticeship*, 63.

141. Slaughter, "Report on emergency posti di conforto," 2, Robert W. Bates Papers, private collection.

142. See also Carlos Baker, *A Life Story*, 43; and Mellow, *Hemingway*, 59.

143. See Slaughter, "Report on emergency posti di conforto," 2–3, Robert W. Bates Papers, private collection; Gamble, "Cucina Report No. 6," 2–3, Robert W. Bates Papers, private collection.

144. Gamble, "Cucina Report No. 6," 3, Robert W. Bates Papers, private collection.

145. Ernest Hemingway, letter to "Dear Ruth," c. June 25–July 8, 1918, in *The Letters of Ernest Hemingway, 1907–1922*, 113. Spanier and Trogdon indicate this letter was written "c. late June–early July 1918." Red Cross reports suggest that he wrote the letter between June 25 and July 8.

146. Ernest Hemingway, letter to "Dear Folks," August 18, 1918, *The Letters of Ernest Hemingway, 1907–1922*, 130.

147. Lynn erroneously refers to "Lieutenant Hemingway" in his discussion of Ernest as a canteen operator. See Lynn, *Hemingway*, 78. Mellow states that "with characteristic exaggeration, [Hemingway] wrote an Oak Park friend, Ruth Morrison, 'you see I'm ranked a soto Tenente or Second Lieut. in the Italian Army and I left the Croce Rosa Americana Ambulance service a while back, temporarily, to get a little action down here.'" While Hemingway should have included the word *honorary* for a precise description of his rank, the comment to Ruth is otherwise an accurate statement regarding his circumstances at the time. See Mellow, *Hemingway*, 60.

148. Nagel also notes that "Hemingway arrived at this new assignment just as the Italians were engaged in a counteroffensive against the Austrian positions, and there was fighting all along the Piave." See Nagel, "Hemingway and the Italian Legacy," 212.

149. The Supreme Command of the Royal Italian Army, *The Battle of the Piave*, 56–82.

150. See also James E. Edmonds, *History of the Great War: Military Operations Italy 1915–1919* (London: The Imperial War Museum, 1999), 221–41.

151. Bates, diary entry, August 22, 1918, Robert W. Bates Papers, private collection.

152. Bates, letter to "Dear Family," June 27, 1918, Robert W. Bates Papers, private collection.

153. Hemingway, letter to "Dear Ruth," c. June 25–July 8, in *The Letters of Ernest Hemingway, 1907–1922*, 113; Ernest Hemingway, letter to "Dear Folks," July 21, 1918, in *The Letters of Ernest Hemingway, 1907–1922*, 118.

154. Robert W. Bates, letter to "Dear Family," July 8, 1918, Robert W. Bates Papers, private collection.

155. Stephen Bates proposes that, "if Hemingway did knowingly court danger" by volunteering to serve in the same vicinity where McKey had been killed, then "McKey's death can be seen as a cause of his injuries." See Stephen Bates, "'An Apostle for His Work,'" 62.

156. Quoted in Gamble, "Cucina Report No. 6," 2, Robert W. Bates Papers, private collection.

157. Hemingway, letter to "Dear Ruth," c. June 25–July 8, in *The Letters of Ernest Hemingway, 1907–1922*, 113.

4. Hero of the Piave

1. Despite extensive studies, controversy surrounding Hemingway's wounding has persisted. Michael Reynolds has stated that Hemingway was "blown up in a forward observation post where he had no business to be." Agnes von Kurowsky has said that "he got the injuries because he did something that was against orders. They told him to keep away from the front because he was just a boy giving out cigarettes and stuff like that." James Nagel has summarized the "central items of dispute: whether Hemingway was 'heroic' in the incident, carrying anyone or performing any other extraordinary action; whether he was hit by machine-gun bullets (the shrapnel wounds are not in dispute); what medals he received; and whether he was ever officially in the Italian army in any capacity." See Michael Reynolds, *The Young Hemingway* (New York: Norton, 1998), 18; Agnes von Kurowsky, quoted in Denis Brian, *The True Gen: An Intimate Portrait of Hemingway by Those Who Knew Him* (New York: Grove Press, 1988), 19; James Nagel, "Hemingway and the Italian Legacy," in *Hemingway in Love and War: The Lost Diary of Agnes von Kurowsky, Her Letters, and Correspondence of Ernest Hemingway*, ed. Henry S. Villard and James Nagel (Boston: Northeastern UP, 1989), 215.

2. See, for example, C. E. Frazer Clark Jr., "American Red Cross Reports on the Wounding of Lieutenant Ernest M. Hemingway-1918," *Fitzgerald/Hemingway Annual* (1974), 131–36; Kenneth S. Lynn, *Hemingway* (New York: Simon and Schuster, 1987), 80; Nagel, "Hemingway and the Italian Legacy," 216; and "Report of the Department of Military Affairs January to July, 1918," ed. Ken Panda, *Hemingway Review* 18, no. 2 (1999): 72–89.

3. Guy Lowell, telegram to Robert W. Bates, June 22, 1918, Robert W. Bates Papers, private collection.

4. Robert W. Bates, "Ambulance Report No. 8: June 1–30," July 8, 1918, 1, Robert W. Bates papers, private collection.

5. Bates, "Ambulance Report No. 8," 2, Robert W. Bates Papers, private collection.

6. Ibid., 1–2.

7. Ibid., 1. Prior to the Battle of the Piave, Red Cross reports mention two incidents that resulted in special commendation as well. On March 31, as Lowell explained, "Lieut. General Sani, commanding the 13th Army Corps, to which Section II is attached, expressed to Colonel Marzocchelli, our chief liaison officer, in terms of the highest praise of his appreciation of the work done by the drivers of that Section under Lieutenant Gillespie." In his report for May, Lowell wrote "it is a pleasure to report the gallantry of Mr. Bayard Wharton of Section One who on the 24th of May with a total disregard for his own personal safety succeeded in saving the life of Lieutenant H. J. Watts an aviator of the English Army who had fallen with his

machine into the River Brenta." Lowell cites the actions of Charles Waldispuhl and John Cloud "who performed conspicuous services on the same occasion" as well. See Guy Lowell, "Report of the Department of Military Affairs for the Month of March, 1918," 5, box 881, folder 954.11/08, Records of the American National Red Cross, National Archives, College Park, MD; and Guy Lowell, "Report of the Department of Military Affairs for the Month of May, 1918," 4, box 881, folder 954.11/08, Records of the American National Red Cross, National Archives, College Park, MD.

8. Bates, "Ambulance Report No. 8," 3, Robert W. Bates Papers, private collection; for additional discussion of Italian decorations in World War I, see Robert W. Lewis, "Hemingway in Italy: Making it Up," *Journal of Modern Literature* 9, no. 2 (1982): 224.

9. Robert W. Bates, "Ambulance Report No. 9," July 25, 1918, 1, Robert W. Bates papers, private collection.

10. Overall, a total of thirty-seven volunteers were recipients of the War Cross by the end of July. See Guy Lowell, *Report of the Department of Military Affairs January to July, 1918* (Rome: American Red Cross, 1918), 29–30.

11. Bates, "Ambulance Report No. 8," 3, Robert W. Bates Papers, private collection.

12. Quoted in "The American Red Cross at the Front," *Red Cross Bulletin*, July 5, 1918, 1. Excerpts from this account were also published in "Red Cross Volunteers Face Shells While Aiding Italians in Battle," *Washington Post*, September 1, 1918, 8.

13. "The American Red Cross at the Front," *Red Cross Bulletin*, July 5, 1918, 1.

14. Guy Lowell, "Report of the Department of Military Affairs for the Month of June, 1918," 3, box 881, folder 954.11/08, Records of the American National Red Cross, National Archives, College Park, MD.

15. "Red Cross Volunteers Face Shells While Aiding Italians in Battle," *Washington Post*, September 1, 1918, 8.

16. Lowell, "Report of the Department of Military Affairs for the Month of June, 1918," 3, National Archives. Lewis also refers to Miller and Agate. See Lewis, "Hemingway in Italy," 215.

17. "Red Cross Volunteers Face Shells While Aiding Italians in Battle," *Washington Post*, September 1, 1918, 8.

18. Lowell, "Report of the Department of Military Affairs for the Month of June, 1918," 3, National Archives.

19. Ibid.

20. For other discussions of McKey, see Charles M. Bakewell, *The Story of the American Red Cross in Italy* (New York: MacMillan, 1920), 82–85; Michael Reynolds, *Hemingway's First War: The Making of "A Farewell to Arms"* (New York: Basil Blackwell, 1987), 147–49; and Stephen Bates, "'An Apostle for His Work': The Death of Lieutenant Edward Michael McKey," *Hemingway Review* 29, no. 2 (2010): 61–73.

21. James Gamble, "Cucina Report No. 6: June," July 30, 1918, 2, Robert W. Bates Papers, private collection.

22. Herbert Scoville, "Minutes of Office Meeting Held at Rome," June 20, 1918, 1–3, box 881, folder 954.04, Records of the American National Red Cross, National Archives, College Park, MD.

23. See "With the Rolling Canteens," *Red Cross Bulletin*, July 5, 1918, 7.

24. See "Lieut. E. M. McKey Killed on the Italian Battlefront," *New York Times*, June 19, 1918, 1; "Lieut. McKey, of Red Cross, Killed by Shell in Italy," *Washington Post*, June 19, 1918, 4. See also, Stephen Bates, "'An Apostle for His Work,'" 61.

25. Quoted in Bakewell, *The Story of the American Red Cross in Italy*, 83.

26. Quoted in ibid., 84. See also, Reynolds, *Hemingway's First War*, 148.

27. F. Cacciapuoti, "Letter from an Italian Liaison Officer," *Red Cross Bulletin*, July 5, 1918, 7. See also, Stephen Bates, "'An Apostle for His Work,'" 67.

28. Lowell, "Report of the Department of Military Affairs for the Month of June, 1918," 6, National Archives.

29. Quoted in Bates, "Ambulance Report No. 8," 2, Robert W. Bates Papers, private collection.

30. Robert W. Bates, letter to "Dear Family, June 27, 1918," Robert W. Bates Papers, private collection.

31. Bates, letter to "Dear Family," June 27, 1918, Robert W. Bates Papers, private collection.

32. Robert W. Bates, "Report of Captain Bates," *Red Cross Bulletin*, July 5, 1918, 7.

33. Guy Lowell, "Report of the Department of Military Affairs for the Month of July, 1918," 3, box 881, folder 954.11/08, Records of the American National Red Cross, National Archives, College Park, MD.

34. Robert W. Bates, "General Notice No. 34 to Sections," June 29, 1918, Robert W. Bates Papers, private collection.

35. Bates, "General Notice No. 34," Robert W. Bates Papers, private collection.

36. Bates, "Ambulance Report No. 9," 1, Robert W. Bates Papers, private collection.

37. Robert W. Bates, letter to "Dear Family," July 8, 1918, Robert W. Bates Papers, private collection.

38. Bates, "Ambulance Report No. 9," 1–2, Robert W. Bates Papers, private collection.

39. Lowell, "Report of the Department of Military Affairs for the Month of July, 1918," 9, National Archives.

40. Peter Griffin, *Along with Youth: Hemingway, the Early Years* (New York: Oxford, 1985), 73.

41. Lowell, "Report of the Department of Military Affairs for the Month of July, 1918," 6–7, National Archives.

42. See also Griffin, *Along with Youth*, 73; James Mellow, *Hemingway: A Life without Consequences* (New York: Houghton Mifflin, 1992), 60; and Carlos Baker, *Ernest Hemingway: A Life Story* (New York, Scribners, 1969), 44.

43. Ernest Hemingway, letter to "Dear Ruth," c. June 25–July 8, in *The Letters of Ernest Hemingway, 1907–1922*, ed. Sandra Spanier and Robert W. Trogdon (Cambridge: Cambridge UP, 2011), 113–14.

44. Ernest Hemingway, "Class Prophecy," *Hemingway at Oak Park High: The High School Writings of Ernest Hemingway, 1916–1917*, ed. Cynthia Maziarka and Donald Vogel Jr. (Oak Park, IL: Oak Park and River Forest High School, 1993), 107. Reprinted from Ernest Hemingway, "Class Prophecy," *Senior Tabula*, (1917): 57–62.

45. See, for example, C. E. Frazer Clark Jr., "American Red Cross Reports on the Wounding of Lieutenant Ernest M. Hemingway-1918," 131.

46. Bates, letter to "Dear Family," July 8, 1918, Robert W. Bates Papers, private collection.

47. Robert W. Bates, letter to "Dear Hemingway," July 11, 1918, Ernest Hemingway Collection, John F. Kennedy Library, Boston. The letter was initially published in Steven Florczyk, "A Captain in Hemingway's Court? The Story of Ernest Hemingway, *A Farewell to Arms,* and the Unpublished Papers of Robert W. Bates,"in *Hemingway's Italy: New Perspectives,* ed. Rena Sanderson (Baton Rouge, LA: Louisiana State UP, 2006), 88.

48. Nagel has explained that "there has been considerable confusion" about the location of the American Red Cross Hospital in Milan, pointing out that "4 Via Cesare Cantù" was the correct address. Bates's indication of "4 Passagio Centrale" refers to a street that borders the hospital on the other side of Cesare Cantù. See Nagel, "Hemingway and the Italian Legacy," 222.

49. Herbert Scoville, "Minutes of Office Meeting Held at Rome," July 11, 1918, box 881, folder 954.04, Records of the American National Red Cross, National Archives, College Park, MD.

50. Lowell, "Report of the Department of Military Affairs for the Month of June, 1918," 8, National Archives.

51. "Wounded on Italy Front," *Kansas City Star,* July 14, 1918, A5.

52. "E. M. Hemingway Wounded," *Kansas City Star,* July 13, 1918, 1. See also, "Wounded on Italy Front," *Kansas City Star,* July 14, 1918, A5.

53. Arabella Hemingway, letter to Grace and Clarence Hemingway, July 15, 1918, Ernest Hemingway Collection, Pennsylvania State University, University Park, PA.

54. See "Three Are Wounded," *Oak Leaves,* July 20, 1918, 1. See also Audre Hanneman, *Ernest Hemingway: A Comprehensive Bibliography* (Princeton, NJ: Princeton UP, 1967), 343–44. Alternatively, Lynn states that "a telegram from Red Cross headquarters in Washington reached the Hemingways on July 15." See Lynn, *Hemingway,* 82.

55. Quoted in "Three Are Wounded," *Oak Leaves,* July 20, 1918, 1. See also *The Letters of Ernest Hemingway, 1907–1922,* 117.

56. "9 Chicagoans Named in Lists of Casualties," *Chicago Evening Post,* July 16, 1918, 1; "Valor Cross to Hemingway," *Kansas City Times,* July 17, 1918, 8. See also, Hanneman, *Ernest Hemingway,* 343. The decoration mentioned in the *Kansas City Times* is most likely a conflation of the War Cross and the Silver Medal. The *Kansas City Times* article is the only report that referred to Hemingway bringing multiple wounded soldiers to safety.

57. W. R. Castle Jr. to "My dear Mr. [Clarence] Hemingway," July 20, 1918, Ernest Hemingway Collection, John F. Kennedy Library, Boston.

58. Clarence Hemingway, letter to "Mr. W. R. Castle, Jr.," July 20, 1918, Ernest Hemingway Collection, John F. Kennedy Library, Boston.

59. "Three Are Wounded," *Oak Leaves,* July 20, 1918, 1.

60. "A. T. Hemingway," *Oak Leaves,* July 20, 1918, 2.

61. See Ted Brumback, letter to "Dear Mr. [Clarence] Hemingway," July 14, 1918, Ernest Hemingway Collection, John F. Kennedy Library, Boston. Brumback's letter was published in Marcelline Sanford, *At the Hemingways: With Fifty Years of Correspondence Between Ernest and Marcelline Hemingway* (Moscow, ID: U of Idaho P, 1999), 161–63. It was also printed in *The Letters of Ernest Hemingway, 1907–1922*, 114–16. Baker notes that Hemingway's arrival in Milan occurred on "Wednesday, July 17th, 1918, at six o'clock in the morning," but Brumback's letter, dated July 14, suggests it was at least three days earlier. See Baker, *A Life Story*, 46.

62. Brumback, letter to "Dear Mr. Hemingway," July 14, 1918, in *The Letters of Ernest Hemingway, 1907–1922*, 115–16.

63. Ernest Hemingway, postscript to Brumback, letter to "Dear Mr. Hemingway," July 14, 1918, in *The Letters of Ernest Hemingway, 1907–1922*, 116.

64. Clarence Hemingway, addendum to Brumback, letter to "Dear Mr. Hemingway," July 14, 1918, John F. Kennedy Library, Boston.

65. See "Wins Italian Medal," *Oak Leaves*, August 10, 1918, 56. See also Audre Hanneman, *Ernest Hemingway: A Comprehensive Bibliography* (Princeton, NJ: Princeton UP, 1967), 344.

66. Ernest Hemingway, letter to "Dear Folks," July 21, 1918, in *The Letters of Ernest Hemingway, 1907–1922*, 117–18. The statement about Bates suggests that the captain made additional contact with Hemingway between July 11, when he wrote his initial letter to Ernest, and July 16, when Ernest sent the cable.

· 67. Hemingway, letter to "Dear Folks," July 21, 1918, in *The Letters of Ernest Hemingway, 1907–1922*, 118. Nagel has also pointed out that Hemingway's comment is "enigmatic" since he served "in the same area where McKey had been killed" and "would certainly have heard of the incident." See Nagel, "Hemingway and the Italian Legacy," 220.

68. Hemingway, letter to "Dear Folks," July 21, 1918, in *The Letters of Ernest Hemingway, 1907–1922*, 118–19.

69. Bates, "Ambulance Report No. 9," 2, Robert W. Bates Papers, private collection. Excerpts from this report also appear in Florczyk, "A Captain in Hemingway's Court? The Story of Ernest Hemingway, *A Farewell to Arms*, and the Unpublished Papers of Robert W. Bates," 68–69; and Stephen Bates, "'Unpopularity Is the Least of My Worries': Captain R. W. Bates and Lieutenant E. M. Hemingway," *Hemingway Review* 29, no. 1 (2009): 55.

70. Despite the title indicating a summary of work for June, the document provides information through July.

71. Gamble, "Cucina Report No. 6: June," 3, Robert W. Bates Papers, private collection.

72. Moses S. Slaughter, "Report on emergency posti di conforto," July 26, 1918, 2, Robert W. Bates Papers, private collection.

73. Ernest Hemingway, letter to "Dear Folks," August 4, 1918, in *The Letters of Ernest Hemingway, 1907–1922*, 124.

74. Ernest Hemingway, letter to "Caro Mio," August 8, 1918, in *The Letters of Ernest Hemingway, 1907–1922*, 128.

75. "With Our Wounded," *Oak Leaves*, September 7, 1918, 22.

76. Quoted in Nagel, "Hemingway and the Italian Legacy," 216.

77. Lowell, "Report of the Department of Military Affairs for the Month of July, 1918," 9, National Archives.

78. Lowell, *Report of the Department of Military Affairs January to July*, 14.

79. Ibid., 29–30.

80. Ibid., 15.

81. See C. E. Frazer Clark Jr., 130. Hemingway's copy of the report is located at the McKeldin Library, University of Maryland, College Park, MD.

82. Ernest Hemingway, letter to "Dear Folks," August 18, 1918, in *The Letters of Ernest Hemingway, 1907–1922*, 130–33. Subsequent quotations from this letter refer to this edition.

83. Nagel has explained that "the X-rays of Hemingway's legs and the machine-gun bullet in his coin purse would seem to support the account." His analysis leads him to conclude that "this evidence would strongly suggest that Hemingway did not invent the machine-gun story to appear heroic and, indeed, with respect to his foot injury, his wounds were even more severe than he reported." On the other hand, he notes that "Ernest's suggestion that even after he was hit by machine-gun bullets he still assisted a wounded soldier, walking 150 yards, cannot be confirmed with certainty." See Nagel, "Hemingway and the Italian Legacy," 219, 221.

84. Hemingway, letter to "Dear Folks," August 18, 1918, in *The Letters of Ernest Hemingway, 1907–1922*, 131–32.

85. Ibid., 132.

86. See Lewis, "Hemingway in Italy," 215.

87. Baker, *A Life Story*, 48.

88. Agnes von Kurowsky, diary entry, August 27, 1918, in Villard and Nagel, *Hemingway in Love and War*, 73.

89. Henry Serrano Villard, "Red Cross Driver in Italy," in Villard and Nagel, *Hemingway in Love and War*, 22.

90. Robert W. Bates, addendum to "Ambulance Report No. 9," Robert W. Bates Papers, private collection.

91. A related incident underscores Bates's dislike for aggrandizement. While serving as an ambulance driver on the western front, he recorded an episode about his driving partner, F. Gray Blinn, whose paralyzing fear while at the wheel of their ambulance resulted in an aborted mission to retrieve wounded during a heavy bombardment. Even so, their vehicle had been shot up, and, when other volunteers saw it, Blinn "immediately began to pose as a hero." Bates recorded in his diary that he "felt humiliated." Robert W. Bates, diary entry, June 14, 1916, Robert W. Bates Papers, private collection.

92. Ernest Hemingway, letter to "Dear Mom," July 29, 1918, in *The Letters of Ernest Hemingway, 1907–1922*, 120.

93. Hemingway, letter to "Caro Mio," August 8, 1918, in *The Letters of Ernest Hemingway, 1907–1922*, 195. Spanier and Trogdon transcribe Hemingway's phrase as "hammy feet." Hemingway's handwriting is difficult to decipher, but it is likely

that he wrote "brawny feet" instead, considering both the context of his comment as well as comparisons to other words in the same document that contain similar letter combinations. See Ernest Hemingway, letter to "Caro Mio," August 8, 1918, Ernest Hemingway Collection, John F. Kennedy Library, Boston.

94. Charles A. Fenton, *The Apprenticeship of Ernest Hemingway: The Early Years* (New York: Viking Press, 1954), 66.

95. Lewis, "Hemingway in Italy," 219.

96. Guy Lowell, "Report of the Department of Military Affairs January, 1918, to February, 1919," 24, Robert W. Bates Papers, private collection.

97. Ernest Hemingway, postscript to letter to "Dear Folks," August 18, 1918, in *The Letters of Ernest Hemingway, 1907–1922*, 133.

98. Ernest Hemingway, letter to "Dear Dad," September 11, 1918, in *The Letters of Ernest Hemingway, 1907–1922*, 139.

99. Ernest Hemingway, letter to "Dear Ivory and Nun Bones," September 21, 1918, in *The Letters of Ernest Hemingway, 1907–1922*, 142.

100. Hemingway, letter to "Dear Dad," September 11, 1918, in *The Letters of Ernest Hemingway, 1907–1922*, 139.

101. Ernest Hemingway, letter to "Dearest Family," November 11, 1918, in *The Letters of Ernest Hemingway, 1907–1922*, 151.

102. See in this volume the photograph, "Portrait of Ernest Hemingway in formal attire."

103. Felice Cacciapuoti, letter to "my dear Mr. Hemmingway [sic]," November 27, 1918, Ernest Hemingway Collection, John F. Kennedy Library, Boston.

104. Ernest Hemingway, letter to "Dear Bill" [Horne], July 2, 1919, in *The Letters of Ernest Hemingway, 1907–1922*, 195–96.

105. Nagel, "Hemingway and the Italian Legacy," 256–57.

106. See Lewis, "Hemingway in Italy," 223.

107. Quoted in ibid., 224.

108. See Appendix IX in Bakewell, *The Story of the American Red Cross in Italy*, 221–25.

109. Nagel, "Hemingway and the Italian Legacy," 248.

110. Ernest Hemingway, letter to "Dear Mom," August 29, 1918, in *The Letters of Ernest Hemingway, 1907–1922*, 135.

111. Agnes von Kurowsky, diary entry, August 8, 1918, in Villard and Nagel, *Hemingway in Love and War*, 67.

112. Baker, *A Life Story*, 54.

113. Quoted in ibid.

114. Ernest Hemingway, letter to "Dear Folks," October 18, 1918, in *The Letters of Ernest Hemingway, 1907–1922*, 147–48.

115. Ernest Hemingway, letter to "Dear Old Sister," November 23, 1918, in *The Letters of Ernest Hemingway, 1907–1922*, 158.

116. Hemingway, letter to "Dear Dad," September 11, 1918, in *The Letters of Ernest Hemingway, 1907–1922*, 140.

117. Quoted in Robert W. Bates, "Memo to Sections," August 21, 1918, Robert W. Bates Papers, private collection.

118. Hemingway, letter to "Dear Folks," October 18, 1918, in *The Letters of Ernest Hemingway, 1907–1922*, 147. On September 29, Joseph M. King "was wounded in the leg during a heavy bombardment while near the Section camp at Bassano." Bates reported that the young man "made light of his injury and would not allow the Italians who picked him up to bind his wound." He "showed the greatest courage and smiled to the last" when he died "probably through loss of blood." King was designated by Bates as "the first American to die in the A.R.C ambulance service in Italy." (McKey was the first American to die in the rolling kitchen service.) That same day, Harry K. Knapp Jr., also of Section One, had been injured while on duty at Mount Grappa. At the end of the following month, Bates mentioned that his "wound, which was in the left arm, has not proved serious." See Robert W. Bates, "Ambulance Report No. 12," October 20, 1918, 3, Robert W. Bates Papers, private collection. See also, Guy Lowell, "Report of the Department of Military Affairs for the Month of September, 1918," 9, Robert W. Bates Papers, private collection.

119. See Robert W. Bates, "Ambulance Report No. 13," November 5, 1918, 1–5, Robert W. Bates Papers, private collection.

120. Bates, "Ambulance Report No. 13," November 5, 1918, 4, Robert W. Bates Papers, private collection.

121. Ibid., 5

122. Hemingway, letter to "Dear Folks," October 18, 1918, in *The Letters of Ernest Hemingway, 1907–1922*, 147.

123. Ernest Hemingway, letter to "Dear Family," November 1, 1918, in *The Letters of Ernest Hemingway, 1907–1922*, 148–49.

124. Hemingway, letter to "Dearest Family," November 11, 1918, in *The Letters of Ernest Hemingway, 1907–1922*, 150–52.

125. Ernest Hemingway, letter to "Dear Folks," September 29, 1918, in *The Letters of Ernest Hemingway, 1907–1922*, 145.

126. Hemingway, letter to "Dearest Family," November 11, 1918, in *The Letters of Ernest Hemingway, 1907–1922*, 150.

127. Ernest Hemingway, letter to "Dear Folks," December 11, 1918, in *The Letters of Ernest Hemingway, 1907–1922*, 161.

128. Baker, *A Life Story*, 56.

129. See Gerry Brenner, "'Enough of a Bad Gamble': Correcting the Misinformation on Hemingway's Captain James Gamble," *Hemingway Review* 20, no. 1 (2000): 90–96.

130. Agnes von Kurowsky, letter to "My own dear Kid," December 1, 1918, in Villard and Nagel, *Hemingway in Love and War*, 135.

131. Hemingway, letter to "Dear Mom," August 29, 1918, in *The Letters of Ernest Hemingway, 1907–1922*, 136; Hemingway, letter to "Dear folks," December 11, 1918, in *The Letters of Ernest Hemingway, 1907–1922*, 161; Hemingway, letter to "Dear Old Sister," November 23, 1918, in *The Letters of Ernest Hemingway, 1907–1922*, 157.

132. When the war ended, Hemingway wrote "I plan to knock 'em for a loop and will be a busy man for several years. By that time my pension will have accumulated a couple of thousand lire and I'll bring my children over to view the battle fields." See Hemingway, letter to "Dear family," November 11, 1918, in *The Letters of Ernest Hemingway, 1907–1922*, 152.

133. Agnes von Kurowsky, letter to "Dearest Mr. Kid," November 3, 1918, in Villard and Nagel, *Hemingway in Love and War*, 124.

134. Ted Brumback, letter to "Dear Mrs. Hemingway," December 13, 1918, Ernest Hemingway Collection, Pennsylvania State University, University Park, PA.

135. See Hemingway, letter to "Dearest Family," November 11, 1918, in *The Letters of Ernest Hemingway, 1907–1922*, 152; See also Agnes von Kurowsky, letter to "My dearest Kid," October 26, 1918, in Villard and Nagel, *Hemingway in Love and War*, 114. Agnes ended her relationship with Hemingway on March 7, 1919, when she sent him a letter from Italy saying that "I know that I am still very fond of you, but it is more as a mother than as a sweetheart." Agnes von Kurowsky, letter to "Ernie, dear boy," March 7, 1919, in Villard and Nagel, *Hemingway in Love and War*, 163.

136. Bates, "Ambulance Report No. 13," November 5, 1918, 6, Robert W. Bates Papers, private collection.

137. See American Red Cross, List of Personnel, 7, Robert W. Bates Papers, private collection.

138. Quoted in Nagel, "Hemingway and the Italian Legacy," 253.

139. "Has 227 Wounds, but Is Looking for Job," *New York Sun*, January 22, 1919, 8. Reprinted in *Conversations with Ernest Hemingway*, ed. Matthew J. Bruccoli (Jackson, MS: UP of Mississippi, 1986), 1–2. See also Reynolds, *The Young Hemingway*, 17–19; and Nagel, "Hemingway and the Italian Legacy," 197.

140. "Two Who Knew Combat," *Oak Leaves*, January 25, 1919, 11.

141. See Roselle Dean, "First Lieutenant Hemingway Comes Back Riddled with Bullets and Decorated with Two Medals," in C. E. Frazer Clark Jr., "American Red Cross Reports on the Wounding of Lieutenant Ernest M. Hemingway-1918," *Fitzgerald/Hemingway Annual* (1974), 135. Reprinted from the *Oak Parker*, February 1, 1918, 13. For further discussion of "the implication" that Hemingway had served as a soldier, see Reynolds, *The Young Hemingway*, 56.

142. Baker, *A Life Story*, 58.

143. Frederick Ebersold, "Hanna Club Has Rousing First Meeting with 'Ernie' Hemingway as Speaker," in Maziarka and Vogel Jr., *Hemingway at Oak Park High*, 117–19. Reprinted from the *Trapeze*, February 7, 1919, 2. Baker describes the Hanna Club as "a school organization which imported speakers from Chicago and its suburbs, many of them with inspirational messages." See Baker, *A Life Story*, 23.

144. Ebersold, in Maziarka and Vogel Jr., *Hemingway at Oak Park High*, 118.

145. Ibid., 119.

146. Ernest Hemingway, letter to Bill [Horne], February 3, 1919, in *The Letters of Ernest Hemingway, 1907–1922*, 167.

147. Ernest Hemingway, letter to "Dear Old Chieftain," March 3, 1919, in *The Letters of Ernest Hemingway, 1907–1922*, 168–69.

148. "Learn this for Assembly," in Maziarka and Vogel Jr., *Hemingway at Oak Park High*, 120. Reprinted from the *Trapeze*, March 14, 1919, 1. The lyrics are also quoted in Nagel, "Hemingway and the Italian Legacy," 199.

149. Edwin Wells, "Hemingway Speaks to High School," in Maziarka and Vogel Jr., *Hemingway at Oak Park High*, 121–23. Reprinted from the *Trapeze*, March 21, 1919, 1.

150. Reynolds, *The Young Hemingway*, 18.

151. Wells, in Maziarka and Vogel Jr., *Hemingway at Oak Park High*, 121–23.

152. Henry Davison, *The Story of the American Red Cross in the Great War* (New York: The Macmillan Company, 1920), 212.

153. Bakewell, *The Story of the American Red Cross in Italy*, vi.

154. Ibid., 80.

155. Ibid.

156. Bakewell, *The Story of the American Red Cross in Italy*, 224–25.

5. *Dopo la Guerra*

1. Arlen J. Hansen, *Gentlemen Volunteers: The Story of the American Ambulance Drivers in the Great War, August 1914–September 1918* (New York: Arcade Publishing, 1996), 183–85; Robert W. Bates, diary entry, August 22, 1918, Robert W. Bates Papers, private collection.

2. "Robert P. Perkins, Ill for Year, Dies," *New York Times*, April 29, 1924, 22.

3. "Justices Receive New Court House," *New York Times*, February 12, 1927, 14.

4. Robert W. Bates, letter to "Dear Family," October 14, 1918, Robert W. Bates Papers, private collection. See also, Stephen Bates, "'Unpopularity Is the Least of My Worries': Captain R. W. Bates and Lieutenant E. M. Hemingway," *Hemingway Review* 29, no. 1 (2009): 58.

5. Gerry Brenner, "'Enough of a Bad Gamble': Correcting the Misinformation on Hemingway's Captain James Gamble," *Hemingway Review* 20, no. 1 (2000): 93.

6. Ernest Hemingway, "In Another Country," *The Complete Short Stories of Ernest Hemingway: The Finca Vigía Edition* (New York: Scribner, 1987), 207. Subsequent references to "In Another Country" are to this edition.

7. Ernest Hemingway, *A Farewell to Arms* (New York: Scribners, 1995), 18. Subsequent references are to this edition.

8. Ernest Hemingway, *Across the River and Into the Trees* (New York: Scribner, 1978), 21; subsequent references to *Across the River and Into the Trees* refer to this edition. Ernest Hemingway, "Introduction" in *Men at War*, ed. by Ernest Hemingway (New York: Bramhall House, 1979), xii.

9. James Steinke, "Hemingway's 'In Another Country' and 'Now I Lay Me,'" *Hemingway Review* 5, no. 1 (1985): 33.

10. Michael Reynolds, *Hemingway's First War: The Making of "A Farewell to Arms"* (New York: Basil Blackwell, 1987), 277–79; see also Carlos Baker, *Ernest Hemingway: A Life Story* (New York: Scribners, 1969), 147.

11. An excerpt from "Along with Youth a Novel" was posthumously published as "Night Before Landing" in Ernest Hemingway, *The Nick Adams Stories* (New York: Scribners, 1972), 137–42. Subsequent references to "Along with Youth a Novel" are to this edition.

12. See Ernest Hemingway, "In Our Time," *Little Review: Quarterly Journal of Art and Letters* 9, no. 3 (1923): 3–5; Ernest Hemingway, "chapter 1," in *in our time* (Paris: Three Mountain Press, 1924), 9; and Ernest Hemingway, "Chapter I," in *In Our Time* (New York: Boni & Liveright, 1925), 13.

13. Ernest Hemingway, letter to Ezra Pound, "c. 5 August 1923," in *Ernest Heming-*

way: Selected Letters, 1917–1961, ed. Carlos Baker (New York: Charles Scribner's Sons, 1981), 91.

14. Ernest Hemingway, "Chapter I," in *The Complete Short Stories of Ernest Hemingway: The Finca Vigía Edition*, 65. Subsequent references to "Chapter I" are to this edition.

15. Milton A. Cohen, *Hemingway's Laboratory: The Paris "in our time"* (Tuscaloosa, Al: U of Alabama P, 2005), 129.

16. Ibid., 99.

17. Julian Smith, "Hemingway and the Thing Left Out," *Journal of Modern Literature* 1 (1970–1971): 169.

18. Ernest Hemingway, "Soldier's Home," in *The Complete Short Stories of Ernest Hemingway: The Finca Vigía Edition*, 111. Subsequent references to "Soldier's Home" are to this edition.

19. See Ernest Hemingway, *Death in the Afternoon* (New York: Scribners, 1960), 191.

20. See also Kenneth G. Johnston, "'A Way You'll Never Be': A Mission of Morale," *Studies in Short Fiction* 23, no. 4 (1986): 429–35.

21. Ernest Hemingway, "A Way You'll Never Be," in *The Complete Short Stories of Ernest Hemingway: The Finca Vigía Edition*, 311. Subsequent references to "A Way You'll Never Be" are to this edition.

22. Charles M. Bakewell, *The Story of the American Red Cross in Italy* (New York: MacMillan, 1920), 157; James D. Brasch and Joseph Sigman, *Hemingway's Library: A Composite Record* (New York: Garland, 1981), 60.

23. Bakewell, *The Story of the American Red Cross in Italy*, 165.

24. See also Johnston, "'A Way You'll Never Be': A Mission of Morale," 432.

25. Joseph M. Flora, *Hemingway's Nick Adams* (Baton Rouge, LA: Louisiana State UP, 1982), 132.

26. H. R. Stoneback, "'You Sure This Thing Has Trout in It?' Fishing and Fabrication, Omission and 'Vermification' in *The Sun Also Rises*," in *Hemingway Repossessed*, ed. Kenneth Rosen (Westport, CT: Greenwood Publishing Group, 1994), 115–28.

27. Ernest Hemingway, "A Natural History of the Dead," in *Death in the Afternoon* (New York: Scribners, 1960), 137.

28. Robert E. Gajdusek, "Set Piece," *Hemingway Review* 14, no. 2 (1995): 127.

29. Paul Smith, "Hemingway's Apprentice Fiction: 1919–1921," in *New Critical Approaches to the Short Stories of Ernest Hemingway*, ed. Jackson J. Benson (Durham, NC: Duke UP, 1990), 143.

30. Hemingway wrote to Maxwell Perkins on May 30, 1942, that "I was an awful dope when I went to the last war. I can remember just thinking that we were the home team and the Austrians were the visiting team." Quoted in Carlos Baker, *A Life Story*, 38.

31. Michael Reynolds, *The Young Hemingway* (New York: Norton, 1998), 180.

32. Peter Stine, "Ernest Hemingway and the Great War," in *Fitzgerald/Hemingway Annual* (1979), 329.

33. Paul Smith, "Hemingway's Apprentice Fiction," 472n20.

34. Michael Stewart, "Ernest Hemingway's 'How Death Sought Out the Town

Major of Roncade'": Observations on the Development of a Writer," *Literary Imagination* 8, no. 2 (2006): 211.

35. Ernest Hemingway, "A Veteran Visits Old Front, Wishes He Had Stayed Away," *Toronto Daily Star*, July 22, 1922, 7. Reprinted in *Dateline: Toronto, the Complete "Toronto Star" Dispatches, 1920–1924*, ed. William White (New York: Scribners, 1985), 176–80. Subsequent references are to this edition.

36. Reynolds, *The Young Hemingway*, 196.

37. "Weather Report," *Ciao*, June 1918, 1.

38. William Adair, "Hemingway's 'A Veteran Visits His Old Front': Images and Situations for the Fiction," *ANQ: A Quarterly Journal of Short Articles, Notes, and Reviews* 8, no. 1 (1995): 27.

39. Ernest Hemingway, "Riparto d'Assalto," in *Poetry: A Magazine of Verse* 21, no. 4 (1923): 195. Subsequent references are to this edition. Reprinted in Ernest Hemingway, *Three Stories & Ten Poems* (Paris: Contact Publishing Company, 1923), 55; and *Complete Poems*, ed. Nicholas Gerogiannis (Lincoln, NE: U of Nebraska P, 1979), 46.

40. Verna Kale, "Hemingway's Poetry and the Paris Apprenticeship," *Hemingway Review* 26, no. 2 (2007): 65.

41. Quoted in Angelo L. Pirocchi, *Italian Arditi Elite Assault Troops 1917–20* (Oxford: Osprey Publishing, 2004), 49.

42. Ibid.

43. Ernest Hemingway, "chapter 8," in *in our time* (Paris: Three Mountain Press, 1924), 16. References to "chapter 8" are to this edition. See also, Ernest Hemingway, "Chapter VII," in *The Complete Short Stories of Ernest Hemingway: The Finca Vigía Edition*, 109.

44. Cohen, *Hemingway's Laboratory*, 158.

45. Ibid., 159.

46. Hemingway began writing "Now I Lay Me" in November of 1926. See Paul Smith, *A Reader's Guide to the Short Stories of Ernest Hemingway*, (Boston: G. K. Hall, 1989), 173.

47. Margot Sempreora refers to Nick as "the soldier of the silkworm night." While his role as a combatant cannot be verified from the details of the story, the observation identifying the protagonist with the nocturnal sounds from the insects gets at a key element of the narrative. See Margot Sempreora, "Nick at Night: Nocturnal Metafictions in Three Hemingway Short Stories," *Hemingway Review* 22, no. 1 (2002): 31.

48. Ernest Hemingway, "Now I Lay Me," in *The Complete Short Stories of Ernest Hemingway: The Finca Vigía Edition*, 276, 279. Subsequent references are to this edition. Earl H. Rovit has described "Now I Lay Me" as a "direct recounting of [Nick's] convalescence in Milan after the Fossalta wound," but, as Julian Smith has pointed out, details from the setting clearly show that Hemingway's protagonist is "back at the front between woundings." See Earl H. Rovit, *Ernest Hemingway* (Boston: Twayne Publishers, 1986), 63. See also Julian Smith, "Hemingway and the Thing Left Out," 176.

49. Carlos Baker, *A Life Story*, 43.

50. Reynolds has also pointed out that "the ambulance drivers who served with Hemingway" are "identifiable sources who contributed to the novel," mentioning Ted Brumback and John Dos Passos in particular. See Reynolds, *Hemingway's First War*, 161.

51. Hemingway's "Captain Paravicini" was also "an architect" prior to commanding at the front. See Hemingway, "A Way You'll Never Be," in *The Complete Short Stories of Ernest Hemingway: The Finca Vigía Edition*, 308.

52. Robert W. Lewis, *"A Farewell to Arms": The War of the Words* (New York: Twayne, 1992), 39.

53. Stephen Bates, "'Unpopularity Is the Least of My Worries,'" 50.

54. James Nagel, "Hemingway and the Italian Legacy," in *Hemingway in Love and War: The Lost Diary of Agnes von Kurowsky, Her Letters, and Correspondence of Ernest Hemingway*, ed. Henry S. Villard and James Nagel (Boston: Northeastern UP, 1989), 263.

55. Also similar to "Al on Permission," in *The Torrents of Spring*, Yogi Johnson tells a story about "a beautiful thing" that happened while on leave in Paris when he was beckoned by a woman to accompany her to a mansion in "a distant part" of the city. See Ernest Hemingway, *The Torrents of Spring* (New York: Scribners, 1926), 79–80.

56. H. R. Stoneback, "Pilgrimage Variations: Hemingway's Sacred Landscapes," *Religion and Literature* 35, nos. 2–3 (2003): 60.

57. As Nagel discusses, "*A Farewell to Arms* is fundamentally *not* a realistic novel about World War I narrated by Ernest Hemingway; it is, rather, a retrospective narrative told by Frederic Henry a decade after the action has taken place for the purpose of coming to terms emotionally with the events." See James Nagel, "Catherine Barkley and Retrospective Narration," in *Ernest Hemingway: Six Decades of Criticism*, ed. Linda W. Wagner (East Lansing, MI: Michigan State UP, 1987), 171.

58. Robert A. Martin has suggested that these drivers "are without personal characteristics or emotion," but Henry indicates their varying degrees of disgust over the war. See Robert A. Martin, "Hemingway and the Ambulance Drivers in *A Farewell to Arms*," in *Ernest Hemingway: Six Decades of Criticism*, ed. Linda W. Wagner (East Lansing, MI: Michigan State UP, 1987), 200.

59. Bernard Oldsey identifies Captain Enrico Serena as the source for Rinaldi. See Bernard Oldsey, *Hemingway's Hidden Craft: The Writing of "A Farewell to Arms"* (University Park, PA: Pennsylvania State UP, 1979), 46. Nancy R. Comley writes about the soldier and poet Gabriele D'Annunzio as an influence on Hemingway's notions of "Italian charm in action." See Nancy R. Comley, "The Italian Education of Ernest Hemingway," *Hemingway's Italy: New Perspectives*, ed. Rena Sanderson (Baton Rouge, LA: Louisiana State UP, 2006), 45. In a related article, Kim Moreland discusses ways that "Hemingway began to develop his Italian identity" while serving in the Red Cross. See Kim Moreland, "Bringing 'Italianicity' Home," in *Hemingway's Italy: New Perspectives*, ed. Rena Sanderson (Baton Rouge, LA: Louisiana State UP, 2006), 52–55.

60. Charles A. Fenton, *The Apprenticeship of Ernest Hemingway: The Early Years* (New York: Viking Press, 1954), 55.

61. Regarding "A Way You'll Never Be," A. E. Hotchner quoted Hemingway as saying that "I had tried to write it in the Twenties, but had failed several times. I

had given up on it but one day here, fifteen years after those things happened to me in a trench dugout outside Fornaci, it suddenly came out focused and complete." See A. E. Hotchner, *Papa Hemingway: A Personal Memoir* (New York: Random House, 1966), 162–63. Paul Smith explains that the story was not completed until "the spring and fall of 1932." See Paul Smith, *A Reader's Guide to the Short Stories of Ernest Hemingway*, 271.

62. James E. Edmonds, *History of the Great War: Military Operations Italy 1915–1919* (London: The Imperial War Museum, 1999), 240.

63. "Patents Applied For," *Come Stà*, March 10, 1918, 4.

64. Martin, "Hemingway and the Ambulance Drivers in *A Farewell to Arms*," 204. Hemingway worked on *A Moveable Feast* from 1956 until his death in 1961. See Jacqueline Tavernier-Courbin, *Ernest Hemingway's "A Moveable Feast": The Making of the Myth* (Boston: Northeastern UP, 1991), xix–xxii.

65. Ernest Hemingway, *A Moveable Feast* (New York: Touchstone, 1992), 29. Subsequent references are to this edition.

66. Ernest Hemingway, "Al Receives Another Letter," *Ciao*, June 1918, 2.

67. See also H. R. Stoneback, *Reading Hemingway's "The Sun Also Rises": Glossary and Commentary* (Kent, OH: Kent State UP, 2007), 5.

68. Paul Smith and Michael Reynolds also discuss this early sketch. See Paul Smith, "Hemingway's Apprentice Fiction: 1919–1921," in *New Critical Approaches to the Short Stories of Ernest Hemingway*, 141–42; Reynolds, *The Young Hemingway*, 33–34.

69. Quoted in Reynolds, *The Young Hemingway*, 34.

70. Ibid.

71. Quoted in ibid., 58.

72. See Reynolds, *Hemingway's First War*, 148–49. McKey was killed on June 16, 1918.

73. The poem was published posthumously. See Ernest Hemingway, "Killed Piave—July 8—1918," *Complete Poems*, 35. Subsequent references are to this edition.

74. Mellow, *Hemingway*, 64.

75. The sketch was published posthumously. See Ernest Hemingway, "Billy Gilbert," in Peter Griffin, *Along with Youth: Hemingway, the Early Years* (New York: Oxford UP, 1985), 126–27. Subsequent references are to this edition.

76. The sketch was published posthumously. See Ernest Hemingway, "Bob White," in Griffin, *Hemingway, the Early Years*, 125.

77. Reynolds, *The Young Hemingway*, 95.

78. Ernest Hemingway, "How to Be Popular in Peace Though a Slacker in War," *Toronto Star Weekly*, March 13, 1920, 11. Reprinted in *Dateline: Toronto*, 10–11. Subsequent references are to this edition.

79. Ernest Hemingway, "Lieutenants' Mustaches the Only Permanent Thing We Got Out of War," *Toronto Star Weekly*, April 10, 1920, 17. Reprinted in *Dateline: Toronto*, 19–20. Subsequent references are to this edition.

80. Adair has likewise observed that Hemingway "does not mention his being wounded in the article; he merely picks up a piece of rusty shrapnel." See Adair, "Hemingway's 'A Veteran Visits His Old Front': Images and Situations for the Fiction," 28–29.

81. Ernest Hemingway, "95,000 Now Wearing the Legion of Honor," *Toronto Daily Star*, April 8, 1922, 13. Reprinted in *Dateline: Toronto*, 123.

82. Ernest Hemingway, "Lots of War Medals for Sale but Nobody Will Buy Them," *Toronto Star Weekly*, December 8, 1923, 21. Reprinted in *Dateline: Toronto*, 401–3. Subsequent references are to this edition.

83. Cohen has similarly observed that Hemingway's article "treats abstract words like 'honor', 'recognition', and 'valor' seriously, not cynically; if its tone is ironical, its undertone is rueful, even elegiac." See Milton Cohen, "War Medals for Sale? Public Bravery vs. Private Courage in Hemingway's WWI Writing," *North Dakota Quarterly* 68, nos. 2–3 (2001): 288.

84. Ernest Hemingway, "chapter 7," in *in our time* (Paris: Three Mountain Press, 1924), 15. References to "chapter 7" are to this edition. The vignette was subsequently published as "Chapter VI" in *In Our Time* (New York: Boni & Liveright, 1925). See also, Ernest Hemingway, "Chapter VI," in *The Complete Short Stories of Ernest Hemingway: The Finca Vigía Edition*, 105. Philip Young has remarked that "it would be quite impossible to exaggerate the importance of this short scene, which is to be duplicated by a new protagonist named Frederic Henry in *A Farewell to Arms*, and to serve as climax for all of Hemingway's heroes for at least the next twenty-five years." See Philip Young, *Ernest Hemingway: A Reconsideration* (University Park, PA: The Pennsylvania State UP, 1966), 40.

85. Kathryn Zabelle Derounian, "An Examination of Hemingway's Chapters 'Nick sat against the wall of the church . . . ,'" in *Critical Essays on Ernest Hemingway's "In Our Time,"* ed. Michael S. Reynolds (Boston: G. K. Hall & Co., 1983), 74.

86. For the composition history of "Soldier's Home," see Paul Smith, *A Reader's Guide to the Short Stories of Ernest Hemingway*, 68. Carlos Baker has noted that "the story might have had Nick Adams as its central character," but Krebs is actually quite distinct from Adams. Hemingway had not yet produced stories that deal with Nick Adams as a veteran, and the portrayals of him vary significantly from the protagonist in "Soldier's Home." See Carlos Baker, *The Writer As Artist* (Princeton, NJ: Princeton UP, 1963), 130.

87. Steven Trout points to Krebs's service in the Marines as a key to understanding his circumstances in the context of "post-World War I American veterans' issues" that are "not readily apparent to readers today." See Steven Trout, "'Where Do We Go from Here?': Ernest Hemingway's 'Soldier's Home' and American Veterans of World War I," *Hemingway Review* 20, no. 1 (2000): 5.

88. Flora has written likewise that "the war itself was not shattering for Krebs. Krebs was shattered after he got home and was not true to what he learned as a soldier." See Flora, *Hemingway's Nick Adams*, 108n5.

89. Ernest Hemingway, *The Sun Also Rises* (New York: Charles Scribner's Sons, 1954), 30. Subsequent references are to this edition. Stoneback discusses various statements made by Hemingway about the specific nature of the wound, one of which notes that Jake was "capable of all normal feelings as a man but incapable of consummating them." See Stoneback, *Reading Hemingway's "The Sun Also Rises,"* 64.

90. The subject of Jake's development is controversial. See, for example, Donald A.

Daiker, "The Affirmative Conclusion of *The Sun Also Rises*," in *Critical Essays on Ernest Hemingway's "The Sun Also Rises*," ed. James Nagel (New York: G. K. Hall & Co., 1995), 74.

91. Allen Josephs explains the significance of the bullfight for Jake. See Allen Josephs, "*Toreo:* The Moral Axis of *The Sun Also Rises*," in *Critical Essays on Ernest Hemingway's "The Sun Also Rises*," 126–40. Stoneback writes about Catholicism and the theme of pilgrimage in the novel. See H. R. Stoneback, "From the rue Saint-Jacques to the Pass of Roland to the 'Unfinished Church on the Edge of the Cliff,'" *Hemingway Review* 6, no. 1 (1986): 2–29. Stoneback also discusses the fishing episodes. See Stoneback, "'You Sure This Thing Has Trout in It?' Fishing and Fabrication, Omission and 'Vermification' in *The Sun Also Rises*," 115–28.

92. Young refers to Jake as an example of the "Hemingway hero," a term which refers to characters who aspire to live up to the principles of a "code hero." Rovit discusses a similar dynamic represented by the "tyro" and the "tutor." Arthur Waldhorn calls them the "apprentice" and the "exemplar." See Young, *Ernest Hemingway*, 64; Earl Rovit, *Ernest Hemingway* (New York: Twayne, 1963), 55; Arthur Waldhorn, *A Reader's Guide to Ernest Hemingway* (New York: Farrar, Straus and Giroux, 1972), 23.

93. Hemingway worked on "In Another Country" from September to November of 1926. See Paul Smith, *A Reader's Guide to the Short Stories of Ernest Hemingway*, 68.

94. Waldhorn, *A Reader's Guide to Ernest Hemingway*, 69.

95. Hemingway completed "Now I Lay Me" in December of 1926. See Paul Smith, *A Reader's Guide to the Short Stories of Ernest Hemingway*, 172.

96. Likewise, Josephs notes that "the trouble with Nick is not that he cannot sleep; it is that he is afraid to sleep because he will have an OBE [Out of Body Experience] and lose his soul." Flora, however, suggests that the title "lets us know that Nick has been traumatized in some deep ways by events of his childhood." Similarly, Kenneth Lynn interprets the story as related to "the hero's childhood" and a "confrontation between his parents." Young writes that Nick is trying to avoid "going crazy." See Allen Josephs, "Hemingway's Out of Body Experience," *Hemingway Review* 2, no. 2 (1983): 14; Joseph M. Flora, *Ernest Hemingway: A Study of the Short Fiction* (Boston: Twayne, 1989), 55; Kenneth S. Lynn, *Hemingway* (New York: Simon and Schuster, 1987), 105; and Young, *Ernest Hemingway*, 58.

97. Flora suggests that Nick "can't go on" because of the "petition that follows: 'And forgive us our trespasses, as we forgive those who trespass against us.' Nick is too inward turning," he states. See Flora, *Ernest Hemingway: A Study of the Short Fiction*, 56.

98. Scott Donaldson observes that Henry "depicts himself as a passive victim inundated by the flow of events." Donaldson argues that Henry does not show bravery in action and sees him as "unwilling—even when telling his story years later—to accept responsibility for his actions." See Scott Donaldson, "Frederic Henry's Escape and the Pose of Passivity," in *Hemingway: A Revaluation*, ed. Donald R. Noble (New York: The Whitston Publishing Company, 1983), 165–66.

99. H. R. Stoneback, "'Lovers' Sonnets Turn'd to Holy Psalms': The Soul's Song of Providence, the Scandal of Suffering, and Love in *A Farewell to Arms*," *Hemingway Review* 9, no. 1 (1989): 38.

100. The image of the house, the stable, and the canal has been the subject of much critical debate. Joseph Defalco calls it a "comforting and alluring manifestation of the death state conjured up by Nick's unconscious" that "suggests the pull toward immortality." Flora refers to the yellow house as "the spot where Nick was wounded" and "the dream prefigurement of his death." Josephs suggest that Nick is not remembering the place of his wounding; instead, his vision has, "replaced the memory of the moment of his wounding" as it becomes the "image of his own mortality." Frank Scafella interprets the yellow house as related to Nick's cowardice. Paul Quick describes the house as a "construct sublimating the memory of the Austrian shooting him." See Joseph Defalco, *The Hero in Hemingway's Short Stories* (Pittsburgh, PA: U of Pittsburgh P, 1963), 118; Flora, *Hemingway's Nick Adams*, 132; Josephs, "Hemingway's Out of Body Experience," 15; Frank Scafella, "The Way it Never Was on the Piave," in *Hemingway in Italy and Other Essays*, ed. Robert W. Lewis, (New York: Praeger, 1990), 184; Paul S. Quick, "Hemingway's 'A Way You'll Never Be' and Nick Adams's Search for Identity," *Hemingway Review* 22, no. 2 (2003): 36.

Conclusion

1. Ernest Hemingway, letter to "Dear Old Chieftain," March 3, 1919, in *The Letters of Ernest Hemingway, 1907–1922*, ed. Sandra Spanier and Robert W. Trogdon (Cambridge: Cambridge UP, 2011), 169.

2. Michael Reynolds, *Hemingway's First War: The Making of "A Farewell to Arms"* (New York: Basil Blackwell, 1987), 276.

3. Hemingway, letter to "Dear Old Chieftain," March 3, 1919, in *The Letters of Ernest Hemingway, 1907–1922*, 169.

4. Ernest Hemingway, letter to "Egregrio Amicissimo" [Bill Horne], March 5, 1919, in *The Letters of Ernest Hemingway, 1907–1922*, 174.

5. Michael Reynolds, *The Young Hemingway* (New York: Norton, 1998), 89.

6. Quoted in Paul Smith, "Hemingway's Apprentice Fiction: 1919–1921," in *New Critical Approaches to the Short Stories of Ernest Hemingway*, ed. Jackson J. Benson (Durham, NC: Duke UP, 1990), 137.

7. Reynolds, *The Young Hemingway*, 98.

8. Ernest Hemingway, "How to Be Popular in Peace Though a Slacker in War," *Toronto Star Weekly*, March 13, 1920, 11. Reprinted in *Dateline: Toronto, the Complete "Toronto Star" Dispatches, 1920–1924*, ed. William White (New York: Scribners, 1985), 10–11; Ernest Hemingway, "Lieutenants' Mustaches the Only Permanent Thing We Got Out of War," *Toronto Star Weekly*, April 10, 1920, 17. Reprinted in *Dateline: Toronto*, 19–20.

9. Ernest Hemingway, letter to Lawrence T. Barnett, April 30, 1919, *The Letters of Ernest Hemingway, 1907–1922*, 187.

10. Reynolds, *The Young Hemingway*, 170.

11. Hadley Richardson, letter to Ernest Hemingway, March 30, 1921, quoted in Reynolds, *The Young Hemingway*, 203.

12. Ernest Hemingway, letter to "Dear Old Gee" [Grace Quinlan], *The Letters of Ernest Hemingway, 1907–1922*, 290.

13. Reynolds, *The Young Hemingway*, 187.

14. Ibid., 224.

15. Hadley Richardson, letter to Ernest Hemingway, April 20, 1921, quoted in Reynolds, *The Young Hemingway*, 224.

16. Ernest Hemingway, "Roosevelt," *Poetry: A Magazine of Verse* 21, no. 4 (1923): 193. Reprinted in Ernest Hemingway, *Three Stories & Ten Poems* (Paris: Contact Publishing Company, 1923), 52 and *Complete Poems*, ed. Nicholas Gerogiannis (Lincoln, NE: U of Nebraska P, 1979), 45.

17. Ernest Hemingway, "Mitrailliatrice," *Poetry: A Magazine of Verse 21*, no. 4 (1923): 193. Reprinted as "Mitraigliatrice" in Hemingway, *Three Stories & Ten Poems*, 49 and "Mitrailliatrice" in *Complete Poems*, 37.

18. See Reynolds, *The Young Hemingway*, 179.

19. Hadley Richardson, letter to Ernest Hemingway, August 24, 1921, quoted in Reynolds, *The Young Hemingway*, 241.

20. Reynolds, *The Young Hemingway*, 252.

21. Carlos Baker, *Ernest Hemingway: A Life Story* (New York, Scribners, 1969), 82.

22. Reynolds, *The Young Hemingway*, 259.

23. Ernest Hemingway, letter to "Sherwood and Tennessee" [Anderson], c. 23 December 1921, *The Letters of Ernest Hemingway, 1907–1922*, 313.

24. Ernest Hemingway, "France Now in Hands of Old Professionals," *Toronto Daily Star*, February 4, 1922, 3. Reprinted in *Dateline: Toronto*, 90.

25. Ernest Hemingway, "Russian Delegates at Genoa Appear Not to Be of This World," *Toronto Daily Star*, April 27, 1922, 9. Reprinted in *Dateline: Toronto*, 153.

26. Ernest Hemingway, "'Pot-Shot Patriots' Unpopular in Italy," *Toronto Star Weekly*, June 24, 1922, 5. Reprinted in *Dateline: Toronto*, 175.

27. Ernest Hemingway, "Did Poincaré Laugh in Verdun Cemetery?" *Toronto Daily Star*, August 12, 1922, 4. Reprinted in *Dateline: Toronto*, 185–87.

28. Ernest Hemingway, "A Silent, Ghastly Procession Wends Way from Thrace," *Toronto Daily Star*, October 20, 1922, 17. Reprinted in *Dateline: Toronto*, 232.

29. Ernest Hemingway, "Turk Red Crescent Propaganda Agency," *Toronto Daily Star*, October 4, 1922, 1. Reprinted in *Dateline: Toronto*, 219.

30. Ernest Hemingway, "Mussolini, Europe's Prize Bluffer, More Like Bottomley Than Napoleon," *Toronto Daily Star*, January 27, 1923, 11. Reprinted in *Dateline: Toronto*, 253; Ernest Hemingway, "Gaudy Uniform Is Tchitcherin's Weakness, a 'Chocolate Soldier' of the Soviet Army," *Toronto Daily Star Weekly*, February 10, 1923, 2. Reprinted in *Dateline: Toronto*, 259.

31. Michael Reynolds and Robert W. Lewis discuss postwar histories as sources for *A Farewell to Arms*. See Reynolds, *Hemingway's First War*, 139–60 and Robert W. Lewis, "Hemingway in Italy: Making it Up," *Journal of Modern Literature* 9, no. 2 (1982): 227–36. Charles M. Oliver calls attention to five books of Hemingway's that "were published early enough to be useful as source material for *A Farewell to Arms*: Charles M. Bakewell's *The Story of the American Red Cross in Italy* (1920); Martin Hardie and Warner Allen's *Our Italian Front* (1920); Douglas Johnson's *Battlefields of the World War, Western and Southern Fronts: A Study of Military Geography* (1921); and two government monographs, *Report of the Department of Military Affairs, January to July*

1918 and *The War in Italy, No. 18* (soldier's edition, published in September in 1918)."
See Charles M. Oliver, "History and Imagined History," in *Teaching Hemingway's A Farewell to Arms*, ed. Lisa Tyler (Kent, OH: Kent State UP, 2008), 5. The volumes Oliver mentions are also catalogued in James D. Brasch and Joseph Sigman, *Hemingway's Library: A Composite Record* (New York: Garland, 1981).

32. Charles M. Bakewell, *The Story of the American Red Cross in Italy* (New York: The Macmillan Company, 1920), 19.

33. Ibid., 22.

34. Ibid., 23.

35. Ibid.

36. Ibid., 24.

37. Warner Allen and Martin Hardie, *Our Italian Front* (London: A. & C. Black, Ltd., 1920), 154.

38. Ibid., 158.

39. Bakewell, *The Story of the American Red Cross in Italy*, 30.

40. *Our Italian Front* also includes Martin Hardie's illustrations. One of them depicts a "Casualty on the Montello" with a caption indicating that the scene is that of "the interior of a church used as a casualty station. Of all the churches in the war zone on both sides of the Piave few were left as anything but a mere shell." The sketch shows two stretcher bearers carrying a wounded man while another soldier sits on a pile of rubble against the broken wall of a church. The picture is remarkably similar to that of Hemingway's vignette describing "Nick" who "sat against the wall of the church" as he surveys the ruins around him and waits for stretcher bearers. See Martin Hardie, "A Casualty on the Montello," in *Our Italian Front*, plate 13. See also, Ernest Hemingway, "Chapter VI," in *The Complete Short Stories of Ernest Hemingway: The Finca Vigía Edition* (New York: Scribners, 1987), 105.

41. For discussion of Pound's influence on Hemingway, see Milton A. Cohen, *Hemingway's Laboratory: The Paris "in our time"* (Tuscaloosa, AL: U of Alabama P, 2005), 16–21. See also Michael Reynolds, *Hemingway: The Paris Years* (New York: W. W. Norton & Company, 1999), 30–31. In *A Moveable Feast*, Hemingway refers to Pound as the "man I liked and trusted the most as a critic then, the man who believed in the *mot juste*—the one and only correct word to use." See Ernest Hemingway, *A Moveable Feast* (New York: Touchstone, 1992), 134. Subsequent references to *A Moveable Feast* are to this edition.

42. Ernest Hemingway, "In Our Time," *Little Review: Quarterly of Art and Letters* 9, no. 3 (1923): 3–5.

43. Ernest Hemingway, "Champs D'Honneur," *Poetry: A Magazine of Verse* 21, no. 4 (1923): 195. See also Audre Hanneman, *Ernest Hemingway: A Comprehensive Bibliography* (Princeton: Princeton UP, 1967), 5.

44. See the back cover of Ernest Hemingway, *in our time* (Paris: Three Mountain Press, 1924). See also Hanneman, *Ernest Hemingway*, 6.

45. Ernest Hemingway, *in our time* (Paris: Three Mountain Press, 1924), 15. Subsequent references are to this edition.

46. Ernest Hemingway, letter to "Dear Ezra" [Pound], c. 5 August, 1923, in *Ernest*

Hemingway: Selected Letters, 1917–1961, ed. Carlos Baker (New York: Charles Scribner's Sons, 1981), 91.

47. Quoted in James Mellow, *Hemingway: A Life Without Consequences* (Boston: Houghton Mifflin, 1992), 152.

48. Ernest Hemingway, "Big Two-Hearted River," *This Quarter* 1, no. 1 (1925): 110–28.

49. Scholars have debated the extent to which *In Our Time* is a unified work. As Michael Reynolds has noted, "we are not yet in agreement on the logic of the book's unity, but we do agree that it has unity." James Nagel offers one explanation in his treatment of the volume as a short-story cycle. Nagel notes that the "background of the war" in other stories and sketches is "central" to understanding "Big Two-Hearted River." See Michael S. Reynolds, "Looking Backward," introduction to *Critical Essays on Ernest Hemingway's "In Our Time,"* ed. Michael S. Reynolds (Boston: G. K. Hall & Co., 1983), 11 and James Nagel, *The Contemporary American Short-Story Cycle: The Ethnic Resonance of Genre* (Baton Rouge, LA: Louisiana State UP, 2001), 246–47.

50. See Philip Young, *Ernest Hemingway: A Reconsideration* (University Park, PA: The Pennsylvania State UP, 1966), 30.

51. Ernest Hemingway, "Big Two-Hearted River," *The Complete Short Stories of Ernest Hemingway: The Finca Vigía Edition,* 164. Subsequent references to "Big Two-Hearted River" are to this edition.

52. Ernest Hemingway, letter to "Dear Charlie" [Charles Poore], January 23, 1953, in *Ernest Hemingway: Selected Letters,* 798.

53. See Ernest Hemingway, *Death in the Afternoon* (New York: Scribners, 1960), 191. Scholars debate the extent to which "Big Two-Hearted River" is a story about the impact of war. See, for example, Robert Paul Lamb, "The Currents of Memory: Hemingway's 'Big Two-Hearted River' as Metafiction," in *Ernest Hemingway and the Geography of Memory,* ed. Mark Cirino and Mark P. Ott (Kent, OH: The Kent State UP, 2010), 166–69.

54. Ernest Hemingway, *The Sun Also Rises* (New York: Charles Scribner's Sons, 1926), 31. Subsequent references are to this edition.

55. Hemingway, *A Moveable Feast,* 29–30. See also the epigraphs in Hemingway, *The Sun Also Rises.*

56. Ernest Hemingway, "In Another Country," in *The Complete Short Stories of Ernest Hemingway: The Finca Vigía Edition,* 208.

57. Ernest Hemingway, "Che Ti Dice La Patria?" *The Complete Short Stories of Ernest Hemingway: The Finca Vigía Edition,* 230.

58. Ernest Hemingway, "A Simple Inquiry," in *The Complete Short Stories of Ernest Hemingway: The Finca Vigía Edition,* 250, 251, 252.

59. Ernest Hemingway, "Now I Lay Me," *The Complete Short Stories of Ernest Hemingway: The Finca Vigía Edition,* 282.

60. Ernest Hemingway, "Introduction to *A Farewell to Arms* (1948)," in *Hemingway and the Mechanism of Fame: Statements, Public Letters, Introductions, Forewords, Prefaces, Blurbs, Reviews, and Endorsements,* ed. Matthew J. Bruccoli with Judith S. Baughman

(Columbia, SC: U of South Carolina P, 2006), 96. Reprinted from Ernest Hemingway, "Introduction," in *A Farewell to Arms* (New York: Scribners, 1948).

61. Ernest Hemingway, *A Farewell to Arms* (New York: Scribner, 1995), 14. Subsequent references are to this edition.

62. Edmund Wilson, "Mr. Hemingway's Dry-Points," in *Ernest Hemingway: The Critical Reception*, ed. Robert O. Stephens (New York: Burt Franklin & Co., 1977), 1. Reprinted from *Dial*, October 1924, 340–41.

63. Ibid., 2.

64. Review of *Three Stories & Ten Poems* and *in our time*, in *Ernest Hemingway: The Critical Reception*, ed. Stephens, 3. Reprinted from the *Kansas City Star*, December 20, 1924, 6.

65. Ernest Walsh, "Mr. Hemingway's Prose," in *Ernest Hemingway: The Critical Reception*, ed. Stephens, 11, 13. Reprinted from *This Quarter* 1 (Winter 1925–26): 319–21.

66. Conrad Aiken, "Expatriates," in *Ernest Hemingway: The Critical Reception*, ed. Stephens, 33, 34. Reprinted from *New York Herald Tribune Books*, October 31, 1926, vii.

67. Allen Tate, "Hard-Boiled," in *Ernest Hemingway: The Critical Reception*, ed. Stephens, 42. Reprinted from the *Nation*, December 15, 1926, 642–44.

68. Percy Hutchinson, "Mr. Hemingway Shows Himself a Master Craftsman in the Short Story," in *Ernest Hemingway: The Critical Reception*, ed. Stephens, 55. Reprinted from *New York Herald Tribune Books*, October 16, 1927, 9, 27.

69. Dorothy Parker, "A Book of Great Short Stories," in *Ernest Hemingway: The Critical Reception*, ed. Stephens, 58. Reprinted from the *New Yorker*, October 29, 1927, 92–94.

70. Clifton P. Fadiman, "A Fine American Novel," in *Ernest Hemingway: The Critical Reception*, ed. Stephens, 84. Reprinted from the *Nation*, October 30, 1929, 497–98.

71. Malcolm Cowley, "Not Yet Demobilized," in *Ernest Hemingway: The Critical Reception*, ed. Stephens, 74. Reprinted from *New York Herald Tribune Books*, October 6, 1929, 1, 6.

72. George Monteiro, "Introduction," in *Critical Essays on Ernest Hemingway's "A Farewell to Arms,"* ed. George Monteiro (New York: G. K. Hall & Co., 1994), 4.

73. Quoted in Monteiro, *Critical Essays on Ernest Hemingway's "A Farewell to Arms,"* 4.

74. Quoted in ibid.

75. Robert Herrick, "What Is Dirt?" in *Ernest Hemingway: The Critical Reception*, ed. Stephens, 89. Reprinted from the *Bookman* 70 (November 1929): 258–62.

76. M. K. Hare, "Is it Dirt or Is it Art?" in *Ernest Hemingway: The Critical Reception*, ed. Stephens, 101. Reprinted from the *Bookman* 71 (March 1930): xiv–xv.

77. Robert W. Bates, addendum to "Ambulance Report No. 9," Robert W. Bates Papers, private collection. See also Stephen Bates, "'Unpopularity Is the Least of My Worries': Captain R. W. Bates and Lieutenant E. M. Hemingway," *Hemingway Review* 29, no. 1 (2009): 58.

78. Monteiro, *Critical Essays on Ernest Hemingway's "A Farewell to Arms,"* 5.

79. Quoted in James Nagel, "Hemingway and the Italian Legacy," in *Hemingway in Love and War: The Lost Diary of Agnes von Kurowsky, Her Letters, and Correspondence*

of Ernest Hemingway, ed. Henry S. Villard and James Nagel (Boston: Northeastern UP, 1989), 251.

80. See Kenneth S. Lynn, *Hemingway* (New York: Simon and Schuster, 1987), 86 and Lewis, "Hemingway in Italy: Making it Up," 216.

81. Ernest Hemingway, letter to "Dear Mr. [Maxwell] Perkins, February 19, 1927," *Selected Letters*, 247.

82. See Ernest Hemingway, letter to "Dear Max" [Perkins], September 3, 1930, in *The Only Thing That Counts: The Ernest Hemingway/Maxwell Perkins Correspondence 1925–1947*, ed. Matthew J. Bruccoli with the assistance of Robert W. Trogdon (Scribner, 1996), 147. "Introduction by the Author" was later titled "On the Quai at Smyrna" in *The Fifth Column and the First Forty-nine Stories* and subsequent editions of *In Our Time*. See Ernest Hemingway, *The Fifth Column and the First Forty-nine Stories* (New York: Scribners, 1938). See also Hanneman, *Ernest Hemingway*, 9.

83. See ibid.

84. Ernest Hemingway, letter to "Dear Max" [Perkins], December 7, 1932, *Selected Letters*, 379.

85. See Nagel, "Hemingway and the Italian Legacy," 251; Lewis, "Hemingway in Italy: Making it Up," 216; and Lynn, *Hemingway*, 86.

86. Clifton Fadiman, "A Letter to Mr. Hemingway," in *Ernest Hemingway: The Critical Reception*, ed. Stephens, 136. Reprinted from the *New Yorker* October 28, 1933, 74–75.

87. T. S. Matthews, "Fiction by Young and Old," in *Ernest Hemingway: The Critical Reception*, ed. Stephens, 145. Reprinted from *New Republic*, November 15, 1933, 24–25.

88. Archibald MacLeish, "Post-War Writers and Pre-War Readers," *New Republic*, June 10, 1940, 790. See also Michael Reynolds, *Hemingway: The Final Years* (New York: W. W. Norton & Company), 24.

89. MacLeish, "Post-War Writers and Pre-War Readers," 790.

90. Ibid.

91. Ernest Hemingway, "Letter in 'War Writers on Democracy,'" in Bruccoli, *Hemingway and the Mechanism of Fame*, 80. Reprinted from *Life*, June 24, 1940, 8.

92. Ernest Hemingway, "Introduction" in *Men at War: The Best War Stories of All Time*, ed. Ernest Hemingway (New York: Bramhall House, 1979), xiii.

93. Ibid., xxvii.

94. Malcolm Cowley, "Hemingway Portrait of an Old Soldier Preparing to Die," in *Ernest Hemingway: The Critical Reception*, ed. Stephens, 298. Reprinted from *New York Herald Tribune Book Review*, September 10, 1950, 1, 6.

95. Ernest Hemingway, *Across the River and Into the Trees* (New York: Scribner, 1987), 39.

96. Ernest Hemingway, "A Way You'll Never Be," in *The Complete Short Stories of Ernest Hemingway: The Finca Vigía Edition*, 312; Hemingway, "Chapter VI," in *The Complete Short Stories of Ernest Hemingway: The Finca Vigía Edition*, 105; see also, Hemingway, *A Farewell to Arms*, 243.

Bibliography

"5,000,000 in Day's Parade." *New York Times*, May 19, 1918, 9.

"9 Chicagoans Named in Lists of Casualties." *Chicago Evening Post*, July 16, 1918, 1.

Adair, William. "Hemingway's 'A Veteran Visits His Old Front': Images and Situations for the Fiction." *ANQ: A Quarterly Journal of Short Articles, Notes, and Reviews* 8, no. 1 (1995): 27–31.

"Aid for Italy Is Hastened by American Red Cross." *Red Cross Bulletin*, November 13, 1918, 2.

Aiken, Conrad. "Expatriates." *New York Herald Tribune Books*, October 31, 1926, vii.

"Al on Permission." *Come Stà*, April 10, 1918, 3.

Allen, Warner and Martin Hardie. *Our Italian Front*. London: A. & C. Black, Ltd., 1920.

American National Red Cross Records. National Archives, College Park, MD.

"The American Red Cross at the Front." *Red Cross Bulletin*, July 5, 1918, 1.

"And Yet More Driving Power." *Ciao*, April, 1918, 1.

"A. T. Hemingway." *Oak Leaves*, July 20, 1918, 2.

Baker, Carlos. *Ernest Hemingway: A Life Story*. New York: Scribners, 1969.

———. *The Writer As Artist*. Princeton, NJ: Princeton UP, 1963.

"Baker Will Be Orator in Italy-America Day." *New York Times*, May 19, 1918, 5.

Bakewell, Charles M. *The Story of the American Red Cross in Italy*. New York: Macmillan, 1920.

Barton, William. *Our Fight for the Heritage of Humanity*. Oak Park, IL: First Congregational Church, 1918.

———. *The Praise of the Wrath of Man and The Rebuilding of the World, Two Sermons*. Oak Park, IL: First Congregational Church, 1918.

Bates, Robert W. Papers. Private collection.

———. "Report of Captain Bates." *Red Cross Bulletin*, July 5, 1918, 7.

Bates, Stephen. "'An Apostle for His Work': The Death of Lieutenant Edward Michael McKey." *Hemingway Review* 29, no. 2 (2010): 61–73.

———. "'Unpopularity Is the Least of My Worries': Captain R. W. Bates and Lieutenant E. M. Hemingway." *Hemingway Review* 29, no. 1 (2009): 47–60.

"Beg Pardon, Ring!" *Avanti*, February 1, 1918, 4.

"Belgium Scorned Peace." *Kansas City Star*, October 29, 1917, 1.

"Blames Italian Leaders." *Kansas City Star*, November 30, 1917, A15.

Brasch, James D. and Joseph Sigman. *Hemingway's Library: A Composite Record*. New York: Garland, 1981.

Brenner, Gerry. "'Enough of a Bad Gamble': Correcting the Misinformation on Hemingway's Captain James Gamble." *Hemingway Review* 20, no. 1 (2000): 90–96.

Brian, Denis. *The True Gen: An Intimate Portrait of Hemingway by Those Who Knew Him.* New York: Grove Press, 1988.

Bruccoli, Matthew J., ed. *Conversations with Ernest Hemingway.* Jackson, MI: UP of Mississippi, 1986.

———. *Hemingway and the Mechanism of Fame: Statements, Public Letters, Introductions, Forewords, Prefaces, Blurbs, Reviews, and Endorsements.* With Judith S. Baughman. Columbia, SC: U of South Carolina P, 2006.

———. *The Only Thing That Counts: The Ernest Hemingway/Maxwell Perkins Correspondence 1925–1947.* With the assistance of Robert W. Trogdon. New York: Scribner, 1996.

Brumback, Theodore. "With Hemingway Before *A Farewell to Arms*." *Kansas City Star*, December 6, 1936, C1-C3.

Buske, Morris. "What if Ernest Had Been Born on the Other Side of the Street?" In *Ernest Hemingway: The Oak Park Legacy*, edited by James Nagel, 209–16. Tuscaloosa, AL: U of Alabama P, 1996.

Buswell, Leslie. *With the American Ambulance Field Service in France: Personal Letters of a Driver at the Front.* Boston: Houghton Mifflin Company, 1916.

Cacciapuoti, F. "Letter from an Italian Liaison Officer." *Red Cross Bulletin*, July 5, 1918, 7.

"The Cavalry Saved Italy." *Kansas City Star*, November 4, 1917, A8.

Clark, C. E. Frazer, Jr. "American Red Cross Reports on the Wounding of Lieutenant Ernest M. Hemingway—1918." *Fitzgerald/Hemingway Annual* (1974): 131–36.

Clark, Col. C. E. Frazer. "This Is the Way it Was on the *Chicago* and At the Front: 1917 War Letters." *Fitzgerald/Hemingway Annual* (1970): 153–68.

Clark, Harvey C. *Report of the Department of the Adjutant General of Missouri, January 1, 1917–December 31, 1920.* Jefferson City, MO: Office of the Adjutant General, 1921.

Cohen, Milton A. *Hemingway's Laboratory: The Paris "in our time."* Tuscaloosa, AL: U of Alabama P, 2005.

———. "War Medals for Sale? Public Bravery vs. Private Courage in Hemingway's WWI Writing." *North Dakota Quarterly* 68, nos. 2–3 (2001): 287–94.

Comley, Nancy R. "The Italian Education of Ernest Hemingway." In *Hemingway's Italy: New Perspectives*, edited by Rena Sanderson, 41–50. Baton Rouge, LA: Louisiana State UP, 2006.

Cowley, Malcolm. *Exiles Return: A Literary Odyssey of the 1920s.* New York: Viking, 1951.

———. "Hemingway Portrait of an Old Soldier Preparing to Die." *New York Herald Tribune Book Review*, September 10, 1950, 1, 6.

———. "Not Yet Demobilized." *New York Herald Tribune*, October 6, 1929, 1, 6.

Culver, Michael. "The 'Short-Stop Run': Hemingway in Kansas City." *Hemingway Review* 2, no. 1 (1982): 77–80.

Daiker, Donald A. "The Affirmative Conclusion of *The Sun Also Rises*." In *Critical Essays on Ernest Hemingway's "The Sun Also Rises,"* edited by James Nagel, 39–56. New York: G. K. Hall & Co., 1995

Davis, Richard Harding. "Lifeboat Drills on Ships in the War Zone." *New York Times,* November 21, 1915, SM15.

Davison, Henry P. *The American Red Cross in the Great War.* New York: Macmillan, 1920.

Dean, Roselle. "First Lieutenant Hemingway Comes Back Riddled with Bullets and Decorated with Two Medals." *Oak Parker,* February 1, 1918, 13.

"Deeper into Italy." *Kansas City Star,* October 28, 1917, 1.

Defalco, Joseph. *The Hero in Hemingway's Short Stories.* Pittsburgh, PA: U of Pittsburgh P, 1963.

Derounian, Kathryn Zabelle. "An Examination of the Drafts of Hemingway's Chapters 'Nick sat against the wall of the church. . . . '" In *Critical Essays on Ernest Hemingway's "In Our Time,"* edited by Michael S. Reynolds, 54–65. Boston: G. K. Hall & Co., 1983.

Donaldson, Scott. *By Force of Will: The Life and Art of Ernest Hemingway.* New York, Viking, 1977.

———. "Frederic Henry's Escape and the Pose of Passivity." In *Hemingway: A Revaluation,* edited by Donald R. Noble, 165–85. New York: The Whitston Publishing Company, 1983.

Dos Passos, John. *The Best Times: An Informal Memoir.* New York: The New American Library, 1966.

———. "Books." *New Masses,* December 1, 1929, 16.

———. *The Fourteenth Chronicle: Letters and Diaries of John Dos Passos.* Edited by Townsend Ludington. Boston: Gambit Incorporated, 1973.

———. *One Man's Initiation—1917.* London: The Anchor Press, Ltd., 1920.

———. *Three Soldiers.* New York: George H. Doran Company, 1921.

"E. M. Hemingway Wounded." *Kansas City Star,* July 13, 1918, 1.

Ebersold, Frederick. "Hanna Club Has Rousing First Meeting with 'Ernie' Hemingway as Speaker." *Trapeze,* February 7, 1919, 2.

"Editorial Staff." *Ciao,* June 1918, 2.

Edmonds, James E. *History of the Great War: Military Operations Italy 1915–1919.* London: The Imperial War Museum, 1999.

Enlistment Card for Ernest Hemingway. Military Records. Missouri State Archives, Jefferson City, MO.

Fadiman, Clifton P. "A Fine American Novel." *Nation,* October 30, 1929, 497–98.

———. "A Letter to Mr. Hemingway." *New Yorker,* October 28, 1933, 74–75.

Fenton, Charles A. "Ambulance Drivers in France and Italy: 1914–1918." *American Quarterly* 3, no. 4 (1951): 326–43.

———. *The Apprenticeship of Ernest Hemingway: The Early Years.* New York: Viking, 1954.

Fife, George Buchanon. "Answering Italy's Cry for Help: With the Red Cross Ambulance on their Dash from Paris to Milan." *Red Cross Magazine* 13, no. 5 (May 1918): 37–41.

"First $100,000 Gift in Red Cross Drive." *New York Times,* May 14, 1918, 13.

Fisher, Laurence. "Editorial Staff." *Ciao,* May 1918, 2.

"Five U-Boats Sunk in a Single Week." *New York Times,* May 16, 1918, 5.

Flora, Joseph. *Ernest Hemingway: A Study of the Short Fiction.* Boston: Twayne, 1989.

———. *Hemingway's Nick Adams*. Baton Rouge, LA: Louisiana State UP, 1982.

Florczyk, Steven. "A Captain in Hemingway's Court? The Story of Ernest Hemingway, *A Farewell to Arms*, and the Unpublished Papers of Robert W. Bates." In *Hemingway's Italy: New Perspectives*, edited by Rena Sanderson, 62–72. Baton Rouge, LA: Louisiana State UP, 2006.

Fussell, Paul. "Ernest Hemingway, Semi-Weirdo." In Fussell, *Uniforms: Why We Are What We Wear*, 132–35. Boston: Houghton Mifflin, 2002.

———. *The Great War and Modern Memory*. London: Oxford UP, 1975.

Gajdusek, Robert E. "Set Piece." *Hemingway Review* 14, no. 2 (1995): 127.

Gandolfi, Luca. "The Outskirts of Literature: Uncovering the Munitions Factory in 'A Natural History of the Dead.'" *Hemingway Review* 19, no. 2 (2000): 105–07.

"George Fife Dies; Newspaper Man." *New York Times*, March 13, 1939, 21.

"German Sea Raider Chased the *Chicago*." *New York Times*, February 23, 1916, 3.

"Go Together from the Star to the Italian Front." *Kansas City Star*, May 13, 1918, 4.

Griffin, Peter. *Along with Youth: Hemingway, the Early Years*. New York: Oxford UP, 1985.

Grimes, Larry. "Hemingway's Religious Odyssey: The Oak Park Years." In *Ernest Hemingway: The Oak Park Legacy*, edited by James Nagel, 37–58. Tuscaloosa, AL: U of Alabama P, 1996.

Guarino, Jean. *Yesterday: A Historical View of Oak Park, Illinois*. Oak Park, IL: Oak Ridge Press, 2000.

Hanneman, Audre. *Ernest Hemingway: A Comprehensive Bibliography*. Princeton, NJ: Princeton UP, 1967.

Hansen, Arlen J. *Gentlemen Volunteers: The Story of the American Ambulance Drivers in the Great War, August 1914–September 1918*. New York: Arcade Publishing, 1996.

"Has 227 Wounds, but Is Looking for Job." *New York Sun*, January 22, 1919, 8.

Hare, M. K. "Is it Dirt or Is it Art?" *Bookman* 71 (March 1930): xiv–xv.

Hemingway, Ernest. *Across the River and Into the Trees*. New York: Scribner, 1978.

———. "Al Receives Another Letter." *Ciao*, June 1918, 2.

———. *Complete Poems*. Edited by Nicholas Gerogiannis. Lincoln, NE: U of Nebraska P, 1979.

———. *The Complete Short Stories of Ernest Hemingway: The Finca Vigía Edition*. New York: Scribner, 1987.

———. "Crossroads–An Anthology." Printed in Peter Griffin, *Along with Youth*. New York: Oxford UP, 1985, 124–27.

———. *Dateline: Toronto, the Complete "Toronto Star" Dispatches, 1920–1924*. Edited by William White. New York: Scribners, 1985.

———. *Death in the Afternoon*. New York: Scribners, 1960.

———. Ernest Hemingway Collection. Harry Ransom Humanities Research Center, Austin, TX.

———. Ernest Hemingway Collection. John F. Kennedy Library, Boston.

———. Ernest Hemingway Collection. McKeldin Library, College Park, MD.

———. Ernest Hemingway Collection. Pennsylvania State University, University Park, PA.

————. *Ernest Hemingway: Selected Letters, 1917–1961.* Edited by Carlos Baker. New York: Charles Scribner's Sons, 1981.

————. *A Farewell to Arms.* New York: Scribners, 1995.

————. *The Fifth Column and the First Forty-nine Stories.* New York: Scribners, 1938.

————. *Green Hills of Africa.* New York: Touchstone, 1996.

————. *Hemingway at Oak Park High: The High School Writings of Ernest Hemingway, 1916–1917.* Edited by Cynthia Maziarka and Donald Vogel Jr., Oak Park, IL: Oak Park and River Forest High School, 1993.

————. Hemingway Mss. III. The Lilly Library, Bloomington, IN.

————. "In Our Time." *Little Review: Quarterly Journal of Art and Letters* 9, no. 3 (1923): 3–5.

————. *In Our Time.* New York: Scribners, 1996.

————. *in our time.* Paris: Three Mountain Press, 1924.

————. "Introduction." In *A Farewell to Arms,* vii–xi. New York: Scribners, 1948.

————. "Introduction." In *Men at War: The Best War Stories of All Time,* xi–xxvii. New York: Bramhall House, 1979.

————. Letter in "War Writers on Democracy." *Life,* June 24, 1940, 8.

————. *The Letters of Ernest Hemingway, 1907–1922.* Edited by Sandra Spanier and Robert W. Trogdon. Cambridge: Cambridge UP, 2011.

————. *Men Without Women.* New York: Scribners, 1997.

————. *A Moveable Feast.* New York: Touchstone, 1992.

————. "Night Before Landing." In *The Nick Adams Stories,* 137–42. New York: Scribners, 1972.

————. *The Sun Also Rises.* New York: Charles Scribner's Sons, 1954.

————. *Three Stories & Ten Poems.* Paris: Contact Publishing Company, 1923.

————. *The Torrents of Spring.* New York: Scribners, 1998.

————. "Wanderings." *Poetry: A Magazine of Verse* 21, no. 4 (1923): 193–95.

————. *Winner Take Nothing.* New York: Charles Scribner's Sons, 1933.

Herrick, Robert. "What Is Dirt?" *Bookman* 70 (November 1929): 258–62.

Hobhouse, Janet. *Everybody Who Was Anybody: A Biography of Gertrude Stein.* New York: G. P. Putnam's Sons, 1975.

Hotchner, A. E. *Papa Hemingway: A Personal Memoir.* New York: Random House, 1966.

Howe, M. A. De Wolfe. *The Harvard Volunteers in Europe: Personal Records of Experience in Military, Ambulance, and Hospital Service.* Cambridge, MA: Harvard UP, 1916.

"Humor." *Soixante Trois,* August 5, 1917, 2.

Hungerford, Eric. *With the Doughboy in France.* New York: Macmillan, 1920.

Hutchinson, Percy. "Mr. Hemingway Shows Himself a Master Craftsman in the Short Story." *New York Herald Tribune Books,* October 16, 1927, 9, 27.

"Italian Line Is Holding." *Kansas City Star,* November 15, 1917, 1.

"Italy and America." *Ciao,* May 1918, 1.

"Italy Calls on America." *Kansas City Star,* November 4, 1917, 1.

"Italy Gets Six Ambulances." *New York Times,* December 17, 1917, 2.

"Italy on Its New Line." *Kansas City Star,* November 19, 1917, 1.

James, Henry. *The American Volunteer Motor-Ambulance Corps in France: A Letter to the Editor of an American Journal.* London: Macmillan, 1914.

Jenkins, Burris. "Italian Front a Keystone." *Kansas City Star,* October 24, 1917, 6.

———. "Italy, a Country of Song." *Kansas City Star,* October 25, 1917, 8.

———. "Trieste Is Key to Victory." *Kansas City Star,* October 26, 1917, A8.

Johnston, Kenneth G. "'A Way You'll Never Be': A Mission of Morale." *Studies in Short Fiction* 23, no. 4 (1986): 429–35.

Josephs, Allen. "Hemingway's Out of Body Experience." *Hemingway Review* 2, no. 2 (1983): 11–17.

———. *"Toreo:* The Moral Axis of *The Sun Also Rises."* In *Critical Essays on Ernest Hemingway's "The Sun Also Rises,"* edited by James Nagel, 126–40. New York: G. K. Hall & Co., 1995.

"Justices Receive New Court House." *New York Times,* February 12, 1927, 14.

Kale, Verna. "Hemingway's Poetry and the Paris Apprenticeship." *Hemingway Review* 26, no. 2 (2007): 58–73.

Keene, Jennifer D. *Doughboys, the Great War, and the Remaking of America.* Baltimore, MD: Johns Hopkins UP, 2001.

Lamb, Robert Paul. "The Currents of Memory: Hemingway's 'Big Two-Hearted River' as Metafiction." In *Ernest Hemingway and the Geography of Memory,* edited by Mark Cirino and Mark P. Ott, 166–85. Kent, OH: The Kent State UP, 2010.

Lewis, Robert W. *"A Farewell to Arms": The War of the Words.* New York: Twayne, 1992.

———. "Hemingway in Italy: Making it Up." *Journal of Modern Literature* 9, no. 2 (1982): 209–36.

"Lieut. E. M. McKey Killed on the Italian Battlefront." *New York Times,* June 19, 1918, 1.

"Lieut. McKey, of Red Cross, Killed by Shell in Italy." *Washington Post,* June 19, 1918, 4.

"Liner *Chicago* Afire, Reaches the Azores." *New York Times,* October 28, 1916, 1.

"Loss of U-Boats Exceeds Output." *New York Times,* May 14, 1918, 3.

Lowell, Guy. *More Small Italian Villas and Farmhouses.* New York: Architectural Book Publishing Company, 1920.

———. *Smaller Italian Villas and Farmhouses.* New York: Architectural Book Publishing Company, 1916.

———. *Report of the Department of Military Affairs January to July, 1918.* Rome: American Red Cross, 1918.

Lynn, Kenneth S. *Hemingway.* New York: Simon and Schuster, 1987.

MacLeish, Archibald. "Post-War Writers and Pre-War Readers." *New Republic,* June 10, 1940, 789–90.

Martin, Robert A. "Hemingway and the Ambulance Drivers in *A Farewell to Arms."* In *Ernest Hemingway: Six Decades of Criticism,* edited by Linda W. Wagner, 195–204. East Lansing, MI: Michigan State UP, 1987.

Matthews, T. S. "Fiction by Young and Old." *New Republic,* November 15, 1933, 24–25.

———. "Nothing Ever Happens to the Brave." *New Republic,* October 9, 1929, 208–10.

Mellow, James. *Hemingway: A Life without Consequences.* New York: Houghton Mifflin, 1992.

Meyers, Jeffrey. *Hemingway: A Biography.* New York: Harper & Row, 1985.

Monteiro, George. "Introduction," *Critical Essays on Ernest Hemingway's "A Farewell to Arms,"* edited by George Monteiro, 1–27. New York: G. K. Hall & Co., 1994.

Moreland, Kim. "Bringing 'Italianicity' Home." In *Hemingway's Italy: New Perspectives,* edited by Rena Sanderson, 51–61. Baton Rouge, LA: Louisiana State UP, 2006.

Morris, Gouverneur. *His Daughter.* New York: Scribners, 1918.

"My Elegy (Grey's Apologies to Me)." *Ciao,* May, 1918, 3.

Nagel, James. "Catherine Barkley and Retrospective Narration." In *Ernest Hemingway: Six Decades of Criticism,* edited by Linda W. Wagner, 171–85. East Lansing, MI: Michigan State UP, 1987.

———. *The Contemporary American Short-Story Cycle: The Ethnic Resonance of Genre.* Baton Rouge, LA: Louisiana State UP, 2001.

———. "The Hemingways and Oak Park, Illinois: Background and Legacy." In *Ernest Hemingway and the Oak Park Legacy,* edited by James Nagel, 3–19. Tuscaloosa, AL: The U of Alabama P, 1996.

Nash, Jack. "From Paris to the Italian Front." *Avanti,* January 1, 1918, 4.

"Need 74 Men for the 7th." *Kansas City Star,* March 26, 1917, 1.

"No Delay on Austria." *Kansas City Star,* December 5, 1917, 1.

"Now It's Come Stà." *Come Stà,* March 10, 1918, 1.

"Oak Park in the War." *Oak Leaves,* April 14, 1917, 6.

"Official Communiqué." *Avanti,* January 1, 1918, 2.

Oldsey, Bernard. *Hemingway's Hidden Craft: The Writing of "A Farewell to Arms."* University Park, PA: Pennsylvania State UP, 1979.

Oliver, Charles M. "History and Imagined History." In *Teaching Hemingway's "A Farewell to Arms,"* edited by Lisa Tyler, 3–15. Kent, OH: Kent State UP, 2008.

"Our Day." *Ciao,* June, 1918, 3.

"Our Part in the Big Drive." *Ciao,* June, 1918, 4.

Page, Thomas Nelson. *Italy and the World War.* New York: Charles Scribner's Sons, 1920.

Parker, Dorothy. "A Book of Great Short Stories." *New Yorker,* October 29, 1927, 92–94.

"Patents Applied For." *Come Stà,* March 10, 1918, 4.

Paul, Steve. "'Drive,' He Said: How Ted Brumback Helped Steer Ernest Hemingway into War and Writing." *Hemingway Review* 27, no. 1 (2007): 21–38.

———. "Preparing for War and Writing: What the Young Hemingway Read in the *Kansas City Star,* 1917–1918." *Hemingway Review* 23, no. 2 (2004): 5–20.

Persons, E. E. "The Ambulance Service." *New York Times,* July 10, 1917, 11.

Pirocchi, Angelo L. *Italian Arditi Elite Assault Troops 1917–20.* Oxford: Osprey Publishing, 2004.

"Plan for Italy Day." *New York Times,* May 15, 1918, 12.

Poor, H. E. "The Seventh Missouri Infantry." *History of the Missouri National Guard,* edited by the Missouri National Guard, 147–48. Jefferson City, MO: Military Council, Missouri National Guard, 1934.

"A Poor Month for the U-Boats." *New York Times,* May 23, 1918, 12.

"President Leads Red Cross Parade." *New York Times*, May 19, 1918, 8.

Quick, Paul S. "Hemingway's 'A Way You'll Never Be' and Nick Adams's Search for Identity." *Hemingway Review* 22, no. 2 (2003): 30–44.

"Recruit for Red Cross." *Kansas City Star*, April 21, 1918, A3.

"Red Cross Aid to Italy." *New York Times*, May 21, 1918, 24.

"Red Cross Benefits." *New York Times*, May 19, 1918, 56.

"Red Cross Calls Men." *Kansas City Star*, February 22, 1918, 3.

"Red Cross Commission to Italy." *Red Cross Bulletin*, August 4, 1917, 1.

"Red Cross Draws Many." *Kansas City Times*, April 23, 1918, 5.

"Red Cross in Italy." *New York Times*, April 14, 1918, E3.

"Red Cross to March by President Today." *New York Times*, May 18, 1918, 11.

"Red Cross Volunteers Face Shells While Aiding Italians in Battle." *Washington Post*, September 1, 1918, 8.

"Report of the Department of Military Affairs January to July, 1918." Edited by Ken Panda. *Hemingway Review* 18, no. 2 (1999): 72–89.

Review of *Three Stories & Ten Poems* and *in our time*. *Kansas City Star*, December 20, 1924, 6.

Reynolds, Michael. *Hemingway: The Final Years*. New York: Norton, 1999.

———. *Hemingway: The Paris Years*. New York: Norton, 1999.

———. *Hemingway's First War: The Making of "A Farewell to Arms."* New York: Basil Blackwell, 1987.

———. "Looking Backward." *Critical Essays on Ernest Hemingway's "In Our Time,"* edited by Michael S. Reynolds, 1–12. Boston: G. K. Hall & Co., 1983.

———. *The Young Hemingway*. New York: Norton, 1998.

Reynolds, Michael S., ed. *Critical Essays on Ernest Hemingway's "In Our Time."* Boston: G. K. Hall & Co., 1983.

"Robert P. Perkins, Ill for Year, Dies." *New York Times*, April 29, 1924, 22.

"Rollins Mixture." *Ciao*, May, 1918, 3.

Roosevelt, Theodore. Introduction to "With the American Ambulance in France" by J. R. McConnell. *Outlook*, September 15, 1915, 125–26.

"Roosevelt Speeds California Men." *New York Times*, May 12, 1917, 11.

Rovit, Earl. *Ernest Hemingway*. New York: Twayne, 1963.

Rovit, Earl H., and Gerry Brenner. *Ernest Hemingway*. Boston: Twayne, 1986.

"Sam Browne Belts Are Barred Here." *New York Times*, October 18, 1917, 18.

Sanford, Marcelline. *At the Hemingways: With Fifty Years of Correspondence Between Ernest and Marcelline Hemingway*. Moscow, ID: U of Idaho P, 1999.

Scafella, Frank. "The Way it Never Was on the Piave." In *Hemingway in Italy and Other Essays*, edited by Robert W. Lewis, 181–88. New York: Praeger, 1990.

Sempreora, Margot. "Nick at Night: Nocturnal Metafictions in Three Hemingway Short Stories." *Hemingway Review* 22, no. 1 (2002): 19–33.

Shealy, Gwendolyn C. *A Critical History of the American Red Cross, 1882–1945: The End of Noble Humanitarianism*. Lewiston, NY: Edwin Mellon Press, 2003.

Simonds, Frank H. "It's Win or Lose for Italy." *Kansas City Star*, November 18, 1917, C14.

"Slavs Still in War." *Kansas City Star,* November 2, 1917, 1.

Smith, Julian. "Hemingway and the Thing Left Out." *Journal of Modern Literature* 1 (1970–1971): 169–82.

Smith, Paul. "Hemingway's Apprentice Fiction: 1919–1921." In *New Critical Approaches to the Short Stories of Ernest Hemingway,* edited by Jackson J. Benson, 137–48. Durham, NC: Duke UP, 1990.

———. *A Reader's Guide to the Short Stories of Ernest Hemingway.* Boston: G. K. Hall, 1989.

Steinke, James. "Hemingway's 'In Another Country' and 'Now I Lay Me.'" *Hemingway Review* 5, no. 1 (1985): 32–39.

Stephens, Robert O. *Ernest Hemingway: The Critical Reception.* New York: Burt Franklin & Co., 1977.

Stewart, Michael. "Ernest Hemingway's 'How Death Sought Out the Town Major of Roncade': Observations on the Development of a Writer." *Literary Imagination* 8, no. 2 (2006): 211–19.

Stine, Peter. "Ernest Hemingway and the Great War." *Fitzgerald/Hemingway Annual* (1979): 327–54.

Stoneback, H. R. "From the rue Saint-Jacques to the Pass of Roland to the 'Unfinished Church on the Edge of the Cliff.'" *Hemingway Review* 6, no. 1 (1986): 2–29.

———. "'Lovers' Sonnets Turn'd to Holy Psalms': The Soul's Song of Providence, the Scandal of Suffering, and Love in *A Farewell to Arms.*" *Hemingway Review* 9, no. 1 (1989): 33–76.

———. "Pilgrimage Variations: Hemingway's Sacred Landscapes." *Religion and Literature* 35, nos. 2–3 (2003): 49–65.

———. *Reading Hemingway's "The Sun Also Rises": Glossary and Commentary.* Kent, OH: The Kent State UP, 2007.

———. "'You Sure This Thing Has Trout in It?': Fishing and Fabrication, Omission and 'Vermification' in *The Sun Also Rises.*" In *Hemingway Repossessed,* edited by Kenneth Rosen, 115–28. Westport, CT: Greenwood Publishing Group, 1994.

Supreme Command of the Royal Italian Army. *The Battle of the Piave: (June 15–23, 1918).* Trans. Mary Prichard Agnetti. London: Hodder and Stoughton, Ltd., 1919.

Svoboda, Frederic J. "On Teaching Hemingway's *A Farewell to Arms* in Contexts." In *Teaching Hemingway's "A Farewell to Arms,"* edited by Lisa Tyler, 16–39. Kent, OH: Kent State UP, 2008.

Tate, Allen. "Hard-Boiled," *Nation,* December 15, 1926, 642–44.

Tavernier-Courbin, Jacqueline. *Ernest Hemingway's "A Moveable Feast": The Making of the Myth.* Boston: Northeastern UP, 1991.

"Test for Home Guard." *Kansas City Star,* March 24, 1918, 4.

Thompson, Mark. *The White War: Life and Death on the Italian Front 1915–1919.* New York: Basic Books, 2009.

"Three Are Wounded." *Oak Leaves,* July 20, 1918, 1.

"Three More Elude U-Boats." *New York Times,* March 5, 1917, 2.

"To Aid Till Italy Wins." *New York Times,* December 13, 1917, 4.

"To Send Troops to Italy." *Kansas City Star,* December 6, 1917, 1.

Trevelyan, G. M. *Scenes from Italy's War*. Boston: Houghton Mifflin Company, 1919.

Trout, Steven. "'Where Do We Go from Here?': Ernest Hemingway's 'Soldier's Home' and American Veterans of World War I." *Hemingway Review* 20, no. 1 (2000): 5–21.

"Two Who Knew Combat." *Oak Leaves*, January 25, 1919, 11.

"Valor Cross to Hemingway." *Kansas City Times*, July 17, 1918, 8.

Villard, Henry S., and James Nagel. *Hemingway in Love and War: The Lost Diary of Agnes von Kurowsky, Her Letters, and Correspondence of Ernest Hemingway*. Boston: Northeastern UP, 1989.

Waldhorn, Arthur. *A Reader's Guide to Ernest Hemingway*. New York: Farrar, Straus and Giroux, 1972.

Walsh, Ernest. "Mr. Hemingway's Prose." *This Quarter* 1 (Winter 1925–26): 319–21.

"War Time Days." *Oak Leaves*, June 23, 1917, 18.

"Weather Report." *Ciao*, June 1918, 1.

Wells, Edwin. "Hemingway Speaks to High School." *Trapeze*, March 21, 1919, 1.

"We're Doing Our Bit." *Oak Leaves*, April 14, 1917, 6.

"We Saw it Ourselves." *Come Stà*, March 10, 1918, 3.

"Who's Who in Section One." *Come Stà*, April 10, 1918, 2.

"Will Review the Guard." *Kansas City Star*, February 18, 1918, 3.

Wilson, Edmond. "Mr. Hemingway's Dry-Points." *Dial*, October, 1924, 340–41.

"Wilson to Be Patron: President Indorses Plan to Celebrate Italy-America Day." *New York Times*, May 13, 1918, 12.

"Wins Italian Medal." *Oak Leaves*, August 10, 1918, 56.

"With Our Wounded." *Oak Leaves*, September 7, 1918, 22.

"With the Rolling Canteens." *Red Cross Bulletin*, July 5, 1918, 7.

"Wounded on Italy Front." *Kansas City Star*, July 14, 1918, A5.

"Young Hemingway: A Panel." *Fitzgerald/Hemingway Annual* (1972): 113–44.

Young, Philip. *Ernest Hemingway: A Reconsideration*. University Park, PA: The Pennsylvania State UP, 1966.

Index